Highland Peoples of
New Guinea

Highland Peoples of New Guinea

PAULA BROWN

Professor of Anthropology
State University of New York at Stony Brook

CAMBRIDGE UNIVERSITY PRESS

Cambridge
London   New York   Melbourne

Published by the Syndics of the Cambridge University Press
The Pitt Building, Trumpington Street, Cambridge CB2 1RP
Bentley House, 200 Euston Road, London NW1 2DB
32 East 57th Street, New York, NY 10022, USA
296 Beaconsfield Parade, Middle Park, Melbourne 3206, Australia

First published 1978

Printed in the United States of America

Typeset by David E. Seham Assoc., Inc., Metuchen, New Jersey
Printed and bound by the Murray Printing Company,
Westford, Massachusetts

Library of Congress Cataloging in Publication Data
Brown, Paula, 1925–
Highland peoples of New Guinea
Bibliography: p.
Includes index.
1. Ethnology—Papua New Guinea. 2. Chimbu
(New Guinea people)
I. Title
GN671.N5B72   301.29'95   77-80830
ISBN 0 521 21748 2 hard covers
ISBN 0 521 29249 2 paperback

TO THE MEMORY
OF MY PARENTS

Contents

Tables

Maps

Preface

I knew very little about the highland people of New Guinea when I arrived at the Australian National University in 1956. Shortly after I arrived there, a group of social anthropologists gathered to discuss their fieldwork findings in New Guinea, and I learned that the highland people of New Guinea were one of the last large groups to be brought into the world community.

When, in 1930, Australian gold prospectors penetrated the heavily forested interior mountains of New Guinea, which they believed were inhabited by only a few small groups, they discovered in this eastern highlands area of New Guinea large village settlements in gardenlands and grasslands that covered broad valleys and slopes at altitudes about 4,500 feet (1,400 m). Further exploration revealed that, totally unknown to the outside world, a population of hundreds of thousands dwelt in the highlands, energetically grew sweet potatoes, raised pigs, competed and fought with their neighbors, exchanged goods, and celebrated their achievements in large festivals. The extraordinary development of this concentrated and specialized highlands culture is the subject of this book. Highlands New Guinea society was an amazing discovery, because most of interior New Guinea consists of groups that subsist on a sparse livelihood provided by shifting cultivation, hunting, and gathering for small groups living in scattered hamlet settlements.

The continuing research of anthropologists, geographers, archaeologists, and many other social and natural scientists has added greatly to our knowledge of the highlands culture, ecology, and society. This book has drawn on their work. Over the years, my debt is to the countless people who, in writing and discussion, have raised and answered questions about the highlands. But I surely owe the most to the Chimbu of Mintima, with whom my own fieldwork was centered. When I arrived in May 1958, the people of Mintima immediately welcomed me, with continuous good will and help in every way. Mintima was my home base, where I knew the names, households, and family relationships of nearly a thousand people, closely studied marriage, kinship, leadership, local, and clan activities. H. C. Brookfield, a geographer, and I collaborated in studying settlement, land use, and agriculture. Mintima also provided a convenient center for the exploration of other areas of Chimbu by road. We could visit other parts of Chimbu to map land and territories, study tribal traditions and regional differences, and attend ceremonies. I revisited Mintima many times between 1958 and 1965, and then returned in 1976.

I am most grateful for this opportunity to express my appreciation to the Australian National University, which supported my research in the field and in Canberra, to my colleagues, especially J. A. Barnes, D. Freeman, M. Reay, and W. E. H. Stanner, and to Sir John Crawford, former Director of the Research School of Pacific Studies. More recently, my research has been supported by the State University of New York.

My initial goods included camping equipment, staple foods, and the salt, tobacco, and other trade materials which I used to purchase fresh produce from my neighbors. I depended almost entirely on local people and supplies, that first year. Mintima is close to the so-called highlands highway, but in 1958 there was no through traffic because heavy rains had washed away the Chimbu River bridge. My mail and supplies landed by air in Kundiawa, and then reached me when a car or truck was passing on district business. In later years, when bridges and roads were improved, more vehicles were in use, and road traffic became hazardous.

I discovered that the boundary of two large clans runs through Mintima, the stream forming a boundary in places, and the ceremonial ground and rest house site are divided by the clan boundary. The first house I occupied had two rooms, each built by and on the land of one clan: I ate in Kombaku and slept in Numambugu. But these names, and the names of clan segments, which are the identity marks for people, group activities, and land divisions, only slowly acquired meaning as I met people, visited gardens and houses, and attended gatherings. We spoke in pidgin English as I tried to learn Chimbu. My first and main informants were men, who were more fluent in pidgin, more accustomed to dealing with Europeans, and more active in political and economic affairs than women and children.

My first important lesson in fieldwork was that what people say is not always what they do. This is not due to intentional misrepresentation on the part of the people, but rather resulted from their attempts to simplify a complex reality. During my first few days several men identified for me the men's house locations in the vicinity and listed their occupants. Only after months of survey and census did I realize to what extent these are idealized statements of memberships, while actual residence is both impermanent and dispersed.

One early experience, which in retrospect is of great significance, was an intertribal gathering organized by the "big men" of what a few months later became Waiye Local Government Council, named for the highest peak in the area. Four of the groups I came to call tribes were involved: Naregu, Nauru, Kamanegu, and Endugwa. I was taken, and at times literally carried on a steep footpath from Mintima to Gor, the Nauru tribal center, by Kondom, the highest ranking big man in Chimbu, and an escort of other Naregu men. Our walk was cheerful and easy-going until we reached a point on the trail crossed with a line of casuarina trees. These had been planted on the advice of a government officer, to serve as the intertribal boundary marks. Once in Nauru territory, the home of traditional enemies, the Naregu were tense and wary. We spent several hours at Gor, the central meeting place in Nauru territory, where several hundred people, leading men of the other tribes, and many men and a few women of Nauru attended the meeting. We were served food by the Nauru. Representatives and speakers of all the groups spoke about the prospects for a council and political and economic development, stressing good relations between the several tribes. A number of the speakers said that formerly, the four groups fought one another, and that this must now cease; in future they would work together and have a single council which would promote the progress of all. Kondom was a prominent speaker; he commanded attention, and his remarks elicited cheers. When the speeches ended, some men were given more food by the Nauru and remained overnight. My escort group returned, another two-and-a-half-hour walk. As we crossed the border, the Naregu men visibly relaxed. I noticed that within Naregu territory all passersby were greeted, and men entered any convenient house if they needed an ember to light a cigarette. Outside tribal territory they were circumspect. The Naregu and Nauru had not been friends.

Much later, and only gradually, I understood the relations between settlement, land, and political relations of the Naregu and Nauru and other Waiye groups in ecological and social terms. The evidence was there, during this walk, but I was not able to appreciate it, or to phrase questions that might elicit the important information from my companions.

I found that life in Chimbu was rarely dull. Each day brought something new. Someone or some group would start a new activity – a garden, a house, a fence – some expansion or development of his personal and domestic estate. The plans and arrangements for personal and domestic affairs involved others, who might have competing plans or be drawn into a group project. A loss, misfortune, a quarrel or illness calls for a meeting and discussion of rights and responsibilities. The intricate considerations – holding back a pig now for a daughter's wedding in a month or two, inviting an affine (in-law) to share in a bean feast, wondering whether it would be expected to repay a debt in shells or money to help a kinsman's funeral feast – always involve a give-and-take with other people. Every person can be seen as the center of a social network. Debts and obligations tie the individual to clan and kin; one man may know just what is owed him, but he must also reckon on competing demands when he plans his daughter's wedding. At every occasion the onlookers calculate their expectation, and look for opportunities to gain support or prestige.

Before the end of my first field season there was a pandanus nut presentation, a *mogena biri:* Kamanegu tribe had invited Endugwa. On the morning, my friends at Mintima labored for hours over the adornment and facial painting of a young Endugwa man who worked for me. Then we all went to Pari, where a huge circle, perhaps fifty yards in diameter, was marvelously arranged with bundles of sugarcane, bunches of bananas, marsupials tethered to posts, fruits, and vegetables stacked all over. The predominant item was large wheel-shaped parcels of pandanus nuts, tied together and decorated with colorful leaves, moss, and flowers. The visiting Endugwa tribesmen, faces painted, wearing feathers and shells, carrying weapons and drums, were a column of dancing warriors who entered the arena in a series of rushes led by men holding spears. Kamenegu also joined together in a mock-fighting formation, to oppose them.

After these preliminaries, leading men spoke of the intertribal exchange relations, and the size of the Kamanegu gift. The gift itself, I discovered, was made up of many hundreds of individual parcels, gifts from one person to another. It took hours for the heap to be dismantled parcel by parcel and for each recipient's name to be called out to come forward and take the parcel. Women, for the most part wives of the recipients and often sisters or daughters of the donors, shouted their appreciation of parcels, acknowledging that their kinsmen had presented a gift to their husband and family. I found that this group and individual character of intergroup gifts was repeated in every form of Chimbu transaction. In this way I began to appreciate the facets of interpersonal and intergroup relations.

Before my departure, I acknowledged the help and hospitality of the Mintima people. We prepared quantities of festive foods, with rice, meat, and vegetables. Speeches were made to tell the assembled group how I had come to live at Mintima and the people had shown me their ways, invited me to their festivities, and I had joined in their activities. The whole quantity of feast food could be admired, and then it was divided among the individuals, families, and groups present. Some distant visitors were told to take their portion and tell their people of the event. Generosity brings prestige in highland society and gifts of food can serve as signs of generosity and as indicators that an important event has taken place. Learning to direct and allocate portions at a feast stands, I feel, as a measure of my understanding of Chimbu. Over the years of my visits to Chimbu, I became a member of the Mintima community, contributing to payments and receiving a share in distributions. In 1976, eleven years after my last visit, my earlier contributions were recalled. If I had once, years before, helped in a marriage payment, I was allocated a share by the husband when he received a gift.

In addition to my gratitude to the Chimbu, I am also deeply indebted to the colleagues with whom I have discussed the highlands, and whose works I have read over twenty years. The bibliographic references are limited to works used directly in the text, and cannot enumerate the sources of all the materials. Most of the ethnographic research was done within the period from 1950–1975, and accounts refer to this period. The reader can assume that, except as mentioned, statements refer to the highland peoples as they existed soon after contact, that is, after 1935 when they had accepted colonial, mostly Australian, administration. Change in the ecological and social system had not yet become definitive. I hope that my use of the works of others, and my own observations, do not misrepresent the highlands way of life during this time.

January, 1978   PAULA BROWN

Introduction

My background, training, interests, and experience are all expressed in my view of anthropology and my aims in this book. I have studied the interrelations of ecology, culture, and society and attempted to demonstrate this interdependence in the New Guinea highland setting.

An ecological view of a people considers the environment and resources available, the effect of environment upon such things as diet and population patterns, and the people's knowledge, use, and effect upon the environment and resources. A cultural study examines beliefs and values and how these are reflected in religious practices, artistic endeavors, the ideology of the habitat and the management of resources, and technology. A social study concentrates upon behavior, group formation, structure, and composition, and interpersonal rights and obligations. No belief, object, or practice is pertinent to only one of these inquiries.

Put most simply, I might say that there is an ecological system of organisms in an environment, a cultural system of beliefs and practices, and a social system of relationships and groups. However, this set of distinctions seems to me formal and of limited analytic value. My book attempts to show how these systems are interdependent.

The stability and change of any system, or the group of interrelated systems I call ecological, cultural, and social, is complex. To stress stability, the concepts of homeostasis and equilibrium are used. They emphasize the continuity and tendency to balance the ecological, social, and cultural systems and to resist the effect of external influences which may alter this balance. But we know that these systems are never wholly isolated or unaffected by new external and internal environmental, cultural, and social events and ideas. The ability of a people or organism to adapt to a changing environment minimizes the disruptive effects of such forces. Evolution or unilineal development is a progressive trend to intensity, complex-

1

ity, increase in size and efficiency. Other reactions to external or internal change may be fluctuating, an absence of direction and perhaps tendency to regain an earlier position, and revolution, a more complete change, destroying some or all of the previous organization and creating many new elements to make a different whole.

Thus, to say that society is an interrelated social, ecological, and cultural system is not to say that it is unchanging or resistant to new ideas. My aim here is to understand the present in the New Guinea highlands, and to achieve this some understanding of the past influences is desirable.

Three broad contexts for studying the highlands as a whole involve: (1) examining its place in the larger region of Melanesia and especially New Guinea; (2) the distinctiveness of the highland culture; and (3) the differences within the highland culture itself.

In terms of the first of these contexts, Melanesia is an environmental and cultural unit, in which some trade and interchange has always existed. There is no sharp boundary between highland and other New Guinea societies. Highland groups and relationships are of the same unstable, fragmented, and competitive character as those of lowland Melanesia. No centralized states, conquests, stratification, specialization of labor or other institutions characteristic of the complex societies, such as are found in Indonesia or Polynesia, emerged in New Guinea.

Secondly, altitude, climate, temperature, and other environmental characteristics set the highlands apart from the tropical lowlands. The interior of New Guinea is mountainous, with steep slopes and deep valleys. Many small and sparsely populated groups inhabit this mountain region. They garden, hunt and gather food at low and high altitudes, and trade goods between lowland and highland regions. I refer to these peoples as the highlands fringe, to distinguish them from the highlands. From their subsistence agriculture, with technical advances, the highlands have a potential for intensifying agriculture and supporting a dense population in some areas. The size of social groups, scale of festivities, and intergroup relations of the highlands are possible because of their efficient food production. Population expansion has produced large language and cultural groups; some ceremonial exchange systems connect over a hundred thousand people, and there are large-scale alliances and warfare.

Finally, as the reports of research have accumulated, many differences between peoples and communities have been noted. Some of these appear to be related to intensification of agriculture and population expansion: Between different communities and areas of a single language and cultural group, there may be one or more centers with more populous clans, larger alliances, more permanent settlements, continuous cultivation of gardens, and closely guarded land boundaries. Such cultural specifics as sorcery beliefs, cannibalism, initiation rituals, tool types, agricultural practices, and settlement types all show some variation from place to place, often appearing in several adjacent, or separated language and cultural groups, but in different form and combination. While each community or tribe is a coherent cultural and social system, there are many variations and differences, which cannot be simply explained as adaptation to differing environments, invention or diffusion. Some contrasts, such as the distinction between eastern-Chimbu settlement in large villages and central-Chimbu scattered-homestead settlement, might be expected to have more cultural concomitants than we have found. Others, such as the gradation of size of Dani confederacies, seem to fit with differences in population density. There are alternative ways of managing land pressure and allocation of resources to people and groups: For example, Chimbu groups, in the denser areas as in the less dense, invite relatives to join and share resources, thus redistributing people according to needs and resources, while Enga discourage such movement especially in the denser groups, thus restricting resources for the use of members.

A wealth of evidence suggests that the highlands people had a remote common origin. They have been in New Guinea for many thousands of years, at first widely dispersed gatherers and hunters subsisting upon the indigenous plants and animals. Their technology and later introductions of agriculture and pigs were developed from Southeast Asia and Melanesia. These reached the highland peoples by ancient trade routes which carried goods and knowledge into the interior. The highlanders have much in common with Melanesian peoples, the most with those of interior New Guinea who were less affected by the Austronesian influences which led to the settlement of eastern Oceania. In the agriculturally favorable central highlands of New Guinea a distinctive cultural type emerged, with centers of dense settlement, local and specialized forms.

New Guinea is the largest island in Melanesia, near Australia and Indonesia. The central highlands are a region about 700 miles (1,120 km) long and 100 miles (160 km) wide, four to seven degrees south of the equator, spanning parts of Irian Jaya and Papua New Guinea (see Maps 1 and 2). The western part of New Guinea is still relatively unknown. It was formerly within Netherlands New Guinea and is now Irian Jaya, a province of Indonesia. The Irian Jaya highland region may contain 400,000 or more people. Papua New Guinea, formed from the former territories of Papua in the southeast and Australian New Guinea in the northeast, became independent in 1975. There probably are more than 900,000 people in the Eastern Highlands, Chimbu, Western Highlands, Enga, and Southern Highlands provinces of Papua New Guinea. The highlands of Papua New Guinea are more well known because of the studies carried out, especially since 1950.

The highlands, with peaks as high as 16,000 feet (5,000 m), are the source of the major rivers of New Guinea. They can be approached from numerous valleys, through steep mountainous terrain which seems increasingly untenanted. Until 1930 only native traders followed routes into and through the highlands. They brought products of the lowland and seashore, and exchanged food and manufactured goods. After the beginning of colonization about 1900, some items of European manufacture were also traded. Highlands culture can only have been developed from resources and cultural forms common to New Guinea and Melanesia. The subsistence base is gardening: Sweet potato, introduced hundreds of years ago from an American origin and taken into the highlands by native trade, has become the staple food of people and their pigs. It is the only vegetable crop known which will grow in these highland tropical climates to provide sufficient food for the population there.

The most distinctive feature of highland culture is agricultural specialization, which supports large concentrations of people and periodic festivals at which thousands of visitors are entertained and feasted. In Melanesia, ceremony, feasts, and exchanges are the high points of social life; the highlanders value pigs, certain stone objects, feathers, and shells for display and distribution. Local groups conserve their land and resources, protect their property, and defend their land and prestige by fighting nearby groups. Highlanders in competition are brilliantly adorned in oils, cosmetic paints, plumes and feathers of bird of paradise, and iridescent shells; they carry bows, barbed arrows, spears, and finely polished stone axes. War, festival, and ceremonial exchanges are the stage for rivalry of men – for individuals and for "big men," the leaders of groups. The competitive activities – with frequent fights and tests of skill and accomplishment – split traditional groups, attract individual followers, and move people to new settlements or associations. There is no static or stable life in the highlands.

The characteristic agricultural practice of most coastal and inland New Guinea peoples, and of many in the highlands, is shifting cultivation – meaning that the people clear land for a garden, and after a single harvest or possibly two harvests, leave the land to bush for many years. When the secondary forest is well established, it may again be cleared for another garden. Thus the community requires enough arable land for a long fallow cycle of twenty to fifty years. However, in Chimbu and several other densely settled areas, a short fallow pattern of land use prevails, with expanded cultivation to provide food to fatten pigs and serve guests at feasts. The core area is fenced and divided into many individually owned and inherited garden plots. These are cleared and prepared with drainage ditches, tillage, mounds, and other special techniques. After a harvest, the plot may rest only briefly, and be planted with another crop. Each owner cultivates for his own needs, leaving some of his land in short fallow for a few months or years. But the plots are never abandoned and any attempt by others to encroach is resisted. These practices, and the land claims, are a form of semipermanent tenure. Many highlanders have a core area which is intensively used and outlying areas where shifting cultivation is practiced. The difference may be one of proportions; in the Upper Chimbu and Grand Valley Balim a high proportion of arable land is in permanent cultivation or short fallow, while in the Wahgi Valley and Western Dani nearly all arable land is in shifting or long-fallow cultivation. Two

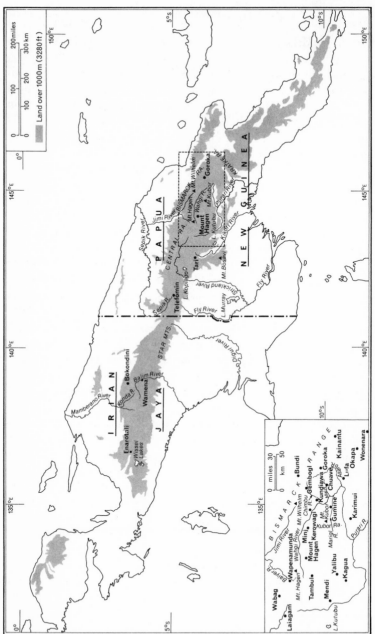

Map 1. The highland area

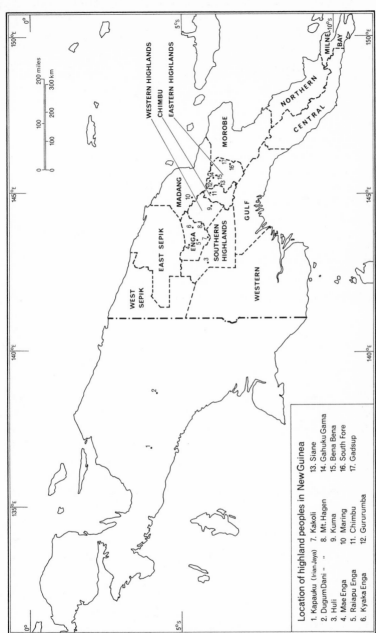

Map 2. Location of highland groups in New Guinea. Provinces of Papua New Guinea are named and outlined.

Location of highland peoples in New Guinea

1. Kapauku (Irian Jaya)
2. Dugum Dani   "   "
3. Huli
4. Mae Enga
5. Raiapu Enga
6. Kyaka Enga
7. Kakoli
8. Mt. Hagen
9. Kuma
10. Maring
11. Chimbu
12. Gururumba
13. Siane
14. Gahuku Gama
15. Bena Bena
16. South Fore
17. Gadsup

characteristics of this situation are notable: the intensity of agriculture in some areas, and the practice of both permanent and shifting cultivation by some groups of people. These variations in agricultural practices clearly show the adaptability and inventiveness of the people and their ability to prepare periodic large feasts. The spacious highland valleys and slopes provide livelihood for communities of hundreds and some tribes of thousands of people. Through intensive cultivation and permanent settlement, highlanders have reached population densities found nowhere else in Melanesia. Four areas: Kapauku of the Wissel Lakes, Dani of the Balim Valley, Enga of Wabag and Chimbu, are each centers of agricultural development, population growth, and large group activities. Between and around these are less-concentrated peoples of the same language groups whose settlements, sometimes large and permanent, are often surrounded by larger areas of fallow land. Peoples and groups have moved about, settling on new or long-unused land, returning to old sites and pioneering. This redistribution of peoples is probably a constant characteristic.

My own fieldwork in the highlands was centered in Chimbu, which today comprises a province, renamed Simbu, of over 160,000 people in six subprovinces in Papua New Guinea. I arrived at Mintima, the center of the Naregu tribe, in Chimbu in 1958. I had an initial impression of patrilineal clans and subclans, because other highlands anthropologists had reported this, and the Chimbu spoke of "house belong Moa," an older man of the locality, "line belong Kagl," a local leader and government-appointed *tultul*, or "Bau-Aundugu," a clan segment of intermediate status. I was readily told the general plan, but my knowledge of the actual boundaries and behavior was built up over many months of observation, questioning, and rechecking. I expected, for example, that there would be localized named groups, that men would own the land and their sons would inherit it. This is patrilineal clan and subclan organization. For the most part men remain in their area of birth, and bring in wives from other clans. Such clan exogamy and patrilocality is the general rule, but in practice there are many individual choices and special cases. Everyone has visited and most people have resided for a time in settlements of other tribes where relatives and affines hold land rights.

Men's houses, on a prominent ridge or hilltop, are the residences of men and older boys, and the gathering place for the local group. Women, girls, and all young children of a family use a small house often located in garden areas near a fence, with pig forage areas outside. The house, with a door at each end, is partitioned into pig stalls and family sleeping and eating sections.

During the first few days after my arrival I was also struck by the differences in the social behavior of men and women. In all public activities, men take the leading part; they plan, announce meetings, speak, travel, visit, and direct activities. Women were not often present at public discussions or men's work or planning activities. If seen at all, they were carrying food, working in gardens, or sitting on the sidelines at gatherings. I later realized that many of the exchanges between men and groups are transactions concerning women; wives, daughters, and sisters are the links between men that establish and maintain exchanges. But women rarely speak or perform in public. I saw little questioning of these roles. However, modern education may well give women and men new occupations and opportunities.

At Mintima the big men of local and subclan groups were introduced as leaders. Several wore the badge of office of *tultuls*, a title used for leaders who had been recognized and appointed by the Australian administration and were responsible to mediate between their people and government representatives. They called out for men to help improve my house and its site, notified people of my presence and requirements, and discussed current issues. These were not hereditary chiefs, but men whose competence and ability gave them influence and respect – in local parlance, "big men." Later, councilors were chosen in local government council elections as representatives of groups; former leaders and the runners-up became committee men, leaders of subgroups. Ageing leaders retired as new abilities were needed in the developing political and economic spheres. In 1958 a remarkable Chimbu named Kondom was the outstanding big man of Naregu, respected by Chimbu in other tribes, and also regarded by the Australian administration as a progressive leader and a government-appointed *luluai*. This headman title, which originated in New Britain, was used throughout New Guinea. By example and leadership, Kondom encouraged the

Naregu in cash cropping, economic, and political development. In the years of successive visits to Naregu, I spent two periods at Kondom's home area, Wandi, which had become headquarters for meetings, discussions of disputes, the primary school, and local government council activities.

Naregu are a Chimbu Valley tribe, who trace their origin to the middle and lower valley of the Chimbu River. They point to former land in territory now held by Kamanegu, another Waiye group. As Kamanegu grew in size and strength, pressed into the lower Chimbu Valley by other expanding tribes, they drove the Naregu out to the southwest, so that the Naregu lost the best land of the Singga Valley, a tributary of the Chimbu, and moved down the slopes into the area of Mintima and other streams which flow southward into the Wahgi River. The Naregu lost very rich limestone land, suited to settlement and permanent cultivation of a variety of crops. Mintima is good land, but below in the Wahgi Valley are grasslands on soil which is only arable on a long-fallow rotation, or for pigs. This land type, with some richer pockets, extends over the slopes and has been used by Nauru and Naregu for occasional gardens and pigs.

The Nauru, who speak a slightly different dialect, say that they have long been at Gor and in the Wahgi Valley area. They have a different tradition from the Chimbu Valley people, and were once a single tribe with Endugwa, whose territory is in the southeastern quarter of Waiye. However, the Endugwa and Nauru quarreled and broke up. While Endugwa land is uneven in quality, most of it is better than that of Nauru. The Nauru are least favored of this group of tribes. Only Gor Peak has valuable land, and very few of the favorite feast foods – pandanus nuts and oil fruit, bananas, and sugarcane – can be grown. Some introduced crops and livestock such as peanuts and cattle may give them new opportunities. The land between Gor and Mintima is comparatively undesirable, used less for gardens than for pig grazing and pig houses. Usually, women tend the livestock and gardens; the men visit the area infrequently. Gardens and social life cluster at Mintima and Gor.

Thus the Nauru and Naregu men had little contact and few common interests. The dialectical difference is indicative of this lack of contact. It was embellished with beliefs about sorcery, theft, attack, and danger from one another, which increased the avoidance. They did not intermarry or attend one another's festivals, so that opportunities to meet and arrange visits and marriages rarely occurred. When the Catholic mission was established at Mingende, they so feared sorcery that they would not share food at religious festivals or attend church together. Accepting food at Gor, and joining together in the Waiye Council, was an important move toward alliance and recognition of common interests among the tribes. Marriage, visits, and exchanges have followed.

During that first season we began the study of Chimbu land and agriculture. We found that the 8.5 square miles of Naregu territory covers a wide range of altitude and land types. Naregu, with around 2,500 people, is at about the median of Chimbu tribes in population density and size, as our later studies show. I quickly became aware of subclan and clan territories; men and their families were associated as members of men's houses and local and clan groups. In my first walks, the transition from the land of one person to another made me think of a patchwork of garden plots of different crops or fallow areas. The distribution of one family's gardens and houses in four or five separate locations was hard to comprehend. As we mapped the individual plots and linked the owners to subclan and clan groups, we discovered clan holdings and group territories. But still there was a patchwork of subclan territories, until we grasped that they were in different kinds of land, and therefore valuable for different things, such as sweet potatoes, sugarcane, vegetables, pandanus nuts, pig forage land, forest products, and materials for manufacturing. By dividing sections of clan land among subclans and individuals all the resources of a territory are allocated, and each has a share. The Chimbu system of land allocation distributes the available land resources so that everyone has access to forest, trees, and arable and forage land within the clan territory, which is for the most part a bloc of land within tribal territory.

On every later trip to Chimbu I saw the central role of transactions in establishing and maintaining interpersonal and intergroup relations. The content of these gifts has over the years come to include peanuts, cans of fish, cows, cartons of beer, and money. Wars begin in quarrels over payment and compensation, and end with exchanges of food and valuables. The small and personal interests of each individual – his chances for a gift of pandanus nuts

from the current harvest, or obtaining a plume to add to a payment –
are only units in a larger exchange system, that between the clans
and tribes. There is a general and broad flow of intergroup transactions in marriages, funerals, harvest, and pig feasts. The men of a
local group act in concert, exchanging with other groups. If they
make a poor showing, every member is ashamed.

On the whole, Chimbus feel they are independent individuals,
deciding the allocations of their time and energy in their own or local
group activities. And yet their obligations to clansmen require participating in group affairs. They cannot neglect these. There is pleasure and pride in group achievements. For Chimbu the scale and
frequency of this participation is very high, and it reaches its pinna-
cle in the largest pig feast. When a feast is under way, it dominates
the interest of all the tribes in the region – both the hosts of the
ceremony and the others who will watch and receive meat. Only
with a concentrated population, intensive agriculture, and pig husbandry, could they achieve such large-scale group collaboration to
build a ceremonial village, accumulate plumes and valuables, and
devote many months to the pig feast, killing at the end thousands of
large animals and distributing them to all tribes in the region. The
connection between the ecological and cultural elements of this system will be explored in this book.

Over the time that I have known highlanders, from my own visits
and reports from others, I have been especially interested in the
region and the changes which have occurred there. By 1960 there
were local government councils and some cash income, from coffee
growing and migrant labor. The highlanders are still primarily subsistence farmers, who sell some produce and purchase some of their
supplies. But they are also now members of the world community.
Since 1960 all Papua New Guinea, including outlying groups, has
been brought into the national development program, with educational, health, and economic services, self-government and independence in 1975. In this development each tribe and cultural group has
retained its language, identity, and traditions. They are often wary
of strangers and more concerned with local rather than national or
world affairs. Interregional and intergroup fighting declined and
nearly disappeared, although there is some recent revival, but pride
and competition continue. The values of wealth and strength are still

important, and we may wonder how these may be redirected in the future.

In addition to my own fieldwork and research, I have drawn on the work of anthropologists and others who have carried out research in the highlands. However, the Chimbu will dominate the discussion, and in dealing with most topics I naturally think of my own experiences and observations first. But the reader will find that a comparative analysis (cf. Brown and Podolefsky 1976) examined some seventeen highland areas and groups, and that my own text will refer to a number of peoples as well. In highland valleys at an altitude of about 5,000 feet (1,520 m), and on the slopes above them, are the settlements and gardens of the highlanders. Between the mountain ranges surrounding these valleys and the New Guinea lowlands are steep slopes; the inhabited area lies between 3,000 feet (900 m) and 7,000 feet (2,100 m). This is the highlands margin and fringe. I distinguish first marginal peoples, some of whom have evidently migrated from the highlands and closely resemble highlanders in language and culture. They may be in trade and other contact with both highlanders and those I call people of the highland fringe. Those I call fringe peoples seem mostly to be between lowlanders and highlanders in culture; many speak languages of groups also found in the lowlands. They are characterized by small and scattered settlements and partial dependence upon hunting and gathering. Inexact as these categories are, they permit some comparisons between peoples and their cultures.

Aside from a few remarks about the people of the Star Mountains, Irian Jaya references are to the Kapauku of the Wissel Lakes, in the far west of the highlands, and to the several subgroups of Dani in the Balim and adjacent valleys. In Papua New Guinea near the Irian Jaya border, the Telefomin, Miyanmin, Sanio, Baktaman, Hewa, and some other fringe groups (cf. Chapter 1) appear to differ culturally and linguistically from the majority of highlands people, who speak languages within the Central New Guinea Macro-Phylum.

Continuing eastward, the Southern Highlands Province is the home of some further fringe groups (e.g., Etoro, Kaluli, Lake Kutubu); among the more well known highlands people are the Huli and Mendi. A nearly continuous region of highland peoples, interrupted only by some uninhabited slopes and peaks, is found in the

Enga, Western Highlands, Chimbu (or, now, Simbu), and Eastern
Highlands provinces. From west to east they include Enga (Mae,
Raiapu, Kyaka subgroups), Kakoli, Mt. Hagen (or Melpa), Kuma,
Manga, Maring (including Tsembaga and the Bomagai-Angoiang),
Chimbu, Sina Sina, Chuave, Gururumba, Siane, Gahuku-Gama,
Bena Bena, Kamano, Fore, Auyana, Tairora, and Gadsup. High-
lands fringe peoples in the central and eastern area include the
Daribi and Bundi.

The book follows a general progression from discussion of the
habitat to the largest group activities, an organization both conventional and, I believe, most conducive to developing my viewpoint on
the relations of ecology and society.

The first chapter, on the environment and the use of resources,
presents an overview of the climate, terrain, plants, and animals of
interior New Guinea. A clearing, settlement, garden, and man-
made bush land has replaced the natural vegetation and wild life in
areas of dense population. An opposition of wild and domestic or
transformation from forest to settlement is a central idea in highlands
thought. A section on prehistory discusses the technological phases
and transition from hunting and gathering to a predominantly agricultural mode of subsistence. A brief section on language classification and physical characteristics follows. Then the discussion turns
to an examination of mountain society on the fringe of the highlands,
ranging from lower to higher altitudes on steep slopes. The fringe
peoples I see as representing the type of society and culture from
which the highlanders have developed. By combining what we know
of highlands' prehistory and the culture of the contemporary fringe
people, we may imagine the background of the highlanders' special
development. After examining the fringe societies, we will move to a
discussion of technology and trade in the highlands and from there
to an examination of diet and disease patterns. Diet will be considered in terms of the foods consumed, irregularity in consumption
of protein and fats, nutritional deficiencies, and resultant physical
conditions. The beliefs of highlanders about the causes and cures of
disease and the link between health and social and cultural
phenomena are also examined.

Chapter 2, on agriculture and population, begins with a general
discussion of modes of measuring agricultural intensity in terms of

the frequency of cultivation and fallow periods, and is a more specific measure of techniques of land preparation, care of the growing crop, and food production. Several varieties of highland agriculture, adapted to environmental and land types, are distinguished and described. A section on pigs – the major domestic animal of the highlands – as a focus of agricultural production and ceremonial follows. The distribution and expansion of the population throughout the highlands, in relation to regional resources and agricultural intensity, is then discussed. A statistical study summarizes the interrelations of agricultural intensity, population density, and land tenure, to show their close association.

Chapter 3 develops the subject of land, territory, and local group relationships. The importance of communal and individual property rights and the high value placed upon ancestral land is discussed. Examples of land tenure and territorial relations are taken from all types of highland societies. The significance of locality, centering on men's house groups, is also examined.

Chapter 4 considers family and kinship. The several stages of social development, adolescence, initiation, courtship, marriage, and family formation are described with examples from various highland societies. The processes of group formation, expansion, and intergroup relations are considered in terms of highland concepts of patriliny, descent, and membership.

The culminating chapter, on cohesion and competition, examines the structure and relationships of the larger groups. The manner in which segmentary forms, opposition, and alliance are affected by the dynamic, big man leadership pattern is described. A study of the population size of exogamous clan groups and largest political units is presented to show how these are both directly associated with population density. It will also be shown that the group which coordinates social, political, and ritual activities occupies a territory of limited size. Competition, fighting, and warfare will be examined on an interpersonal, intertribe, and intratribe basis. Finally, festivals – the high point of group productivity and achievement – will be examined in terms of their social and cultural significance.

1

Life in the highland habitat

An ecological approach to anthropology involves studying society as part of a system in which natural resources and environment, technology, the division and type of labor necessary for human subsistence, culture, and social groupings and relationships all constitute interdependent elements of the system. When we examine the forms of community, family, and kinship groups, we can see that they are adapted to the environment and vary according to regional or local circumstances. The people's evaluation of their situation as shortage or abundance, restricted, competitive, or expanding affects their behavior. These beliefs about man and environment appear as themes in social and cultural activities – such as, the significance of locality and settlement as an interdependent and sharing group, the separation of men and women, and the special training and protection of young men to fight for community preservation and expansion. In this study of the highland society of New Guinea, the density and distribution of population will be considered in its geographic dimension and in relation to resources and agricultural systems. Diet, health, and disease patterns will also be examined from an ecological perspective, as will the particular cultural and social dynamics that have evolved within the highland habitat.

The people of interior New Guinea practice many kinds of subsistence economy. They range from the small groups of collectors and shifting cultivators of the highland fringe to the central highland tribal groups, who are permanently settled in broad valleys and mountain slopes and intensively cultivating and raising pigs for large ceremonies. All fringe and central highlanders live on their land, manage its resources, and see their welfare as dependent upon favorable environment.

Within the central highlands area, local societies range from small scattered communities to concentrated settlements of thousands of people. Agricultural intensity and population density are also found

16

with certain property and land tenure forms – close settlement of households, individual and closely guarded land rights, permanent claims, and defense of territory.

Local groups are in some respects self-sufficient, but must cooperate to conserve their land and resources and to defend themselves against expanding outsiders. Their ties of kinship to other communities preserve local exchange, provide assistance and sources of new or needed goods and ideas. The great food festivals are a culmination of local and tribal cooperation in food production and the accumulation of valuables. In these festivals the tribes proclaim the use of resources to achieve wealth and renown.

Most of the highland people, and those who have been most studied, are in the highlands of Papua New Guinea, a newly independent nation. The highland area spans the central sections of both Papua New Guinea and Irian Jaya, the western half of the island which is now a province of Indonesia.

AN ECOLOGICAL OVERVIEW

The New Guinea highlands is a distinctive geographical and cultural region. Its rocks, soils, and vegetation are based on the characteristic natural materials of the region. The lands of Southeast Asia, Australia, and Melanesia were once interconnected, but the deep ocean trough known as Wallace's Line has long separated Southeast Asia, the Philippines, and Indonesia (the Sunda Shelf) from Celebes, east Indonesia, New Guinea, and Australia (the Papuan Shelf). This deep ocean trough is a major biological dividing line. The native fauna of the Papuan Shelf is composed of invertebrates, fish, amphibians, reptiles, birds, and marsupials. No true mammals except, perhaps, rats, mice, and bats reached New Guinea until man came traveling over water. The large mammals of Southeast Asia are wholly absent. Pigs and dogs were probably introduced as domestic animals. The land of central New Guinea is continental in type, having complex land forms and geological development with vulcanism, earth movement, erosion, and sedimentation. The natural vegetation has been greatly modified by human use over a long period of occupation. Australian continental mass and base rocks underlie the highlands. Present configurations are of late Mesozoic and Tertiary origin, with mountains arising in the last one-hundred million years. Further, vigorous tectonic and volcanic activity has characterized the last fifteen million years, with frequent earthquakes and volcanic eruption at present. The land of the highlanders is topographically and geologically young.

In the uplifting of the central highlands, limestone deposited on the ocean floor in Miocene and Pliocene times became folded and faulted into mountains. These have subsequently been eroded and shifted, covered with volcanic ash, weathered, and transformed. The present highlands are composed of a complex of igneous, metamorphic, and sedimentary rocks. Many distinct soil types are found, varying throughout the region, and soil differences are recognized by the people within their settlement area. These variations are important to understanding and assessing land use practice and values and in estimating the carrying capacity, that is, the capacity of the land to continue to provide subsistence to a population.

The region which we consider here has no precise physical boundary, and any social boundary would be arbitrary, cutting social linkages and trade routes. The central cordillera includes mountain ranges, peaks over 12,000 feet (3,700 m), high plateaus, and valleys. This mountainous interior extends through the island's center both in Irian Jaya and in Papua New Guinea. Its length is about 700 miles (1,120 km) from approximately 136° to 145° east longitude, and its width varies, running from 3° in the northwest of New Guinea to 7° south latitude in the southeast, but reaching its greatest, about 200 miles (320 km), in the center. Between the central mountains with their wide valleys and the coast are steep slopes and narrow valleys inhabited by small groups of fringe people.

Many things distinguish this central highland region from low-lying places at the same equatorial latitude. Generally, Melanesia is an intensely humid, rainy region, but the highlands are distinctly less wet and sometimes seasonally variable. The climate is best described as subtropical, above 3,000 feet (900 m) in altitude. Both drought and frost sometimes strike the high altitude gardens. The inhabited highlands are in the lower Montane rain forest zone, a range from 3,500 feet (1,100 m) to 9,000 feet (2,700 m) in altitude. Heavy rainfall in the low-lying tropics draws off soil nutrients, but the cooler and drier highlands have a slower rate of loss of organic material in the soil. Compared to low altitude tropics, these highland valleys and slopes are fertile. Rainfall in the highlands varies both seasonally and regionally, but on the whole the highlands are well watered, with at least eighty inches a year, and often over one hundred inches. At times, heavy rain erodes or floods the region.

In some areas below 5,000 feet where rainfall is heavy, that is, 150 or more inches (400 cm) a year, weeds overcome cultivated plants in gardens, and growth is so rapid that cultivators seem to prefer to move to places where the regrowth is taller, more developed, and easier to clear than to attempt to replant a recent garden plot. The combination of warmth at lower altitudes and high humidity make for rapid weed growth, leaching, and poor agricultural soils.

The higher altitude slopes are less humid, better drained, and at lower temperatures the weeds grow more slowly; humus and weathered rock combine in better soil. Above 4,500 feet (1,400 m) with adequate sun and rain there may be soils capable of producing food crops for several plantings before being abandoned to fallow. It is in this zone that some very intensive agricultural practices have developed into permanent garden plots in regular use.

Above 7,000 feet (2,100 m) cooler temperatures, occasional drought and frost, and the slow growth of food crops as well as weeds may restrict the potential for settlement. But these conditions are not linked to altitude alone; they involve the complex interrelations of temperature, amount of rainfall, cloud coverage, and composition of soil. Specialized cultivation techniques have been developed to improve agricultural productivity by controlling landslips, drainage, and temperatures of growing plants.

Natural forest here is oak, as in Southeast Asia, beech, as in southern temperate zones, and pine. The dominant forests have been removed by burning and cutting for cultivation, and after harvest are followed by grass, reeds, shrubs, cultivated trees, and secondary forest or recultivation. Above the cultivation zone is high altitude moss or cloud forest, and alpine vegetation to the highest peaks.

The natural vegetation is rich and complex, varying according to and within soil, altitude, and climatic zones. The natural montane forest has a canopy of trees from thirty to sixty or more feet (nine to eighteen m) in height and a lower level of shrubs, plants, vines, young trees, and plants. To make a garden, some or all of this is cleared. Grass replaces both after cultivation, and in some areas becomes thick. Then woodlands may form above the grass. Often, the people transplant seedlings to gardens, especially encouraging useful trees such as pandanus and casuarina. The inhabited parts of the highlands are now a mixture of human settlement, cultivation, grassland, and disturbed forest. Undisturbed forest remains at higher altitudes, in areas difficult of access, or on the fringes in sparsely settled regions.

The forest zone supported a nonagricultural population for thousands of years, and the undisturbed forest contains much edible vegetation – the nut-bearing and the oil-fruit pandanus, and nuts or acorns of *Elaeocarpus, Castanopsis, Quercus* and some other trees. Seeds of breadfruit, vines with edible fruits and leaves, *Pueraria* roots, edible fungi, tubers, leaves, and fruits of many shrubs, can provide a varied and nutritious diet. Sago, which grows in the lower altitudes, may be processed as palm pith and traded to the highland people. The less disturbed forest zone also supports a great variety of animals which may be used as food. The largest birds are flightless cassowary of several species; sizable doves, parrots, cockatoos, crows, pigeons, and many smaller birds may be eaten. In recent times many birds, especially the birds of paradise, have been more valued for their colorful plumes and feathers than as food, and these are widely traded. One type of chicken has been semidomesticated; nowadays chickens and some other fowl are commonly kept, but not often used for eggs or food.

Of the true mammals, pigs, rats, mice, and bats have long been found in the New Guinea countryside. There is evidence of pigs dating to 10,000 years ago. Until recently archaeologists believed that pigs were brought by man over water, most probably as domestic animals. It is possible that pigs reached New Guinea by swimming (Bulmer 1975). Wild pigs have mated and reproduced in New Guinea forests for thousands of years, to be hunted and eaten by man. In archaeological sites the bones are not identifiable as domestic or feral. In the deep forest pigs are still the most important game, although marsupials are numerous in the trees and on the ground: Varieties include tree kangaroos, cuscus, wallabies, bandicoots, and possums (Bulmer 1968). Smaller game is even more common –

snakes, reptiles, frogs, lizards, insects, larvae, eels, fish, snails, and grubs. Recently introduced domesticated animals include cattle now being developed for milk and meat, a few goats, horses, sheep, cats, chickens, ducks, turkeys, and new varieties of dogs and pigs.

The combination of naturally occurring plant and animal food sources provides sustenance for a small hunting and gathering population, and many contemporary groups obtain an important proportion of their foods from wild sources. But where the population is dense, permanent settlement and continuous cultivation have greatly reduced the wild food available.

Grass may be burnt to clear the land for cultivation, as a protection against surprise attack, in hunting, and for other purposes. The natural woodland which has been cleared does not regenerate quickly. Consequently, certain areas, especially in the eastern highlands, have become permanent grassland. In such places, there is a shortage of wood for building and sometimes of other forest products, except in places too steep or inaccessible for gardens. The Chimbu and some western highlanders preserve and transplant casuarina seedlings and other trees in fallow farmland, to be used later in building and for firewood. Casuarina trees have valuable effects on the soil in that they fix nitrogen. Where highly valued trees, such as pandanus, stand permanently, they are often individually owned or claimed by a family group and any gathering of their products by others is considered theft.

In the inhabited zones, a wide variety of natural and induced plants is present, usable for food, manufacturing of clothing, tools, shelter, or containers. These include ferns, mushrooms, the roots, stalks, leaves and fruit of plants and shrubs, and nuts. Dyes, poisons, medicines, cosmetics, stimulants, gums, salts, flavorings, smoking materials, and magical materials in great variety are prepared from wild and cultivated plants. Minerals, clays, and animal products provide some of these materials, too.

Gourds, vines, grasses, reeds, bamboo, wood, bark, and fibers from wild plants are used in manufacture. Stone, bamboo, bone, and wood are fashioned into striking, chopping, digging, grinding, or cutting tools. These bush and forest products have always been important to the highlanders. The craft uses of plants include use of woods, fiber, resin, oil, tannin, bark, gum for net bags, baskets, carvings, containers, musical instruments, tools, weapons, ornaments, fence and house building, and clothing. Animal bones, teeth, pig tusks, bird bills, skins, pelts, and plumes have been used as tools, ornaments, and in trade.

Some rare colored clays, bird feathers, stone for axe blades, salts, and tree products are highly valued both in their usual habitat and by people in other areas where the material is unavailable. Exchange networks, long trading expeditions and localized barter or exchange put these goods into circulation so that their final consumption or use is often far from their origin. Many of the plants which were used before general settlement and cultivation have become semidomesticated: Naturally occurring seedlings are transplanted, seeds or shoots are planted. Those found in gardens and near houses are protected and staked.

Only in the last few years have some town-dwelling highlanders become almost wholly dependent upon manufactured tools, clothing, household goods, and nonindigenous foods. For them, their Westernization is a matter of prestige and display of wealth and accomplishment.

PREHISTORY

The prehistory of the highlands can be partly reconstructed by combining archaeological, physical, and linguistic data. The very existence of these hundreds of thousands of people was unsuspected by outsiders as recently as fifty years ago. The first foreign visitors, in what was at the time Netherlands New Guinea, Papua, and Australian New Guinea, found large populations with no knowledge of Western technology or peoples. Between the coast and the highlands were small settlements and scattered groups. The highlands had lived in partial isolation, with only trade links out of the highlands, for many thousands of years. The prehistory of New Guinea was virtually unknown until about fifteen years ago. Excavations of the last few years tie the cultural development of New Guinea to the Southeast Asian cultural center. There are many important discoveries, particularly in the highlands, which make it possible to indicate dates for some major cultural advances.

The first men crossed from Asia into Australia and New Guinea more than 30,000 years ago. In New Guinea, the earliest site so far is at Kosipe in the Papuan highlands dating to about 25,000 years ago. At this time in the Pleistocene, the highest New Guinea mountains were glaciated. Glaciation reached its greatest extent 17,000 years ago, and then retreated.

Archaeology, historical linguistics, and physical anthropology have reached only partial and tentative conclusions about the origins and development of these peoples. The first human arrivals in New Guinea may have occupied coastal sites where both sea and land resources were plentiful. Penetration inland and occupation of the cool, steep, and mountainous areas may have taken some time; the mountainous areas did not have sea foods, coconuts, and other familiar coastal resources. Food collection was the dominant mode of subsistence for many thousands of years, providing a mixed and varied diet of plant and animal foods. The settlements were most probably small, temporary shelters. Pandanus nuts and fruits were available in the mountains. Both natural rock and cave shelters and huts might have been used, as they are now by the more mobile peoples of the interior. It is difficult to imagine permanent local groups of large size; there could be only short-lived supplies sufficient to feed more than thirty people at any place. However, a small and dispersed population could exist on natural products of the forest.

The first Melanesians were hunters and gatherers. Their tools were rough and unspecialized, pebbles and flakes used as choppers and scrapers. A wide variety of wild vegetables, nuts, and fruits were available at this time. The largest animal was the cassowary, a flightless bird which is still a favored food although very rare. Most of the food was probably collected plants and small insects, amphibians, birds, reptiles, rats, and marsupials. The flake tool industry apparently continued until 6,000 years ago.

Research in Southeast Asia indicates that plants were domesticated by 12,000 years ago. In Southeast Asia, this was accompanied by the development of ground stone tools, pottery, the domestication of pigs, and probably also cattle. These neolithic advances did not immediately reach New Guinea. In the highlands, which must have received these influences some time after they arrived at coastal and western New Guinea, rock-shelter excavations reveal a flaked-stone industry, with edge-ground axes and waisted, flaked blades, indicating hafting. Some rock-shelter sites were occupied, probably intermittently, over a very long period of time.

The ground stone axe or adze which became the basic and characteristic tool for land clearing and building appears about 5,000 to 6,000 years ago. The stone tools at this time consisted of flaked stone artifacts, waisted blades which may have been used as hoes, scrapers, edge-ground artifacts, as well as the ground stone axe-adzes. Such tools could be used for forest clearing, house building, fence building, and to fashion wooden implements.

From examining the archaeological remains, a transition from hunting and gathering to agriculture and pig domestication is evident. Probably associated with gathering and early agriculture are some distinctive ground stone tools no longer made in the highlands. Stone club heads, figurines, mortars, and pestles were ground by a similar technique. They may have been used in fighting, grinding seeds or nuts, and in a cult concerned with the bird and animal figures, but no direct evidence or stratified excavation is yet available. The ground-stone implements, which might be hafted as an adze or as an axe, are found in many excavations. In cross-section they vary from oval to lenticular to quadrilateral, and are apparent precursors of the fine ground-stone axes of recent time which are general tree cutting, brush clearing, and building tools.

Evidently forest clearing for shifting cultivation occurred some 5,000 or 6,000 years ago, when agriculture and pig domestication were first practiced. Grasslands were created by burning and clearing for gardens, hunting, and defense, and cultivated foods replaced wild foods as the mainstay of the diet. The main food crops were probably taro and yam, both brought from Southeast Asia. Taro, a tuber which is still a major food in the highland fringe, became the most important. Other crops may have included bananas, leaf and stalk vegetables, cucurbits, greens, beans, and sugarcane – some of which may have been native to New Guinea, where wild varieties are found. Many New Guinea peoples still grow these crops in gardens.

Pollen analysis from early sites in the Wahgi Valley suggests that shifting agriculture was practiced over 5,000 years ago. At a later date, 2,000 to 3,000 years ago, the swamplands were extensively drained with ditches for intensive cultivation; fence posts and wooden spades were utilized there. Because swamp gardening is technologically far more complex than shifting cultivation, such an intensive technique implies the existence of a large and settled population, stable communities with houses, and a social system to protect property rights. The widespread systematic water control and swamp drainage gardening in the Wahgi Valley associated with specialized techniques, using spades, is believed to have been used in taro cultivation. On the slopes, other crops, most probably yams, bananas, sugarcane, stalk vegetables, greens, and beans, could have been grown. It is probable that the valley population increased to require more permanent forms of agriculture, and the moist valley bottom beds were adapted to the requirements of growing taro. However, the swamps were not continuously occupied, and the population shifted to the slopes at times.

Sweet potatoes are now the most important food crop in the highlands. Large-scale pig production, which is basic to feasts, group activities, and exchange, depends upon them. Sweet potatoes were first domesticated in Central or South America, where they became an important tropical highland staple food crop. They apparently were introduced in New Zealand, Easter Island, and Hawaii hundreds of years before Columbus and became the most important food crop in those areas, but it is not known for certain when or how they reached Melanesia and New Guinea. Most people have thought that the Portuguese and Spanish brought sweet potatoes to the western Pacific and the Philippines in the sixteenth century, and they reached New Guinea after that.

In the Wahgi Valley, the swamp drainage fields at Kuk seem to have been largely abandoned about 1,200 years ago and then resettled about 300 years ago, the time when most people believe that sweet potato was established in the highlands. The ability of sweet potatoes to thrive at higher altitudes made the mountain slopes available to the increasing population. If sweet potato was known and adopted before 1600 A.D. in Papua New Guinea and in Irian Jaya, the present population concentrations might have developed more slowly and at higher altitudes. A later introduction would suggest greater dependence on the altitude-limited taro by highlanders, and perhaps a rapid change in location when sweet potato entered.

A few years ago anthropologists and geographers often spoke of the highlands as if it were an enclosed region, a single isolated group of languages, with a more or less separate tradition based upon the development of pig and sweet potato agriculture, competitive feasts, and warfare. Recent language and cultural studies have shown the ties of highland to other inland language groups, the extent of trade, and the complex, varied, and interrelated cultural traditions of highland and interior peoples. This variety is evident in the highlands fringe. It is neither possible nor of any value to think of the highlands people as an isolated cultural type. The variations we find within the highlands are as great as any between highlands and fringe or inland peoples. Our understanding of these variations will be best advanced by considering ecology, the distribution of peoples, society and culture in this highland region.

LANGUAGE AND PHYSICAL TYPE

While once the variety of separate languages in New Guinea bewildered scholars, most recent analysis reveals some relationship among the great majority of languages spoken in the interior, although a number of unconnected and apparently isolated language groups remain. Traditionally, Melanesian, mainly coastal languages, were classified as Austronesian and related historically to Malayan, Polynesian, and Micronesian languages. The Melanesian groups probably appeared in New Guinea subsequent to the settlement of the interior. But that great variety of Papuan or non-Austronesian languages, sometimes evidently overlain by Austronesian, have in the majority now been classified as the Central New Guinea Macro-Phylum.

Of this group, the first to be recognized, and the most widespread, is the East New Guinea Highlands Language Phylum. Nearly all the people of five Papua New Guinea provinces, the Eastern Highlands, Chimbu, Western Highlands, Southern Highlands, and Enga, and some in adjacent districts, speak languages in this group. Other Phyla include: Central and South New Guinea, West New Guinea Highlands, and probably related stocks and families – Anga, Sepik Hills, and Upper Sepik – which surround the highlands center. Most of the fringe peoples speak languages of these other phyla. Now some scholars would include most of highland

New Guinea in the Central New Guinea Language Macro-Phylum. However, the Macro-Phylum includes people of other cultural groups, not only highlanders.

Although distant linguistic connections between the East New Guinea Highlands Language Phylum and other languages are now established, languages within this group are more closely related than any with outside language stock and are classified as one stock and several families (Wurm 1961). The approximate and rounded-off population figures of this language group as of 1960, are presented in Table 1.

Table 1. *The East New Guinea Highlands Language Phylum*

Language families and sub-families	Number of speakers 1960 population
Eastern family	30,000
Gadsup-Agarabi sub-family	15,000
Auyana-Usarufa	5,000
Awa	1,000
Tairora	9,000
East-Central family	158,000
Gende sub-family	8,000
Siane sub-family	20,000
Gahuku sub-family	33,000
Kamano sub-family	68,000
Fore sub-family	29,000
Central family	292,000
Hagen sub-family	91,000
Wahgi sub-family	43,000
Jimi sub-family	24,000
Chimbu sub-family	144,000
West-Central family	269,000
Enga sub-family	123,000
Lembun sub-family	600
Huli sub-family	54,000
Mendi sub-family	77,000
Wiru sub-family	14,000
Karam family	17,000
Duna family	6,000

Closely related families – Mikaru (7,000), Foi (3,000), and Pawaia (2,000) – are in the highlands fringe to the south of the central and western groups.

Population and language analysts who have studied the highland people of Irian Jaya have established a West New Guinea Highland Phylum consisting of four language families: Wissel Lakes–Kemandoga, Uhunduni-Amung, Dem, and Greater Dani. These appear to be related to the Eastern group, and part of the Central New Guinea Macro-Phylum.

In terms of physical anthropological studies, the people of the highlands bear a general resemblance to a physical type sometimes called Papuan, related to but distinct from coastal Melanesians who show, physically as in their language, a tie to Polynesians and Malays. A connection between Papuans and Australians has been suggested, but this is more distant.

The physical anthropological studies of highlanders have not made the same measurements, blood analysis, or presented other biological data on all peoples, and few conclusions have been reached. Aside from common origin and general resemblance, local populations appear to be mainly distinct, partly isolated, and rarely interbreed beyond the region.

Thus both language and physical type suggest the same conclusion. The interior peoples have a remote common origin. Their relations to Australians and Malayo-Polynesians are of two sorts: possible common origin, perhaps 50,000 years ago; and intermittent trade and migratory contact, which became more active in the last 3,000 years when new techniques, agriculture, population growth, larger groups, closer settlement, and exchange developed and intensified trade. People of the highlands and the highland fringe share a cultural base, with related languages. With favorable living conditions and intensification of agriculture, the central highlands people have become numerous, secure, and expansive. They have migrated in all directions from centers of population growth to occupy new lands on the margins of this territory.

SOCIETY IN THE HIGHLAND FRINGE

The interior mountain people surrounding the highlands, whom I shall call the fringe people, have been the last to be studied because they are sparsely distributed in relatively inaccessible areas. Yet their life is probably much like that of the whole interior region before intensive agriculture and population growth stimulated concentrated settlement in the central highlands. Thus, the fringe may serve as a base point for understanding the specialized development of the highlands.

The small communities and fragmented groups of the fringe area utilize a variety of food sources, none providing surpluses or allowing the expansion of groups. Populations are very small. Ritual and behavior of fringe societies suggest a deep feeling of insecurity. These societies surrounding the highlands have always been intermediaries and traders, bringing new ideas and techniques into the highlands from outside. Their own resources and capacity to expand are limited. The highlanders were dependent upon regular trade for very little. For the most part their technology used highland resources with skill and selectivity. In the highlands polished stone tools reached a high level, and agricultural tools were developed for specialized uses. The climate required warm houses, but clothing was sparse. Body decoration, painting, and adornment had many local specializations, such as elaborately shaped wigs and shell trimmed headbands. Pigs, stones, feathers, and shells were used in ceremonies and payment.

Before the 1960s, the fringe had not been closely explored; no government posts or services were established. Hardly anything was known of the groups living there, their population, and culture. Reports and first studies indicate great diversity among these isolated small language and tribal groups. But so far, the information available does not invite generalization, except perhaps as in contrast to the intensity, size, and complexity of highland culture. The ecological adaptation, culture, and social structure of the fringe area resembles that of lower altitude New Guinea societies in many ways. We might suppose that, prehistorically, the people of the highlands fringe had a food-collecting and mixed-agricultural subsistence. Many had access to several altitude and ecological zones with varied resources, including sago palms. Each small hamlet or village was a group of related families, perhaps with the men forming a continuous line of descent and wives coming to join their husbands' groups. Several small hamlets or scattered settlements made for rather isolated language and culture areas of a few hundred people.

There was visiting, interchange, and ceremonies linking communities within the linguistic group, and some with other groups. Group fragmentation characterizes all of interior New Guinea. This interpretation might further suggest that the densely settled, larger, and more complex cultural and social forms of the highland peoples have developed from such a base, with sweet potatoes, intensification of agriculture, developed pig husbandry, and the circulation of valuables and growth of local or tribal groups under big men as leaders. The varieties and combinations of practices and beliefs are very numerous indeed, yet some such process is plausible in the light of our present knowledge of New Guinea prehistory and contemporary social life.

Numerous distinct groups of the fringe region will be referred to in this section. Some are in the Sepik-Fly headwaters area around Telefomin and in the Star Mountains, between the concentrated highland peoples to the east and west. Recent social, cultural, and ecological studies of the central New Guinea peoples show each small local language and cultural group having access to a variety of ecological zones at different altitudes. A wide range of hunting, fishing, trapping, and collecting techniques are used. Among the Miyanmin and others, it can be said that hunting the larger marsupials and pigs is a man's favorite occupation. Game is most plentiful far from settlement and garden sites. Men join together to hunt in the forest. Group and individual movement are adjusted to the accessibility of forest for hunting. A sparse and dispersed settlement pattern is the preferred form, and a greater reliance on cultivated vegetable food is not desired.

SUBSISTENCE

In the fringe areas, breadfruit trees produce leaves and edible fruit at lower altitudes, where betel, elaeocarpus, pangium, and other nuts and fruits are valued. The ripening of fruit is closely watched for its future consumption by people, who also know the preferences of game animals. Concentrated groves of pandanus and some other trees are important; they may be claimed by territorial groups. The wild vegetables, fruit, and nuts are often restricted by altitude and seasonal variations, but the more accessible sources are closely watched and used. Groups and individuals move to harvest fruit, nuts, and other wild foods.

One important food source, sago, is restricted to altitudes below 3,300 feet (1,000 m) with moist swamp soils conducive to sago palm growth. The natural stands of trees are visited by sago collectors, who may also grow the palms from seedlings or shoots. Cultivated sago is privately owned. The slow process of growth is noted and individual trees selected for future use. Sago palms reach a height of thirty to fifty feet, a trunk twenty to thirty inches in diameter, in eight to fifteen years. They must be cut before flowering destroys the starch. One tree produces hundreds of pounds of starch. Wild pigs are attracted by cut sago logs and may be killed or captured in the area. In some areas domestic pigs are confined in a natural or fenced enclosure where sago palms are felled to provide food. Sago grubs are eaten by pigs as well as by people, and both the extracted starch and the pith are eaten by pigs.

The process of making food from sago is laborious, but a great quantity of starch is obtained. A Sanio woman can produce enough sago in one day to provide 16.7 people with their daily sago food needs. For human consumption, the palm is cut down with an axe or adze. Men usually cut the trees and may then work with women or move to other tasks. Sago pith is then grated and crushed with a stone and piled on a platform. Near a stream or pool the pith is washed and kneaded. The starch and liquid flows down a trough, is strained through fiberous matting, and the remaining starch is collected in another trough to settle. After draining and drying, the starch is wrapped in leaves, stored, or transported for future use. It is usually mixed with other foods in a baked cake or boiled pudding. Leaf-wrapped packages of dried sago, which are long-lasting, are traded to other people for food or goods and may be the main staple food. While sago is not a fully satisfactory or nutritious food by itself, accompanying plant and animal foods, wild and domestic, complete dietary needs. The Sanio, for example, consume mostly sago pudding: It provides 85 percent of their dietary calories. Another 5 percent is wild and cultivated vegetable food, including breadfruit seeds, pandanus fruit, greens, bananas, and tubers. The remaining 10 percent of the diet is composed of meat from feral and domesticated pigs, small game, fish, insects, and larvae (Townsend

1974). Some sago is cut and left to collect grubs and larvae, an important source of protein and fat. Among the Gadio, a fringe group whose language is related to Enga, sago is less important than cultivated food. It serves as a seasonal staple and support while new gardens are prepared. The Saiyolof transplant and cultivate sago palms, and also collect wild sago, from group-owned territory. These sago producing techniques are also practiced by lowland people, for whom cultivated foods are also important.

Both wild and domestic pigs are prized. Some domestic pigs are fed on sago. However, few pigs are kept, in some areas none; the domestic sows interbreed with wild boars, and young wild pigs may be captured and kept for a feast. The low-density, small hamlets, impermanent settlements, and frequent movements to collect varied food sources do not foster development of large pig herds. Thus pig feasts on the scale of central highlands ceremonies are not possible. Ceremonials are relatively small and infrequent, involving the slaughter of one or a few pigs, cassowaries, birds, and other game. Fighting between groups is somewhat akin to hunting: Enemy dead who are taken add to the meat supply of some peoples.

SETTLEMENT AND COMMUNITY

Site selection in the highlands fringe is based on a variety of criteria – access to wild plant resources, hunting land, sago, old hamlet sites, and friendly neighbors. A site may be chosen because it is far from dangerous enemy groups, or areas associated with sickness and misfortune. The quality of the soil is another consideration; river alluvium or other areas of rich soil or land less liable to erosion are preferred.

In shifting cultivation, after a garden site is chosen, its existing trees, shrubs, grasses, and other plants must be partly removed to provide a clearing for the garden crop to be planted.

Kaluli in the Southern Highlands Province (Schieffelin 1975) have an unusual procedure. Bananas, breadfruit, and pandanus are planted after a rough clearing of underbrush. The garden canopy is felled after the seedlings are established. However, fallen trunks are not removed. For sweet potatoes, tubers, sugarcane, and vegetables the plot is cleared of undergrowth and trees, and also fenced against pigs. A sloping site may be selected, and beginning at the bottom, the trees are notched on the downslope side. Forest clearing is a difficult job, as stone axe or adze chopping takes about four times as long as steel axe cutting. At the top of the slope a large tree is felled, and as it falls it topples the others. Large branches and underbrush are removed. These other tasks are little shortened by steel tools. When the vegetation is sufficiently dry and more clearing is required, some vegetation may be burnt. Felled trees are used for house building and firewood. Fencing is needed where domestic pigs are numerous.

New planting requires some clear place for planting the tubers of taro or sweet potato, and adequate light as it grows. But the new planting is interspersed among stumps and fallen logs. Some weeding may be done while the crops are young. Other cultivated foods, in gardens or hamlets, are banana, sugarcane, yams, and some local forms of leaf greens, beans, stalks, cucurbits, and other vegetables. Newly introduced food crops, such as tapioca, cucumber, pumpkins, papaya, melons, corn, and peanuts are readily adopted. The crops mature at different times, with a main crop of taro or sweet potatoes in six to eight months. Before this some vegetables may be gathered, whereas banana and sugarcane grow more slowly. A family collects wild and cultivated foods from several sites, returning to nearly abandoned gardens for some and new gardens for others. Food sources are very widely distributed. Large areas are gardened by a house group, but the crops are not closely planted. Thus the yield from this area may be less than in more intensive systems.

Moving to a new area requires house construction and land preparation, while the group must depend upon stored, wild, or cultivated foods until the new gardens have begun to produce. Old garden and hamlet sites with food plants or trees are visited to collect ripening fruits. People live in separate garden houses from time to time. Thus, a family and larger group has a number of places they know and where they have rights to resources which they have planted or previously gathered. The main residence of the community is built near sources of water and suitable garden land as well as sago or other wild foods.

The communal extended family house type settlement is built by a number of peoples in the region. The house is raised on posts, with fires, which provide warmth and some protection from mosquitoes, on internal platforms or beneath. The Kaluli and Etoro of the Mt. Bosavi region have a village-long house occupied by several nuclear families, members of different lineages and clans.

This house form is also found among many peoples of the Fly-Sepik head waters, but its relation to settlement and ritual center varies. The Australian administration has encouraged the construction of central-village settlement forms here, as they did in the central highlands shortly after first contact. But cultivators and collectors here are habituated to moving about their territory. No one settlement site can be convenient to all their needs. Territories are over one hundred square miles, and villages often a day's walk apart.

Before contact with the Australian government a few years ago, the Saiyolof people of the highland fringe were highly mobile. A group occupied a large extended family house, about thirteen meters by ten meters, built above ground in the trees with women and children sleeping on one side, men and boys on the other, in a communal room with fireplaces. Houses were built at a cliff's edge for protection from enemies (Hatanaka and Bragge 1973). The house served as the family's base, but the family would be seminomadic, moving every few days to gather new wild foods, and returning to the house for garden cultivation and harvest. New gardens were dug frequently, and after a year or two new houses were built, often distant from the last. Some crops, such as banana and tree fruits, were harvested after another garden was established; thus a visit to the old house and garden was included in the traveling round.

Some people of this area site their houses in scattered garden hamlets. Others have a separate men's cult house that women and uninitiated boys are forbidden to approach. Where a central village with a plaza is built, as among the Faiwolmin, who include Baktaman, one or more men's sleeping houses and cult houses are distinguished, while women's houses are separate and a menstrual hut is set aside. This type of village is used especially for ceremony; when gardening and collecting, most groups occupy garden hamlets or scattered houses.

The Baktaman, who number less than 200, have a territory of about 250 square kilometers of mountain slope and valley ranging from 1,800 feet to 6,500 feet (500 m to 2,000 m) in altitude (Barth 1975). Villages are newly located every few years; gardens last about two years, with a fifteen- to twenty-year fallow. Much of the Bakta-man's territory is permanent forest, used in hunting and collecting. Rights to sago palms and collecting areas are vested in a person who may allocate them to others. The village is a public arena from which people withdraw to garden houses for privacy and men to cult houses for secret ritual. Men of several clans, who are initiated to-gether, share the men's houses. The leaders of the men's houses do not command or direct people in everyday activities.

In this fringe area a political community, composed of a village or group of hamlets with a territory, may have 100 to 250 members. Such a group maintains internal peace while in a constant state of enmity or tension with respect to all others, with occasional fights and killing but no institutionalized peace. Ritual, especially male initiation, is an important force for male solidarity and the com-munication of knowledge about man, nature, and the spirits.

The largest language and cultural groups number several hundred people, and the usual group living together in a house or hamlet is fifty or fewer people who are mostly interrelated through the male members. General density may be less than one person per square mile, rarely over ten per square mile (4/km²). The people's contacts with others are irregular, and as likely to be hostile as festive. Some trade friendships transcend language differences, but gatherings are rare and brief. Neighbors are distant family groups; a marriage might be arranged with a group that is two to three days' walk away. Territories are large and general, with the valued resources closely watched and other sections rarely visited. Family membership changes with death or departure to other areas and recombination of members in marriage exchange. Since the government has estab-lished a station in the area and controlled warfare, the people fear raids less. They have become more settled and have begun to accept strangers as neighbors.

Large stretches of forest remain; they are used for hunting and collecting but considered unsuited to settlement or cultivation. It is questionable whether a larger population would be supportable in this ecological and subsistence system where high rainfall, poor soils, and difficult terrain greatly limit the arable land. Wild resources may be exhausted while the land declines in productivity. Settled village life must increasingly depend upon cultivated food, and fewer wild plants or animals can be found where garden land has replaced the forest to any extent. Whereas, in the past, concentrations of population were only temporary, the normal form of short-lived small hamlets has recently changed with government influence and population growth: Settlements are becoming larger and more permanent. This may disrupt the ecological balance.

Before colonization by the Australian government, settlement in the fringe area was integrated with a mobile subsistence ecology and occasional brief concentrations for trade and ceremony. Normal food sources could not sustain larger or more permanently settled groups. An estimate of maximum size and duration of residential groups, or frequency of ceremonial concentration, can only be approximate. In the fringe area the population which speaks one language is frequently less than 1,000, and these rarely, if ever, gathered as a whole. Where, as in some Telefomin area groups, Lake Kutubu, the Star Mountains, Daribi, and Kaluli language and cultural groups are somewhat larger, group gatherings were nevertheless infrequent and did not bring together the entire population. Such sparse populations would have to travel for days to reach a central point for the entire group, and food supplies could not sustain a gathering. The Kaluli maintain continuous relations of trade in dog's teeth, hornbill beaks, string bags, black palm bows, tree oil, tobacco, salt, and pubic aprons, which were available in Bosavi and adjoining regions. Some remote objects also reached them from the south (Schieffelin 1976).

In some of the larger language and cultural groups, kinship groups or clans are recognized units which include several residential units. Thus the Hewa have clan territories containing several family groups. Clans are exogamous, and men generally bring wives to live in their own clan territories, two to three days distant from their family territories. A neighborhood group, households of one or more clans, gathers for occasional feasts and trade.

Where exogamous patrilineal clans are territorial units, marriage between communities stimulates intervisiting, and extends social connections and trade partnerships. In visiting and change of residence after defeat or difficulties, clansmen move to new communities. Important interconnections are fostered by clan bonds, when segments of clans share an interest in shrines and cults. The clan tie may also be invoked for sanctuary or adoption. Many of the fringe people have a complex set of ritual initiations for boys and men, and the seclusion of initiates is required. For special rites, several communities and their ritual specialists may collaborate. Cult houses are decorated with carved boards, the ritual representations of taro and ancestor spirits. At Telefomin, for example, more elaborate cults and cult houses are centers for large ceremonies, with participants from other cultural groups. Some of these activities – such as seclusion and instruction of boys – are more reminiscent of Sepik area practices than of highlands to the east or the west of Telefomin.

The people of the Lake Kutubu area live in more permanent villages. A village men's house is used by men and boys for sleeping and storage, while each woman, her daughters and infant sons has a separate house. More permanent settlement has involved clan group ownership of sago swamps and individual patrilineal inheritance of the most valuable long-lived trees: pandanus, breadfruit, and the oil-producing tigaso. Men cut sago from mature trees in the clan grove, but the work of extraction and preparation is done almost entirely by women. Gardens are of less importance for food, but the diet is enhanced by meat from hunting, domestic pigs, and fish. One or more patrilineal exogamous clans are represented in each village. The men live together in a communal house, but have separate clan land and sago rights. No general men's or boy's initiations are found but there is a cult, Usi, whose practitioners must be initiated and taught the preparation and use of medicine and may be engaged by patients.

Intercommunity visits among the Kaluli are occasions of ceremony (Schieffelin 1976). Hosts prepare food and the guest group performs dances in elaborate costume, striking in their dramatic effect. The relations between communities are occasioned by marriage and other ceremonies with visits, dances, and gifts of food. Food must be specially grown, or marsupial meat smoked, to provide for guests. Relations between communities are reciprocal.

In the Star Mountains area of Irian Jaya are a larger and more settled people, whose basic social group is a hamlet usually of fewer than one hundred persons. A group of nearby hamlets are joined together, with a traditional founding hamlet that was the origin of others. This pattern suggests a population growth in recent generations. The central village is also a ritual center where youths are initiated and men gather for ceremony and political planning and discussions. It is a stable center for the short-lived garden and hamlet groups which frequently re-form in different parts of group territory.

Barth (1975) found the Baktaman to have a series of seven male initiation rituals in which the symbols and meanings are successively revealed to boys and men. His is the first description and interpretation of this system of knowledge. Sacrifice is of central importance: An animal is presented to the ancestors and then may be shared with them or burnt. Prayers always accompany the sacrifice. Fire is the center of the ritual sacrifice. The eating of meat or vegetables together signifies sharing and mutual trust. This is most clearly expressed in the series of initiation rituals.

The Baktaman are most concerned with fertility and man and his relation to nature. The formal initiations are the key to all ritual knowledge, collectively held for sets of males in the village community. First a group of novices, whose ages range from about five to fifteen years, are taken from their mothers into the forest, rubbed with dew and pork fat, kept in seclusion during their instruction in ritual secrets, emblems, and objects, made to observe food and other taboos, and given ritual meals of game and pork fat. This group may shortly thereafter proceed through the second degree initiation, with pig sacrifice and a brief instruction concerning the clan ancestor cult; the true nature of the ritual thus emerges. A long ritual, sacrificing a number of pigs, marks the third degree initiation, which may be two to five years later. This cult is associated with warfare, preparing and strengthening the novices, and involves another set of symbols of marsupials, meat, and the ancestors. However, the major features of the cult are not yet revealed. Fourth degree initiation concerns male adulthood, evidenced by the appearance of the beard. The emphasis is upon adult sexuality and its symbols. By stages, then males enter into participation into adult life and secret knowledge.

While secret hunts were made to provide meat in other initiations, the hunt is the focus of the fifth degree initiation, when all men try to bring in as much marsupial and wild pig as possible. At this point the initiates are adult. The sixth degree initiation is the preparation of a shrine, and both feast and myth express the close relation between marsupial, ancestors, and taro. The final, seventh degree initiation is at the shrine associated with taro, women, and motherhood. The initiates reach the status of fully authorized seniors, who know the secrets and have taken part in every phase. Not all the men survive to the seventh degree, but the whole village has a share in the feast when the ritual is made.

The initiation series – which Barth views as a system of communication – involves the most elaborate set of symbols of the Baktaman culture. The major rites concern the cult of the clan ancestors, the association of forest and game, taro, the village temple, and the ancestors. This is the foundation of the communal cult. Secrecy, ignorance of the uninitiated, and authority of the senior cult leaders are further themes. The cult leaders and senior men direct ritual activities, including sacramental meals. They are responsible for transmitting sacred knowledge; if it dies with them, it is irreplaceable. Occasionally a local group loses a shrine and cult leader; then they may attend that of a neighboring friendly group, but cannot easily reconstitute the cult. This has happened to some communities and to some groups. The activity of initiation and cult ritual is a measure of community prosperity: The people share in planning and holding feasts of game and taro and gain confidence in community and regional relations. Group survival and continuity depend upon these resources, which are ritually secured. In contrast, the community suffers severe losses in death, sorcery beliefs, warfare, killing, abduction, all of which weaken the group and threaten survival. When an important cult leader or warrior dies, the community may not find a successor. Community isolation in the fringe area makes recovery from such losses difficult. The insecure and delicate state of the fringe societies is emphasized. We will see how the power and strength of highland society is a marked contrast.

TECHNOLOGY AND TRADE

The highlanders know their immediate environment and the resources of their community territory very well. They all recognize

that some materials make better tools than others. With very few
exceptions, basic needs can be satisfied with local goods. Yet some
materials obtained by trade from other areas are acknowledged as
superior in some ways. Access to these sources is valued, even if the
materials are not always essential to survival. Of particular value are
some salts, mineral clays, oils from oil seeps and from certain trees,
and resins. Wood, which is used to make a great variety of tools, is
widely available, but special varieties are favored for some uses.
Black palm is favored for bows, and there are other specific preferences. Trade has always linked isolated sparsely distributed people
to one another. They recognize the value of some natural products
not locally available and take interest in the goods and practices of
others. Inventions and discoveries, knowledge, and products are
spread by occasional trade contact between communities. But at the
same time, contact with strangers is considered dangerous. The unfamiliar is not trusted, for illness, sorcery, and dangerous spirits may
come from these strangers.

The most courageous men engage in trade activities, visiting associates in distant and hostile groups. They obtain rare valued
goods, and their adventures are the source of new ideas as well as
goods. Such men reinforce their ties with trade partners by arranging marriages between the groups. These continue the relationship
into the next generation, increasing the exchanges and knowledge of
other peoples. Trade ties interconnect communities in all directions
to form a complex mesh in which goods and ideas are transmitted
between geographical zones and cultural regions.

Everywhere in the highlands, people have access to some forest
plants and trees. They set traps and snares to catch animals and
birds. This is a most important occupation and food source in areas
with few permanent gardens and sparse settlement, but even the
Chimbu and Dani who have the least such territory, caught some
birds and forest animals and trapped eels in the streams. It is
noteworthy that plants and animals are not used to make cloth or for
their hide.

The New Guinea peoples mostly used a fire-saw method for making fires: Dry tinder is ignited with friction when a length of bamboo
or a rope is rapidly pulled back and forth through the tinder. Ordinarily, burning sticks or embers are carried, sometimes between
wooden tongs, to bring fire where it is used.

Tobacco, in a bamboo pipe or leaf cigarette, is commonly smoked by men, and often by women and boys. Smoke of tobacco and other plants is often an element used in curing.

SALT

In the interior of New Guinea, minerals as found in the natural or cultivated foods are generally adequate for normal health. Sea water is not available, but water from salt ponds is sometimes used. Salts are processed in several ways for consumption and trade. Sodium salt occurs naturally in mineral springs. Water from the spring is evaporated into a dry sediment, sometimes boiled, and kept in a bamboo or gourd container which may be traded outside the local area. Another technique of preparation begins by soaking grasses, plant stalks, and leaves in salty springs or ponds. The plants are then dried and burnt. The ash is again wetted down, strained, evaporated, and the sediment formed into a cake to trade or preserve until used. For the highlands, the most important salt springs are in the lower Wahgi Valley, a source of widely traded salt cakes, the Simbai Valley, Enga, and the southern highlands. Salt from these springs is distributed in trade throughout the highlands. But only near the springs is it consumed frequently. In most places sodium salt is a rare addition to food cooking for a feast. The human body's need for sodium is not clearly established, for many highlanders consume very little.

In the absence of these sodium salts, a salt high in potassium is prepared from the ash of selected plants by many people for consumption and trade. Many varieties of plants can be used for this ash-based salt. The knowledge of technique and labor of preparation, more than limited access to a salt spring, makes salt a product valuable and worth trading. The association of salt with feasts and its ceremonial use requires making, keeping, or acquiring salt for such special occasions.

The human need for salt requires further medical study, but the substitution of manufactured salt sold in trade stores for traditional local salts may change the mineral content with serious effects. This seems to have brought serious iodine deficiency and cretinism to the Maring in the 1960s (cf. pp. 59–60).

STONES, TOOLS, AND WEAPONS

Many useful implements are made of stone, and stone is used flaked or ground and polished to make tools for hammering, drilling, scraping, cutting, chipping, and shaping, Ground stone mortars, pestles, figurines, club heads, and other forms have often been found but the making and use of these by highlanders is not known in recent times. Axes and adzes are made from hard, tough, and fine-grained metamorphics and shales: Greywacke siltstone, argillite, granodiorite, and hornfels have been identified in axes and adzes.

Stone axes and adzes, now almost everywhere replaced with steel axes, are the highlanders' most important tool for garden clearing, house and fence building, and exchange. Sources of good stone – such as mountains and fallen rocks – are recognized and extensively quarried. In Papua New Guinea, important sources are several quarries in the upper Jimi Valley, in the Wahgi Valley at Abiamp and Dom, and to the east at Kafetu on the Asaro River. Stone from these sites was traded in a wide area, and the trade network is integrated with local exchanges to provide a means whereby rare and valued goods were widely dispersed. The products of minor stone quarries supplement the more important, but are not so widely traded. Of the considerable collection of axes examined, measured, and studied, a few found in the highlands are evidently imported from lowland quarries, further demonstrating the extent of trade.

The rocks in the quarry are cracked and broken, then removed. Some rough shapes may be traded to be finished elsewhere. To finish, rocks are laboriously shaped on wet sandstone into blades; a thick work axe planilateral or nearly rectangular in cross-section and a thin flat ceremonial axe were the main types. People of the area, the owners of the quarry territory, had the right to quarry, work, and trade the stone axes. Each quarry area produced characteristic shapes and styles. The Kafetu axe is oval in cross-section, while a planilateral, lenticular, or straight-edged oval is made in the Jimi Valley. With use, the cutting edge of a work axe or adze becomes dull and must be sharpened by the owner. Ceremonial axes are valued for their size and thin cross-section.

An adze is hafted at a right angle to the handle, an axe perpendicularly. A wooden handle and reed or fiber binding, sometimes strengthened or padded with tree gum or other materials, holds the blade in position.

Every man needs a work axe, and carries it with him much of the time; he uses it every day. Size and shape preference for different jobs exists, but few men regularly keep several axes. Men who quarry stone and make axes do so primarily to exchange them; they have no need to accumulate axes. In some highland areas an adze is the more common tool. Occasionally a small adze or chisel is required for more delicate jobs, but not every man has one. Stone is sometimes seen in other shapes to be used as a knife, hoe, drill, or bark pounder. Stone for these jobs is not necessarily the hard and fine-grained type preferred in axes. It may be an adaptation from a river stone or local rock. Axes, adzes, and some other tools are hafted onto wooden handles and bound with grass, fiber, or reeds available in every area. Ceremonial axes are stored and exchanged, rarely used or carried except in warfare and dancing. They are collected for presentation at a marriage, pooled, given, and then distributed by the recipient group so that accumulation is only temporary.

Bows are made of a hard wood, probably black palm, or, more quickly, of strong bamboo, and strung with a bamboo strip. Arrows have a reed shaft, the point attached by fiber, or split-reed binding and gum. They are not feathered. Some arrow points are hardwood, cut sometimes into elaborate barbs or notched. Fighting arrows are sometimes pointed or barbed with animal teeth or other sharp objects. Sharp bamboo points are made for hunting, and a three-pronged or four-pronged bamboo tip can be used in bird hunting. Large wooden shields are used in warfare.

In the central highlands of Chimbu and Wahgi, spears of nine-foot or ten-foot long hardwood are carried in war and in ceremonies. They may be notched or barbed, made with wooden prongs, and decorated with fur, feathers, or carving. Spears and arrow points are scraped and shaped by stone, bone, tusk, and other materials.

Cutting, scraping, and butchering are done with stone or bamboo knives. A bamboo knife can be quickly made by splitting a reed, and sharpened by removing a strip. Such tools are still often preferred to a dulled steel knife. Sharp, pointed implements, or daggers, are made of the long leg bones of cassowaries, pigs, and other animals. A needle made of bone was used in making netting, sewing leaf mats, and weaving armlets. Now when these traditional crafts are practiced some modern materials such as steel needles and cotton thread may be used.

Those peoples whose agriculture involves clearing and tillage use sticks shaped or fire-hardened for heavy use in prying up grass and roots. A small digging stick is used for breaking the soil and planting seeds. Axes or adzes are the main tool in tree cutting and fence building, with steel axes quickly replacing stone. Paddles or spades of wood were used for digging ditches before the introduction of steel shovels. A pointed wooden hoe, hafted on a handle, was also used by the Chimbu. Hoes, blades, or spades of stone, probably hafted on wooden handles, were used in tilling, ditch digging, and other garden work.

Vegetable fibers have a multitude of uses. Some of these are found in the forest, others planted near houses to use as required. The inner fibers of vines, shrubs, bark fibers, roots, and so on are stripped and separated. A woman keeps a constant supply of fiber in her bag, and twists or spins cord against her thigh while she sits resting or visiting. Cord may be colored with vegetable dye. The cord is then fashioned into net bags, netted hats, net aprons, string skirts, and other accessories, often decorated with bits of fur or patterned in different colors. Fibers are also made into lashings, pig-tethering ropes, belts, armbands, and other useful or decorative goods. Bridges of vine and rope span streams where people live and garden on both sides, but a river which forms a boundary between enemy groups may not be bridged.

Mats are made of pandanus leaf stitched into rectangles. They serve as bedding, rain capes, and to support a baby while it is being carried or is resting in a net bag. Women always carry one or more net bags on their heads to use for carrying and as shawls. They are suspended from the forehead, resting on the back when babies, firewood, food, and other things are carried. A woman returning from a garden may support a load of fifty pounds or more this way. Designs and materials of fiber and bark for clothing and ornament have been developed into many different forms. Barkcloth, pounded strips which may be decorated with dye and incising, were used as back coverings by Chimbu women. A bark belt, sometimes carved and colored, was made in some places. Bark cord may be loosely wound about the waist to suspend a net apron or string skirt. Design elements on wood, bark, in woven mats, on wooden and gourd containers, and on bamboo pipes are dyed, painted, carved, burnt, etched, plaited, or woven. They represent many natural objects such as animal tracks, insects, flora, nuts, shells, teeth; others are geometrics such as triangle, chevron, zig-zag, squares, and so forth. Special symbolic designs, which designate the owner or some other purpose, are used on ritual objects.

Bamboo cylinders, which serve as containers and carriers for water, oil, and other fluids, are sometimes decorated by cutting and burning. Bamboo is also used for flutes and jews harps. Drums are hollowed wood, usually decorated, and skin-covered. Pottery is not developed in highland New Guinea, appearing only in a musical instrument, rather like an ocarina, and in trade.

CONSTRUCTION

Highlands houses, especially at the higher altitudes where night temperatures are often below 50°F (10°C) and sometimes freezing, are built close to the ground, with thick insulated walls and heated by fire. In contrast, there is no evidence that coastal New Guinea people ever constructed houses to retain heat. The general shapes varied from rectangular to round to ovoid, or straight at one end and rounded at the other. The normal highland dwelling house for a woman and children, or men and boys, was constructed in the same way. In some fringe areas, large partitioned houses for several families, raised buildings, and other distinctive forms of group dwelling were found.

House building, at new sites or replacements, is part of the flux and change of location and activity of highland people. The house is habitable for perhaps two to five years, but may not be used regularly all of this time. Although varying somewhat in size and floor plan, the mode of construction is similar. The main house wall is usually one or more layers of upright wood slabs pointed at both ends, placed in a rectangle, ring, or oval with a gap for a doorway. The men's house is a long oval or rectangle and has several stout tall posts, about six feet high, in the center for the roof support. A long pole rests on the posts as the roof center beam. House walls are about waist-high, and insulated with leaves and reeds between the upright slabs. There may also be an inner and/or outer wall of woven

These round houses with outer walls of woven pitpit and roofs of kunai grass are typical of hamlets in the eastern highlands.

split "pitpit" (reed). The insulation and padding is lashed to the pointed wood slabs forming a wall several inches thick. At higher altitudes the walls are thicker and nearly air-tight so that the inhabitants can keep warm at night. Sloping roof structures are built up of bamboo and pitpit poles tied together with vine and cord. Then *kunai* grass clumps are folded and overlapped to make a rainproof roof. More leaves may also be piled on top and an accidental or decorative addition of ferns and plants often sprouts from the roof. Smoke from one or more fires seeps through the roof, and some air enters through the open door.

Doorways can be barred with slabs of wood or lightly covered with grass and leaves suspended over a bar across the top. A door on a rectangular house is at one or both of the gable ends; on a round house it is an opening in the curve. Still others have a gable end with a door and a rounded end without an opening. The design depends partly on purpose; where the house adjoins a fence and pigs enter a fenced track to grazing land, one door is used by pigs while the other opens to a garden, sitting area, or footpath. Large men's houses may have two entrances, while the small round village houses usually have only one.

Traditionally, the highlands family did not ordinarily sleep under one roof. For the most part, sexes were separated. However, in the eastern highlands, men's houses are now rarely built and elsewhere they may not be used exclusively by males. A woman's house, whether in the village, hamlet, garden, or pig grazing area, is rarely a man's sleeping place. Dwelling houses are often partitioned into space for sleeping, hearth, cooking and sitting, and pigs. Weather and convenience decide the placement and use of family houses. Most married women sleep with their children and sometimes with the pigs; any other women in the house are close relations, or temporary visitors. Men and older boys share larger men's houses with other male members of the community or one-blood group, and short- or long-term visitors. Central fireplaces, sections, and sleeping platforms are built inside. Men's and women's houses may be clustered, strung along a ridge or street, or scattered in the occupied part of the group territory. A few plants, or a vegetable garden, are usually planted nearby. Men's houses are usually prominently sited, with an open or tree-shaded space for gatherings. There are often some separate or secluded buildings for livestock, fowl, coffee hullers, women in childbirth or menstruating, latrines, and outliers used for guarding boundaries or resources. Highlanders are often on guard against enemy communities nearby, and some settlements are built with deep ditches, steep approaches, stout fences, removable ladders, escape tunnels, and other defenses. The separation of livestock, women, and infants is part of the defense pattern.

Special ceremonial buildings and dance grounds are erected by the Chimbu and western highlands people whose ordinary settlements are dispersed. People and pigs are concentrated for only the last weeks of the ceremony. Houses for ceremony are specially decorated with carvings, leaves, and ferns. The open space is planted or surrounded with rows of trees, outlined with colorful, flowering plants.

Where pigs and people are few, and agriculture is less intensive, the protection of gardens is not a major concern. But in the areas of concentrated settlement, where pigs break through fences and can destroy large sweet potato gardens, they must be contained. The main pattern evolved has been to build a fence around the garden and to allow pigs freedom to forage in grass and forest. This pig forage area may be far from the main village settlement. A domesticated pig returns to a house for feeding and sleep. Thus garden-border pighouses are the most convenient place for a gardener to feed the pigs. If a small garden is planted within a fallow area, this must be fully fenced. Where a large stretch of gardens and temporary fallow are usual, as in the densely settled parts of Chimbu, this whole area is fenced and the fences kept up by communal effort.

Fence styles vary with the available materials. In the eastern highlands wood is scarce, and fences are often of pitpit reed. In the Chimbu and western highlands casuarina trees are planted in fallow land to be used for houses and fences. These fences consist of a double row of upright slabs and posts spaced along a line with horizontal poles lashed between them, or a stout close line of pointed slabs tied to horizontal reeds. One line of fence may be built in several styles and have supports where the terrain favors this.

Since steel tools have become common the shaping of posts and splitting of wood is much easier. Nails have replaced lashings and many buildings are straight-walled and higher with raised floors, hinged doors, padlocks, and other new materials. Outer walls are of woven pitpit or bamboo, and the inhabitants are dependent upon blankets and clothing for warmth because fires are not built on the floors. Among other things, furniture, iron roofs and walls, brick, finished wood siding, and kerosene lamps have followed with the introduction of wages and cash crops.

CLOTHING AND ADORNMENT

The first outside observers found highlanders wholly dependent on local materials and some traded goods. Their clothing was derived from plants: Cord and netting as skirt or apron were predominant pubic coverings. In the western and Irian Jaya highland area the Telefomin, Star Mountain, and Balim Valley men wear long gourds as penis sheaths. Body and face may be tattooed by cutting designs with a sharp point – nowadays glass or razor blade – and rubbing with oil and charcoal to make a dark pattern. Nasal septum and ears are cut so that ornaments may be attached, and plumes are sometimes put in holes on the nose. As a rear covering bunches of cordyline leaves, grass, ferns, other leaves, or barkcloth strips are used. The pubic and rear covering is fastened to a belt of woven fiber, bark, or other material, from simple to elaborate, decorated or with many strands.

Aside from the pubic area, little of the body is covered. But it is decorated with armbands, leg bands, and on the head or around the neck with netting caps, wigs, feather head ornaments, shell, fur, bone, pig tusks, dog's teeth, snakeskin, leaves, flowers, and ferns. Nose and ears are pierced to hold feathers, shell, and bone. Many people have face and body incised and rubbed with charcoal to make tattoo-like skin decorations. Charcoal and colored clay and minerals are applied to the face. The more elaborate clothing, necklaces, headdresses, and paints are worn at ceremonies. At the time of discovery, shell ornaments were rare, having come to the highlands from remote coastal sources. But feather, tooth, bone, and fur ornaments were more common.

While face decoration, feathers, shells, and traditional clothing are revived for ceremonial occasions, most male highlanders now have wardrobes of shirts and shorts, with some cloth wraparounds (laplap), long trousers, and sweaters. Women wear blouses and skirts or cotton dresses more often than traditional netting skirts. Footwear has been a recent addition.

Ceremonial objects often have a religious significance, representing ancestors, spirits, and magical qualities. The wearing of wickerwork or painted wooden boards, barkcloth emblems, certain plants, feathers, shells, and animal parts conveys the wearer's belief, success, wealth, or special ritual status.

In several areas, but with strikingly different variations, men wear wigs made of matted human hair mounted on a frame. Highlanders' hair is tightly curled, so that it holds its shape when attached to a frame. A full wig is kept for ceremonial use. In Enga there are many styles, often large and rounded; in Mendi Napoleonic-like caps with wings rising on the sides are worn. In Huli a crescent rounded over the head with thick lower ends on each side is predominant; at Porgera very wide and upturned wigs are worn. In Hagen and in Chimbu an open-topped hood hanging straight to the shoulders is common. Wigs are adorned with flowers, leaves, small and large shells, green beetles, animal teeth, fur, clay, paint, and feathers. Elaborate coiffures, tied with fur or grass, greased ringlets, and other hair-dressing styles are also reported. For the most part these were worn by men; the women keep their hair short and cover their heads with net bags, which are often filled for carrying.

The dancer also attaches iridescent shells, fur, bird of paradise plumes, and feathers to his forehead, nose, top of head, neck, belt, and armband, so that a moving line of dancers is a brightly colored and light-reflecting mass of movement. Bodies are anointed with oil and sometimes colored with charcoal, paint, or clay.

At marriages and exchange ceremonies these goods are displayed to proclaim the wealth of the participants. Some are given for payment or compensation; others form a return gift when the elaborately decorated bride is presented to the groom.

The preparation of valuables and personal decoration for a feast or exchange occupies the whole group for some time. Dance grounds must be cleared, and often buildings are constructed. Plants are placed for decoration, and leaves, ferns, and flowers are collected to use in adornment. Making wigs is laborious, and decoration requires collecting many materials. The ointments, feathers, furs, and other decorative materials often must be traded from friends in other areas, or obtained on loan from kinsmen.

Ceremonial participants themselves only produce or gather part of their display goods; the presentation of rare imported goods and foods is a matter of pride. The prestige of the ceremonial participants derives from the goods they show and give their exchange partners. Every group's ideal is to make impressive displays, and this occupies much time and effort. Many items are kept and traded for adornment and exchange, borrowed, or presented at ceremonial occasions. Some decorative items, paints, cosmetics, and fresh leaves, for example, can only be used on one occasion and are obtained for these special uses.

At dances, drums, axes, and weapons are carried; these enhance the activity with sound and motion, as well as demonstrate the strength of the dancers. A large ceremony is a time when people of different communities come together for a somewhat tense competitive interchange, display, and gift prestation. Goods are traded between people who have access to products of different environments and trade routes. Also, those who have finished a dance and killed all their pigs trade dance ornaments which are no longer required for young pigs and then begin accumulating goods for the next ceremony.

With contacts and as roads have developed, coastal goods, especially shells, have become more plentiful. There has been a great increase in the amount of shell, especially goldlip mother of pearl, displayed and exchanged. Cloth, plastic beads, leather, and other clothing and ornaments have augmented and supplemented many traditional forms. Colored paints are used in traditional patterns (Strathern and Strathern 1971). Many ceremonies are larger and more frequent. At the same time the exchange values have changed. Money is used in transactions, and there has been some diversion of interests into cash cropping and labor for wages. All this has drastically changed the quantity and variety of goods worn, used, and exchanged. Some groups lost interest in traditional exchange, at least for a time. But the highlanders take great pride and pleasure in self-adornment at large festivals in which the group's beauty and wealth are displayed.

DIET, HEALTH, AND DISEASE

The highlanders grow most of their food. However, all people consume some uncultivated plants and captured or hunted insects, birds, marsupials, reptiles, and other game foods.

While there is much variation between areas, seasons and individuals, the highlands people's diet is dominated by the sweet potato which everywhere provides over 70 percent of the calories. The woman prepares food for her children and usually for her husband. In the morning any leftover cooked sweet potato tubers are eaten, and fresh sweet potatoes and other foods may be roasted in embers. The husband may have his own supply, obtain some from his house-mates, or go to his wife's house for some breakfast. During the day small snacks are taken: uncooked bananas, peanuts, sugarcane to chew, and perhaps children catch or pick insects, grubs, lizards, wild or cultivated fruits, nuts, and vegetables, only occasionally heating these on a fire. The men often pause in their work to smoke,

using any nearby fire to ignite a handrolled cigarette. Women usually carry some food in their bags. The nutritional value of these
casual snacks is the most difficult to measure and evaluate. The diet
nearly everywhere in the highlands is now supplemented with imported foods, of which the most common are rice, bread, biscuits,
meat, fish, salt, and sugar.

The largest meal is eaten in late afternoon or evening. It consists
usually of sweet potatoes, washed and peeled, and a variety of other
foods, all steam-cooked in a drum or earth oven with hot stones and
leaves. This meal is shared by the family, visitors, and pets. Pigs also
eat uncooked food, discards, and peelings. Sweet potatoes are the
main food at every meal, with other tubers rarely eaten in any
quantity.

Seasonally, the proportion of greens, nuts, and other foods varies.
Oil pandanus and nut pandanus rich in fat and protein are shared at
seasonal feasts. At a feast, perhaps once a month, there may be up to
a pound of meat or some special vegetable food, but most people
have no more than a few ounces of protein and fat-rich foods on
festive occasions. The daily average is a few grams.

A much greater variety of food is eaten among the lower altitude
and fringe peoples who grow more taro, yam, and banana than the
highlanders. These people may also eat a wider variety of fruits,
vegetables, and animal foods from both cultivated and wild sources.
Central highlanders' diet is predominantly sweet potato. The remaining foods include leafy greens, edible stalks (pitpit), yams, taro,
manioc, beans, bananas, sugarcane, corn, pumpkin, and miscel-
laneous plant and animal foods; all of which are nutritionally very
important (see Tables 2 and 3).

Most important, from the nutritional standpoint, are the total
calories, carbohydrate, fat, protein, and essential nutritional elements of the diet. A predominantly sweet potato diet is deficient in
protein and fat and lacks some essential amino acids. People on this
diet may have an adequate calorie and carbohydrate intake, vitamins
and minerals, but be undernourished as measured by weight-height
proportions and muscle tissue. The nutritional value of highlands'
beans, greens, nuts, and other foods is not fully known. Some recent
studies indicate that some of these are rich in protein and fat.

In highland society, infants are nursed for an unusually long time,

Table 2. *Percentage weight in diet of various foods*

	Tsembaga Maring (Rappaport) 1968	Modopa Enga (Waddell) 1972	Pari Chimbu (Hipsley & Kirk) 1965
Sweet potato	21	63	77
Taro	26	—	6
Yam and manioc	10	9	—
Banana	8	—	4
Green leaves	10	7	3
Pork	1	1.5	2
Beans and corn	—	5	3
Sugarcane	—	7	—
Other vegetables, fruits, and nuts	21	5	5

Note: The several studies grouped foods somewhat differently, so that the blanks do not necessarily mean that none of the food was available–only that it was not separately noted. Different studies in the same region may have striking variations: e.g., Sinnett reports for Enga 90 percent sweet potatoes with only 5 percent nontuberous vegetables (1972).

and given solid food, usually green stalks (pitpit), leaves, banana, sweet potato, and other soft foods as a supplement at the age of six months or older, after some teeth have erupted. From the ages of six months to three years the amount of breast milk in the infants' diet declines and that of solid food increases. Weaning is gradual, usually complete at three to five years. These practices may result in depletion of calcium, vitamin D, protein, and calorie deficiency in lactating women. The conditions may persist in pregnancy, leading to oedema and weight loss.

Highland babies apparently thrive for their first few months on mother's milk. As they grow they must adapt to the normal diet of vegetables, and the quantity of watery carbohydrate sweet potato consumed may strain their stomachs without adequately nourishing them: Young children often have protuberant abdomens and thin limbs. A baby's first solid foods are not highly nutritious, and there has been some attempt to introduce peanut paste, rich in protein and fat, or other legumes as a supplement. Peanuts are a new crop,

Table 3. *Dietary nutrients*

	Chimbu[a]		Maring Tsembaga[b]		Modopa[c] Enga	Tukisenta[d] Enga	
	Male	Female	Male	Female		Male	Female
Calories	2,360	1,605	2,130	1,735	2,400	2,300	1,770
Protein (gm.)	19.9	16.9	32	32	32	25.3	20.2
Fat (gm.)	5.5	7.2	—	—	15	6.2	7.4
Calcium (mg.)	811	558	640	640	400	—	—
Iron (mg.)	15.8	11.8	—	—	15.5	—	—
Carotene (I.U.)	14,050	11,620	—	—	5,000	—	—
Thiamin (mg.)	2.1	1.4	—	—	2	—	—
Riboflavin (mg.)	1.2	.9	—	—	1.1	—	—
Niacin (mg.)	12.1	8.9	—	—	13	—	—
Vitamin C (mg.)	542	368	—	—	430	—	—

Note: Where no figure is given, author did not give this information.
[a]Hipsley & Kirk 1965. [b]Rappaport 1968. [c]Average of 2 periods. Cf. Waddell 1972, p. 126. Data are for both males and females. [d]Sinnett & Whyte 1973.

grown for consumption and sale. The preparation for infants requires roasting in the shell, shelling, taking peanuts to a community grinder, preparing the paste, and storing it for regular feeding to infants and toddlers. This is a great change in family feeding habits, and one which parents only follow under careful supervision. General nutritional education is necessary. More recently, increased quantities of beans have been recommended for children. These may require less special preparation than peanut paste and be better adapted to family practice.

Poor infant nutrition results in slow growth and liability to infections, dysentery, worms, and liver damage. These nutritional problems are more serious in some localities where poor soils, inadequate salts, or other mineral shortages are present and in others where an extreme reliance upon sweet potato, absence of other foods, or periodic food shortage has occurred. Some foods rich in needed elements – such as nuts, meats, legumes – may be given primarily to adults, thus depriving youngsters of foods otherwise available. Ailing babies suffering with gastroenteritis and dysentery may suffer from shortage of liquids and be unable to digest the foods they are given at a crucial time. Thus temporary nutritional deficiencies may contribute to serious illness and infection, with long-term effects.

Food preferences and practices which restrict the food eaten by certain individuals and groups often have an important, if sometimes temporary, beneficial or damaging effect on nutrition and health. Short-term taboos during ritual periods are commonly enforced, often resulting in greater supplies for a feast. During initiation of groups of boys in New Guinea, liquids may be withheld to develop stamina. Certain foods believed to promote masculine strength are provided the boys, and others are prohibited. Pregnant and lactating women may eat leaves, sugarcane, or other foods thought to be good for mother and baby. Girls at first menstruation are given certain varieties of sweet potatoes, grubs, and leaves to prevent excessive loss of blood and give strength. Pigs are fed certain foods and mineral soil to make them healthy and fat. Such special feeding is often accompanied by spells to ward off evil spirits or gain spiritual assistance for health, recovery, or success. People in delicate health, or recovering from childbirth, are given special foods such as the meat of birds, rats, chicken or pig, and certain varieties of banana. Foods are given to celebrate changes in status and achievements. Ginger and salt are added to flavor meat at feasts. Some rare foods are especially grown for such occasions, and game is provided for some ceremonial feasts.

Very rarely, perhaps two or three times in a lifetime, a highlander may eat a great amount of meat at a feast. The ill effects of these excesses may be serious when pig-bel (*enteritis necroticans*), an acute inflammation of the small intestine, results. This disease, whose effects resemble those of food poisoning, was identified and treated by radical surgery and antibiotics in the 1960s. It follows large-scale feasts, in which children and adults consume unaccustomed quantities of pork infected with *Clostridium bacilli*. Apparently, boys are most affected by the disease, which has been found in many communities after feasts when pork cooked in traditional earth ovens is eaten some days afterwards. A vaccine has now been developed to prevent it.

The multitude of food practices – presenting and eating certain foods or varieties and prohibiting others at particular times or life events – shows a great development of beliefs about the qualities of particular foods. But the reporting of these beliefs is not enough to draw conclusions about the extent and effect of these special practices on the general health of the highlanders. If anything, only short-term effects may follow the special ritual meals and medicinal plants given to the ill, pubertal, or participants in a ritual. But the small amounts of meat, nuts, beans, fruits, greens, fats, salts, and other wild or domestic foods containing nutrients not found in sweet potatoes may be essential to health. Women and children may eat more nutritious snacks of insects and small animals than do men, who get a larger share of pig meat. A comparison of adult size and diet studies in highland communities is shown in Table 4.

The figures in Table 4 vary seasonally, in different regions, and according to the number of women who are pregnant or lactating. In general, however, compared to other New Guinea diets, the highland sweet potato diet is least supplemented by other foods.

Cooking methods also affect food choices. The tubers may be dry roasted alone in embers, whereas small vegetables, leaves, beans, and so forth are included with sweet potatoes in earth-oven cooking in which hot stones and leaf wrappings are used. A metal pot for boiling, and use of rice and canned meats and fish are all very recent. Their effect on nutrition is not yet known. However, the study by Lambert in 1975 found an increase in height and weight of Chimbu children and adults compared to 1956.

Sweet potatoes are rich in phosphorus and sodium and contain some calcium and other minerals. Carotene and niacene content varies with variety; ascorbic acid content is high, thiamine low to moderate. In general, children and adults eat adequate quantities of food, and while they have less of many elements than other peoples, they rarely experience nutritional deficiencies. However, especially

Table 4. *Height, weight, and diet of men and women*

	Weight in kg.	Height in cm.	Average daily calories	% Sweet potato
Men	47–61	154–161	1900–2400	71–94
Women	46–56	145–153	1290–2540	72–89

in times of illness, shortage or failure of mother's milk, infants and young children may be undernourished and permanently damaged. Two very serious diseases, marasmus and kwashiorkor, have been observed in children, and liver cirrhosis may be a result affecting adults. A high infant mortality rate may be a secondary effect; a malnourished child is prone to respiratory or other infections. Nonetheless, in many areas the population has recently been increasing at over 2 percent annually.

Studies of nutrition and health in the highlands have found serious deficiencies in a few areas. Some of them may be temporary, seasonal, or result from a change in diet. For example, in preparing for a feast especially large amounts of sweet potatoes are used to fatten pigs and great quantities are also served to the guests at the feast. A community may then experience a shortage until newly planted gardens begin to produce. Frosts and dry periods slow the ripening and may kill part of the growing crop. The food supplies may be affected by weather or by demands of other activities, which cause temporary or longer shortages. From day to day the amount and kind of food consumed varies with the amount of work, harvesting, and celebrations. While general practices of reciprocity and sharing usually distribute the food available, some individuals and families may be inadequately fed because of some incapacity. In times of warfare families and communities are sometimes driven off their home lands and lose their gardens, perhaps to seek sanctuary with neighbors and relatives with inadequate food resources. This produces both short-term and long-term effects in terms of diet and health.

Studies of children and mothers at times of food shortage show that they are most severely affected – the children malnourished and the mothers having oedema in late pregnancy and during lactation. Liver cirrhosis and other protein deficiency diseases in children and adults can also be traced to early malnutrition.

A study of growth rates and patterns in the Bundi area shows what may be an extreme case. Here some dietary deficiency was found but little malnutritional disease, although growth rates are slow and height and weight levels are low. Full growth is reached between the ages of twenty and twenty-nine. The girls of Chimbu reach menarche at the average age of 17.5; those of Bundi at 18.6.

This compares with twelve to thirteen years in Europe and fourteen to seventeen in Africa. While these processes may be genetically determined in part, supplementary feeding and dietary changes have a remarkable effect upon those treated in hospitals and residing at boarding schools. Life expectancy at Bundi is low, and liver damage, from malaria and perhaps inadequate protein, is prevalent, especially among men (Bergmann, personal communication, 1976).

Studies of physical condition, health, and strength all show adult New Guinea highlanders, and particularly those of the Wahgi Valley area, to be remarkably healthy. Physical fitness measured in standard tests is generally good, and the adjustment to living and working in the highland environment seems excellent. Tests of middle-aged and elderly people show some effects of a low-protein and low-fat diet in low-cholesterol levels and a decrease in weight and in height with age. The reduction in fat and muscle is greater for females than males, an indication of the effects of pregnancy and lactation with low protein and fat consumption.

Observers of highland people wondered how they could perform so well in tests of physical fitness when their diet, by Western standards, was so poor in protein and fat. Further studies of nitrogen balance, metabolism, and the analysis of chemical content of food and excreta had some unexpected results. One study suggests that nitrogen, the element usually associated with protein foods, may be produced in the body of highlanders because little is present in their foods. The nitrogen may be produced by heat, the storage of nutrients, or in a bacterium, *clostridium*, found in the small intestine. The nitrogen production may be an adaptation to a low-protein diet, and when pork is eaten in quantity at a feast this may affect the bacteria so that *enteritis necroticans* develops. This suggests that the health and vigor of highlanders is adapted to their usual diet and a great increase in meat protein would require a new biological adaptation (cf. Hipsley 1969; Oomen & Cordon 1970).

This brings into question some nutritional assumptions about pig raising and feasting. The feasting patterns have been regarded as giving people inadequate protein most of the time and excessive or wasteful quantities at feasts. Rappaport regards rare pork feasts and sacrifices as providing valuable nutritive additions to the normal diet at times of crisis, stress, and illness (Rappaport 1968). Pork is shared by relatives of the newly married, new born, pubertal, and bereaved when a pig gift or exchange is required to mark a change in status. Intergroup exchanges and compensation payment on a smaller scale similarly distribute small amounts of pork and sometimes other luxury foods such as cassowary, marsupials, eels, pandanus nuts, oil pandanus, and nowadays peanuts, canned or fresh beef, horse meat, and fish.

These occasions of smaller distributions probably do contribute to health by providing more frequent small quantities of protein and fat-rich foods. It is probable that men receive more of this festive food than women and children do, sharing it among the residents of the recipients' men's house and inviting kinsmen to share the meal. The social and psychological effects of pork consumption are also important; the donor and recipient both benefit, and many people enjoy a rare festive meal. The excessive quantity eaten by some at the largest feasts, however, surely contributes mainly to social and psychological satisfactions, and the possible ill effects are now recognized in particular diseases such as *enteritis necroticans*.

The largest feasts and overindulgence occur in a few areas only: Chimbu, the central Wahgi Valley, Dani of the Balim Valley, Kapauku of Wissel Lakes, central Enga in *te* festivals, Melpa in *moka* festivals, and heavily settled highland areas where agriculture is intensive and sweet potatoes are used as pig food. Possibly having fewer pigs and smaller feasts are Maring, most of the eastern and southern highlands of Papua New Guinea, and marginal peoples of the highlands where agriculture is less intensive and fewer pigs are raised.

Many highlanders eat little salt, and the occasional additions of salt to festive meals are often potassium salts which are prepared from plants and ash. Potassium is plentiful in the vegetable diet, so that the added salt does not fill a nutritional need. Sodium salts are prepared from salt springs, traded, and used in exchanges and feasts. These may be more significant in terms of nutrition. Native prepared salts have now been almost wholly supplanted by imported salt.

Special local conditions may also affect health. In New Guinea, in the Jimi and Simbai area, among the Maring, high rates of goiter and endemic cretinism were found in the 1960s. When patients were treated with iodinized oil, dramatic improvement resulted. Further study here shows that the native forms of salt contain adequate supplies of iodine, but when manufactured salt was first introduced, iodine deficiency and its effects were apparent. The continued provision of iodine in some form appears to be required.

DISEASE PATTERNS

The central highlanders are notably heavier and more muscular than most of the mountain people, some of whom have been called pygmy. However, improved health and diet have a marked effect on increasing size and weight of these people once believed to be undersized by genetic factors. The general condition of inland New Guineans is a high incidence of enteric and respiratory disease, especially among children. The traditional house has a central fire and little light or fresh air, nights are cold, and neither people nor their scanty body coverings are often washed. Respiratory diseases –colds, pneumonia, epidemic influenza, and some tuberculosis – are a major cause of illness and death in the highlands. At one survey 14.3 percent of adults in Tukisenta, Enga had respiratory disease. This percentage increases as the age of the population being studied increases. Other common diseases are dental caries, periodontal disease, meningitis, eye diseases, and liver enlargement. There are some parasite and worm infections, including *ascaris*.

Malaria is found throughout New Guinea, but apparently has not always been present in the highlands. The mosquito which carries the disease breeds in warm and moist places, and in the same region those who occupy and remain on higher slopes suffer less. Malaria in the highlands may be seasonal and many areas are little affected. People may contract malaria when traveling or visiting malarial areas and then become ill on their return home. The wet mountain fringe and low-lying river basins are more infected than the upland central highlands. As the moist land of the Wahgi Valley has been drained and houses sprayed to destroy mosquitoes, much new land has become available for settlement. Previously these areas were avoided for fear of illness. Children often have enlarged spleen and liver connected with malaria. Yaws was prevalent, but has been nearly controlled by modern treatment. Leprosy is irregularly distributed, and unusually common in the Karimui area. A study of exposure shows that those in the closest physical contact with a diseased person are in the greatest risk of infection. In a community where males and females occupy separate sections of the house or separate houses, transmission is more commonly to contacts of the same sex.

A most puzzling disease syndrome, kuru, the "laughing disease," was discovered among the Fore of the eastern highlands in the 1950s. It is a neurological disorder affecting children and women, rarely men, which involves trembling, progressive deterioration, with loss of muscular control, usually ending in death within a year. The disease is mostly restricted to the Fore but has spread somewhat to their neighbors. Early studies considered genetic causes but cannibalism by relatives is now known to be the mode of transmission of the pathogenic agent as Gajdusek and others have shown (Glasse 1967). A long period of incubation made tracing this most difficult. Since the practice of cannibalism has virtually stopped, kuru is disappearing. The selective susceptibility of women and children seems due to their practice of eating the brains of a deceased person, where the pathogenic element is concentrated. Men rarely consumed human flesh and only a few were the victims of kuru. The Fore held mourning ceremonies for their kinsmen, and then dismembered and cooked the corpse, dividing the meat among women and children. Among some eastern highlands people, men consumed the bodies of enemies. They did not eat women. Desire for meat, and pleasure in eating meat, is the main reason advanced for cannibalism in Fore. But pork is fairly plentiful here, too. As will be explained later, Fore believe that kuru is the result of sorcery.

Public health services, with regional hospitals and local aidposts supervised by trained orderlies, have improved diagnosis and treatment of many ailments. Latrines, personal hygiene, pest controls, improved housing, clothing, and cleanliness in food preparation are all affecting health and disease control. These changes are the results of health and welfare service, education, and the blankets, soap, and other manufactured products which are now imported and used. They are part of the development program which also results in increased life expectancy and population increase.

BEHAVIOR AND BELIEF ABOUT ILLNESS

In the highlands, few ailments are believed to be of "natural" causes, that is, uninfluenced by sorcerers, ancestor ghosts, or spirits. Many accidents as well as illness are considered due to the malevolent actions of sorcerers, witches, or spirits. Headaches, dizziness, or mental aberrations, and running amok may be caused by ghosts and spirits. Each area and language group knows numerous local forest, water, and bush spirits which may attack and harm people, causing specific or general illness, skin rash, swellings, fevers, and death.

In Chimbu, the *dingan* spirit is in swamps and soft ground. It will take mucus or blood which is allowed to fall, then cause grave illness to the victim – especially eye disease, weakness, emaciation. The ghosts of angry ancestors who have not received sacrifice are also believed to cause illness. Thus a pig may be killed at a cemetery and the ancestors, appeased, alleviate the illness. The Chimbu may invoke the sun, as a god, to cure a sick person.

Women during menstruation are believed to be especially liable to pollute food and water, which can cause illness to men who eat or touch such things. It is believed that an angry wife may deliberately harm her husband by giving him such food; if they have intercourse while she is menstruating, he may become seriously ill.

The Hewa explain misfortune and death by the actions of cannibal witches (Steadman 1975). The witches accused are mostly women and old men. These may be allowed less meat in family and public meals, so may be assumed to crave human flesh. Miyanmin of the Telefomin area are said to practice enemy cannibalism and raid neighboring peoples to obtain meat. Jalé, a Dani group, say they eat enemy dead: The body of a victim is carried back home by the victors, cooked, and eaten in a feast which celebrates a successful revenge killing (Koch 1974). A known person is not eaten. Such cannibalistic practices might be classed nutritionally as sharing of game, with a small addition of meat to the diet. Neither pets nor friends can be considered game. Cannibalism, both of kinsmen and of enemies, is reported as of sporadic distribution in New Guinea, and has mostly ceased. Its former frequency cannot be assessed. No fully documented account has been presented. Its occurrence does not follow any rule: Some people with the least meat regard the practice with horror, and others with more pork and game say they relish human flesh, too.

A curious form of affliction or madness, or amok behavior, is described as affecting individuals in different areas. It is often said to be the result of eating a rare food – certain mushrooms in the Wahgi Valley, pandanus nuts in Chimbu, seeds or other foods elsewhere – but similar behavior may be exhibited without eating anything unusual. Attack by ghosts or spirits is sometimes thought to be the cause. The afflicted appears out of contact with his surroundings, deaf, excited, and dazed. It may be said to be hereditary, especially in men. They demand and take goods, brandish weapons, threaten bystanders, and chase about for hours. The bystanders may flee and view the spectacle at a distance. Some observers think the behavior may be simulated to attract attention and divert an audience, and little damage is caused. The afflicted individual relapses into ordinary behavior after this attack. No specific toxic substances have been identified in the foods considered responsible, but the frenzied behavior does resemble that induced by certain chemicals elsewhere. One is inclined to conclude that the belief and practice may have some occasional chemical origin, but most frenzy behavior is culturally learned and practiced for release and diversion, both of the person apparently afflicted and the onlookers.

The belief that illness may be caused by accidental injury, demons or spirits, ghosts, or breaking taboos is reported in many highland societies. The Enga attribute most injuries, illness, and death to malevolent ghosts, usually a father or brother of the victim. Appeasement of the ghost by killing a pig is the proper response; if that fails, a diviner may find that the sacrifice is insufficient. Kyaka also blame ghosts for illness and kill pigs to placate them. However, among other highlanders, serious illness and death are attributed to witchcraft or sorcery most frequently.

The sorcery beliefs are varied and complex, with many forms of divination and diagnosis, treatment, and attempts to remove the evil agent and cure the patient. Sorcery may use personal leavings of the victim. Commonly, a form of poison is thought responsible; the underlying idea is that disease is caused by the action of the poison in the body. There is a wide range of beliefs about magical properties of plant and animal substances, how a victim's soul can be attacked, what kinds of disabilities can be produced, and how the malevolent sources of power can be eliminated and the victim restored to health.

Witchcraft, the belief that a witch has magical powers not involving the use of poison or other substances to harm others, is also common among highlanders. Among highland peoples in the Chimbu area and adjacent parts of the eastern highlands, witchcraft is thought to occur within the group. They commonly accuse witches in the same local group as the victim, whereas most others feel that sorcerers and witches operate from enemy groups. The distinction is important, for a sorcerer or witch in the community endangers mutual trust and cooperation, and thus all efforts are made to identify and remove or incapacitate the attacker. In Chimbu a married woman accused of witchcraft may be exiled from the community, killed, or forced to return to her kin group. Elsewhere, the danger is from a witch of an enemy group, and retaliatory sorcery or war may be the possible responses. Divination to determine the cause and witch responsible for a death is reported in many cases. Where witches and sorcerers are always believed to be outsiders, the enmity between communities is reinforced and intragroup solidarity is not threatened, but no cure or disease control results (see Chapter 5).

While these beliefs are prevalent people exercise some care, preserving, concealing, or destroying any personal leavings so that sorcerers may not use them. But those forms of wizardry that depend on spells, smoke, and propelling objects into the victim cannot be so controlled, and the many peculiar techniques of sorcerers remain esoteric and unpredictable. For this reason beliefs may persist and new forms may be imagined without any evidence of sorcery practice. The prevalence of kuru disease in Fore made it an important focus for sorcery belief; in this case, accusations were made against nearby enemy districts. But other diseases and deaths are also attributed by Fore to sorcery. They try to prevent enemy sorcerers from obtaining personal leavings or contaminating water holes. Accusations of sorcery are sometimes the beginnings of fights and migrations.

An accident, sprain, cut, burn, or sore may be treated by leaf bandages, vegetable infusions, and smoke. Therapeutic plants may be applied to wounds mixed with pork grease and blood. Plant and animal materials are also prepared to be eaten. At times a serious illness calls for a pig sacrifice, in which the victim and his family have a meal of pork and vegetables, including special herbs, salt, and ginger. A diviner or specialist whose ability is recognized may be called in to divine the cause and to recommend and prepare the treatment. Spells often accompany the medicine. Smoke and breath are common symbols in diagnosis and treatment of illness, including those thought to be caused by witchcraft.

Among many highland groups there is a close association between the presence or loss of blood and sexual maturity. Thus women menstruate at puberty, and young men must purge themselves of "bad" blood by forced nose bleeding or other bloodletting. The operation may be repeated to cleanse men of the polluting contact with women and restore their masculinity.

Healing is not always limited to the patient, but often requires the cooperation or assistance of family to provide the materials, participate in a therapeutic meal, pay a practitioner, or avenge the death. The practices show how a sick person is part of his family and local group: If he is incapacitated, all must suffer; if a sorcerer has killed him and is unavenged, others in the group will be the next victims. In the New Guinea highlands, sickness and death are group concerns; the dependence or loss of a member affects the group's capacities. Thus the group needs to correct its loss by cure, when possible, or revenge to equalize groups once again.

2

Agriculture and population

This chapter presents the main ecological data and analysis of the book: the relationship between population and agriculture in the highlands. In the last chapter, environment, resources, and technology were viewed as basic to highlands culture. The setting for highlands cultural development can be seen in time perspective as agriculture and technology become distinct and more intensive, in contrast to the fringe peoples who continue to live in small, widely-separated communities, subsisting upon a variety of foodstuffs, wild and domestic. Highlands agriculture is more complex and specialized in the cultivation of sweet potatoes and raising of pigs. On this subsistence base the population of the highlands increased, and reached high densities in some areas. This was accompanied by the development of intensified agricultural practices and the individualization of land tenure. This chapter shows the interrelationship of land, agriculture, and population.

It begins with a general discussion of agricultural intensity, measures of agricultural production, and land use; then describes and compares highlanders' agriculture and pig raising. The next section considers population, the distribution of peoples, and population density. It examines the relationships between competition, population growth, and agricultural intensity, and shows that four areas have become centers of agricultural development and population growth. A statistical analysis of the relationship, with a measure of agricultural intensity, settlement form, land tenure, density, and group size is presented at the end of the chapter.

AGRICULTURE

MEASURING AGRICULTURAL INTENSITY

To understand and evaluate a subsistence agricultural economic system, a number of elements may be examined. While many measures and approaches can be used, the final consideration is the yield or productivity of the land. This can be defined or measured in several ways, to produce somewhat different results. The many forms of agriculture practiced by the world's farmers, and even by gardeners in New Guinea, show how different aims and living conditions are managed. For example, we can suggest ways of measuring the output – how much is produced in a standard area such as per acre or per hectare (about 2.5 acres or 10,000 square meters) – over a specified period of time, usually a year to correspond with outputs of temperate regions where the annual variation in weather usually results in a single crop season.

The yield, in weight or bulk, of a particular crop can be measured or compared if a standard is used. Sweet potatoes or other tubers can be weighed in pounds or kilograms while some yields can also or alternatively be measured in bushels, gallons, or some other bulk measure. But we might measure either the corn cobs as harvested or the kernels as processed. Studies have shown that some crop varieties have a higher usable yield. The yield could be evaluated in other terms, for example, calories per area. Sweet potato yield might be evaluated in terms of food requirements: How many people can be fed from the land? This could be compared to a population that is supported on another crop, in another place or in the same environment.

Where one community grows several major crops, the productivity of one may be much more than that of another – more weight, more bulk, more calories, more people fed. There may also be more food value – more calories, more protein, more vitamins or minerals – in some crops or some varieties than in others. This may not be known to the cultivators; they may prefer the taste or the texture of a low-protein variety, or they may not eat the mineral-rich outer husk of a plant. Thus our measures of the food content and yield of crops may not be measures of the nutrition of people who consume it. This could only be accurately measured by a complete study of agricultural practices, food preparation, and diet. Yet our real concern is how many people are and can be nourished by the food which is and can be produced on the land used and available.

The measurements of yield or productivity may be made in terms of all the land available, which would include much land not in cultivation. The whole territory might consist of farms in cultivation and production, farms temporarily out of cultivation, all forms of grassland, fallow, wasteland, grazing land, forest, settlements, rocky slopes, ponds, lakes, rivers and their banks, swamps, and sites used for special purposes such as cemeteries, ceremonial grounds, industrial areas, and areas used for crops which are sold and not consumed, such as rubber or coffee. When the total area is considered, there is an enormous variation in productivity. Such a study in a sparsely settled region where less than 1 percent of the land is in cultivation will show an extremely low productivity. But where little forest, bush, grass, or wasteland remains and most of the land is regularly cultivated, a far different productivity will appear. This does not necessarily mean that the land is well managed or intensely cultivated; the particular agricultural practices in use may result in high or low yield per area of land in cultivation.

If the study concentrated on measuring the yield per acre of land in cultivation – weighing the produce or counting the calories – the results might show how much food is produced in different agricultural systems. If the same foods, or at least the same type of foods, are grown, different conditions or techniques can be compared as to their productivity. But to compare different techniques and different crops would show a general productivity without demonstrating its causes. To take such general productivity measures as a recommendation to change crops and techniques is to suggest that the local conditions of environment and tradition are negligible. In order to understand the interrelations of environment, agricultural practices, and land use, we may compare these throughout an area where there are general similarities, and examine the local differences. Even in the same community, different practices may be adapted to different land types, crops, and weather conditions with measurably different results. Because of his land, his work habits, timing, or choice of planting material, one farmer may produce more food than his neighbor who uses much the same agricultural technique.

Comparisons, then, may not produce understanding because they do not compare the same areas, crops, or practices. The comparison of yield or productivity figures needs careful analysis of the bases of the measurements being compared. There are many elements, and it may be more informative or valuable for prediction to use certain elements rather than others.

The most important elements in an agricultural system and the evaluation of productivity are land, technology, and labor. They lead to different kinds of productivity measures, and may be appropriate to different situations of population and technology. However, it can also be claimed that land use can be intensified only up to a point of permanent use, and any further increases in productivity must be by intensification of labor and technology.

LAND AND FALLOW

The agricultural technique known as extensive, shifting, or swidden, which consists of clearing or partially clearing the land to be cultivated from forest or bush, planting one or a mixture of crops, harvesting each as they ripen, and allowing wild plants to reestablish themselves, is the least intensive. The fallen brush may remain, and garden crops be sparsely planted with a low yield. In such areas as the mountains of the highland fringe of New Guinea, such gardens may occupy .001 percent of the land at any time, and never be made in exactly the same place. Or, more intensively, at an average one year of cultivation is followed by fifty years of forest regeneration. A succession of herbs, grasses, shrubs, and trees grows in the former garden. Some of these are used for food or manufactures. Such an area may never contain all the vegetation and size of the primary forest. Permanent grasslands, or a slow regeneration of secondary forest, may develop. Some favored spots may be cultivated more often because they are more convenient – closer to other areas of activity, better sited, or protected – whereas less desirable sites are never used. Water supply, wood, fruiting trees, insects, enemies, and other nonagricultural considerations may determine garden sites. The more direct considerations are the difficulty of cutting different kinds of forest growth, the availability of sunlight, soil differences, and altitude and slope of land in different parts of the territory. Such considerations are resolved both by individuals and small groups who choose between the alternatives available in terms of their knowledge and desires.

Some land is never cleared for gardens, being considered inaccessible, unsuitable, or otherwise undesirable and not required; for the people concerned, this land may be defined as nonarable or uncultivable. Certainly, other people using other techniques or other crops may define it differently. But in any area, from the point of view of the local population, some land may be nonarable. Such land may be highly valued for its stones, trees, woods, vines, fruits, or other products, or set aside for residential, industrial, hunting, or sacred use. It is then an important part of group or private territory but not cultivated.

All land defined as arable is available for cultivation, and it may be planted with crops continuously, frequently, or rarely. From the examination of cultivation practice over time and the alternation of cultivation and fallow or frequency of use we can measure the intensity of land use in terms of frequency of cultivation. Such a measure is needed for studies of population density and intensity of agriculture. The categories or types of intensity can be scaled or classified, for example, as in Boserup (1976:15–16): (1) forest fallow, shifting cultivation or long fallow – one to two years cultivation and twenty to twenty-five years fallow; (2) bush fallow or short fallow – one or more years of cultivation followed by six to ten years of fallow, thus a rotation of fallow and cultivation; and (3) short fallow – fallow period short and grass rather than bush is usual.

In this classification the time of fallow rather than the kind of wild growth is the criterion. But there are other correlates of this: Certain plants may continue or be encouraged in the fallow to provide herbs, fodder, food, other goods, or wood. Thus the fallow period may actually provide for alternative types of land use in a land production cycle. This leads also to permanent land ownership, where the use of fallow or rotational crops is controlled by the landowner. On the other hand, in long fallow the boundaries of a former garden are lost and the next cultivation in the cycle is likely to be by another gardener. Boserup's other categories of use are most likely to be in systems of individual landownership and some sort of continuous use: (4) annual cropping – land left uncultivated for only a few months, with perhaps a rotation of crops which may include a grass fodder; and (5) multicropping in which one plot bears two or more successive crops a year – may be the same crop or a rotation, but land is rarely left in fallow and is usually nourished by fertilization or irrigation.

This system provides a scale of frequency of land use from extensive or shifting to intensive or permanent cultivation. Other classifications and further distinctions are possible, and the study of any region may suggest a typology more specific to the practice there. Shortening fallow is only one form of agricultural intensity. The relationship between shifting gardens and shifting settlements is not exact: A people with a regular fallow cycle and limited land do not necessarily move their residence frequently, and may continuously reside at the same place.

Fallow time is an essential element in the assessment of the capacity of an agricultural system to provide food to subsistence farmers. But it may not be consistent, even within a region. The comparison of systems on this basis alone is insufficient to our understanding. Furthermore, as Boserup and others have noted, the same people may have different intensity practices for different crops, land, and situations. Particularly common in sites of permanent or long-term settlement is a small mixed garden adjacent to the house where fresh greens, vegetables, and fruits are continuously available and often multicropped, whereas the staple foods are grown in an extensive cropping system to be harvested seasonally or irregularly in larger quantities. Fallow time may not be the same in extensive cropping. The houseyard garden may be made more productive by fertilization with household rubbish or by watering. Not only are different crops and practices followed, but they also may provide different parts of the diet.

ENERGY INPUT AND TECHNOLOGY

Another aspect of agricultural intensity is the energy output: How much work is required to produce a given quantity of a crop or to feed one person? The work may be measured in time, including the production or repair of tools, land clearing, digging, planting, tending, harvesting, carrying, preparing, and cooking. It could include some subsidiary activities such as gathering materials and building fences and collecting herbs, water, and firewood. Rather than measuring time we might measure human energy in metabolism, since we know that people need and use more calories when they chop trees and carry loads up mountains than when at rest. Studies of energy use can only be estimates from experiments, but we can set out some general considerations in labor for agriculture.

Different crops and techniques require very different labor practices, but any estimate of work input must consider the time needed for different agricultural operations. The tools used must also be considered. In New Guinea the highlanders used stone axes or adzes for the heaviest jobs – gardening and felling of forest trees to clear the land – until a few years ago. As soon as steel axes became available, they replaced stone. Tests of timing have been made with swidden cultivators who have used both tools, and it was found that it takes about four times as long to fell a tree with a stone axe as with a steel one. The size of trees, which varies between long-fallow and short-fallow systems, also affects the time ratio.

The variable labor input in a New Guinea subsistence agricultural system can be seen by following a garden from its inception through the crop and fallow. The site may be selected by a group, when pioneering or establishing a new settlement, and some activities may be cooperative. Cooperative labor is sometimes called upon by settled highlanders in reopening a large area or for fencing. However, most projects are done by hand, with an axe or stick, so that a group's effort is by the accumulation of individual efforts, not a change in type. The sociable work-group encourages greater effort, but there may be more rest periods with this type of effort.

If it is heavily forested with large trees, the underbrush may be more easily removed and main branches lopped off, or the trees on a slope may be toppled by a "domino effect" after trees are partially cut and the area made ready. But clearing may be minimal, and plants or seeds placed among the fallow or slashed bush. The bush may be cleared later, or never. Obviously fewer garden plants will grow in such a partial clearing; the density of garden plants will be low.

Many swidden cultivators use an axe to chop wood and a stick to uproot grass. They dry and burn grass and bush to make a clearing. Burning destroys some weeds and seeds. The resultant ash acts as a fertilizer to the new garden. The extreme of clearing is clean-weeding. Not a leaf or blade of the fallow or forest cover remains: A bare soil surface results. This can be tilled with a hoe or spade to make ridges, level, furrows, mounds, ditches, or any other form for planting. A plough may do the same, and results in a characteristic leveling, furrowing, or ridging. At this point a compost, mulch, or fertilizer may also be used. In the New Guinea highlands one stage of land preparation may involve leading pigs into the area where they are allowed to consume any remaining food crops, roots, insects, and other herbage. In the process, they both overturn and fertilize the field. Some specially adaptive forms of ridging, ditching, mounding, and mulching are practiced by highlanders. In land preparation the highlanders' agriculture is labor intensive; sweet potatoes receive especially intensive care.

Where pigs are reared in numbers and settlement is dense, the pigs must be kept out of the fields of growing sweet potatoes. Fence patterns vary with density and community land-settlement patterns. Thus, fencing is often a concern of a group of farmers on adjacent plots who must protect their crops. The wood and vines used for fences may be taken from the land in clearing or from nearby bush. Both the construction and repair of fences involve much time, although the work is not always arduous. Differences in fence types, and the time of construction, is a variable in the highlands.

ENVIRONMENT, WATER, AND NUTRIENTS

Water and drainage control may be practiced and adapted to certain crops and types of terrain. Thus taro, a probable precursor to sweet potatoes in New Guinea, requires moist growing conditions and is often planted where water collects, whereas yams do best in well drained or raised beds. Sweet potatoes need moderately dry conditions and are often planted in mounds or ridges so water does not stand in gardens. The mounds are also adapted to the growing habits of sweet potatoes, as a length of vine is laid flat, covered with a mound, and tubers grow at nodes on the vine. Swampy areas and slopes are trenched to remove excess water and run-offs, preventing overall erosion of steep slopes. In Chimbu, soil on steep slopes is held firm with rows of sticks and small fences, which are a simple form of terracing. Large-scale terraces and irrigation channels are not found in the New Guinea highlands. The Chimbu and Wahgi Valley people make a grid of drainage ditches about ten feet (3 m) apart, and plant on the resulting raised mounds. Wooden paddles were used before steel shovels were introduced.

The nutrient content of soil varies with the mineral content of its rock base and organic surface composition. This may include ash from burnt vegetation, fertilizing additives, enriched soil, and the effects of rotational or fallow crops. The soil texture is also affected by these conditions and additions; it affects the size and nutriment of crops as well. Casuarina trees, planted in the highlands when a garden is being left to fallow, improve the soil by fixing nitrogen, and also provide wood for houses, fences, and other uses. The Dani, Chimbu, Wahgi Valley, Huli, and other people who trench their gardens add nutrient-rich soil to the garden beds. Composting and mulching with vegetation improves the mounds in which Enga plant their sweet potatoes.

Other factors affecting crop growth are the distribution of rainfall, shade, and sunshine, which may vary regionally and seasonally. Altitude and temperature affect plant growth rates, often to a marked degree: The same crop may grow very much slower in some conditions, and some crops or varieties may not grow at all at extremes of temperature, moisture, and sunshine, even within an area where these are traditionally the staff of life. In unusual seasons dryness or cold or excessive moisture affect productivity to such a degree that some people experience starvation. These rare conditions may reduce the population to that which can be supported within a restricted area less subject to such extremes; the survivors may move to more favorable locations. Unexpected crop loss from pests and plant diseases may have the same effect.

CROP SELECTION AND CARE

The previously discussed climatic and soil conditions and preparatory activities are known and evaluated by the highland people. They select and plant their food crops in light of their knowledge of the crops and their most favorable siting. In the highlands, large fields dominated by sweet potatoes take the largest area. Often other crops – bananas, sugarcane, taro, and yam – are planted in the same gardens, at the edge or in sections. Dozens of varieties of sweet potatoes are recognized; they differ in color, taste, texture, and the conditions required for growth. Varieties of the other crops are also cultivated, and may be chosen for special purposes – for gifts, treatment of illness, feeding infants and adolescents, or preferred tastes. Flowers, shrubs, and trees which are planted may be used for personal adornment, fibers, dyes, for food, or for manufacturing.

During the growing period, plants may be trained, weeded, pruned, transplanted, fertilized, sheltered, shaded, watered, and pests controlled. Again, the labor input in tending the growing plant is a measurable variable which results in differences in usable yield. Small and infected produce has a less edible portion. It is difficult to calculate the amount of crop that has been lost as a result of pests and disease.

Harvesting, carrying, and storing are all common types of labor associated with the care of crops in the highlands. Some crops ripen seasonally and must be picked quickly and moved into suitable storage containers for proper preservation and protection against spoilage, infestation, or pests. Other crops, such as sweet potato and fresh vegetables, can be harvested selectively as they ripen and deteriorate quickly. They are only available seasonally or if continuously planted and harvested. In the moist tropics many vegetables can be successfully planted and harvested at almost any time, but most tree fruits and nuts have a limited season.

The harvested crop may require processing and cleaning to remove toxic or inedible elements, and cooking can also be laborious. But some foods – sugarcane, fruits, and some banana varieties – are usually eaten fresh and raw.

As crops are taken from a field, some slower growing plants or trees may remain for future use. Bananas and sugarcane mature more slowly than tubers or vegetables, and nut, fruit, or oil-bearing trees may be planted by sedentary agriculturalists to provide for the future. Some highlanders transplant casuarina trees and decorative cordylines or bushes into old gardens for future use, as a mark of ownership and for timber. Casuarina appears in New Guinea where the forest has been cleared and gardens planted. Casuarina is particularly beneficial as a fallow cover in that it fixes nitrogen in the soil, enriching it. A fallow garden in valued land is not abandoned but closely guarded for future family use. Other gardens are harvested gradually, and over a period of months or years partly or fully recultivated with the same or other crops. This practice serves to perpetuate the productive cycle: A convenient or desirable garden site may be kept in continuous use for years.

These practices constitute forms of land use that bridge the categories of bush-fallow, short-fallow, annual cropping, and multicropping. When a farmer's activities in his land are of this great variation and adaptation to needs, the rigid categories based upon period of cultivation and fallow cannot be applied. Only a general estimate of the average fallow for land of a particular type can be attempted.

Agricultural intensification may take many forms. Boserup is chiefly concerned with the relationship in time of cultivation and fallow. Other forms of intensification are the techniques and labor input at various stages of gardening. These include the clearing and preparation of the plot, selection and planting of the seeds or cuttings, care of the growing crop, fertilizing, and erosion and water control. Protection from pests, care and timing of harvest, and storage to prevent deterioration all affect the usable yield of a garden. The varieties and processes of intensification of agricultural practice are summarized in Table 5.

ACREAGE IN CULTIVATION

Another approach to agricultural intensification has been taken by Sahlins (1971, 1972), who compares acreage in cultivation per gardener. His interests are in economic subsistence and surplus, which he considers in terms of the division of labor by sex and age, the use of technological aids such as machinery or animals, and the input of labor by gardeners providing for large or small family-units. Data from several societies including Maring and Kapauku in the New Guinea highlands are used. Sahlins examines labor intensity (acreage/gardener) in relation to the ratio of consumers to worker. The Chayanov theory that labor intensity varies directly according to the number of consumers per worker – the more consumers in the household per worker, the more they work – was tested by Sahlins in terms of acreage cultivated per worker. This theory applies especially to subsistence, where surplus production has no outlet or advantage. It is assumed that in a subsistence economy, households

Table 5. *Intensifying agricultural practices*

Practice	Definition
Enclosure	Protecting field from livestock and encroachment with wood, reed or metal fence. Also defines boundary.
Fallow	Varied length of fallow, planting casuarina or other trees and long term crops as fallow cover, crop rotation, livestock foraging.
Ground preparation	Clearing trees, shrubs and grasses, tillage, plowing, mounding, ridging, trenching.
Erosion control	Terracing, walling, drainage, selective planting and transplanting.
Water control	Trenching, diverting streams and runoff, ridging. In low rainfall areas, irrigation.
Fertilization	Mulching, composting, adding nutrient soil, selected crop rotation and fallow planting, manuring, applying ash.
Crop care	Seed and crop selection, rotation, pruning, weeding, pest control, sheltering, transplanting.

produce for their own consumption, and that the techniques are the same within a community. Yet Sahlins's analysis found variations: Maring may produce a surplus for exchange and festivals, and some ambitious Kapauku produce many times more than others and may use their produce for prestige activities. Sahlins emphasizes the factor of surplus production for displays, distributions, pig production, and festivals as differentiation in the productive activities of households within the samples from Maring and Kapauku.

Among the Chimbu and Sina Sina, in pig feast preparations the whole ceremonial group increases its land in production so that many large pigs are produced for a feast every seven to ten years. In the period following a feast, all the people drastically reduce their gardening efforts. When a population is growing, there is a high proportion of children to adults; the number of consumers per worker is high and increased supplies of food must be provided. Agricultural intensification is a likely result.

This increase of production may result from farming more land or from increasing the yield by changing the agricultural techniques to grow more on the same area. There is, as we will see, a close relationship between the density of population – a result of population growth at some time in the past – and the intensity of agricultural practices.

NEW GUINEA HIGHLAND PRACTICES

Sweet potatoes have changed the distribution of people in the highlands and increased the population in general, allowing settlement at higher altitudes – up to 2,600 meters or 8,500 feet. The now densely settled Dani, Chimbu, and Enga areas could not have supported these people with previously available food crops. Since adoption of the sweet potato staple, then, family size may have increased and population shifted and expanded, at altitudes between 4,600 feet (1,400 m) and 8,500 feet (2,600 m).

The procedure followed in growing sweet potato, which has become the staple food, eaten by children and adults and providing 70 percent or more of the diet of most highlanders – except at lower altitudes where taro is the major crop – varies somewhat. Many varieties, distinctive in size, shape, leaf form, color, texture, taste, and nutritional composition are known and grown. Variety is valued, and some types apparently grow well in certain conditions only.

A fallow area is chosen for preparation by the owners, who evaluate the site in terms of accessibility, convenience, and fertility of the soil as determined by the fallow vegetation. Mixed fruit and vegetable gardens need more fertile land than do sweet potato gardens. A group of men may jointly decide to clear an area for several family gardens. Initial ground preparation is mainly by men: Heavy pitpit reeds, canes, bush, and grasses are cut with a bush knife and pulled out, and tree branches cut or trees felled. In some areas – for example, Lufa – clearing is incomplete, with some trees remaining. Large pieces of wood are used for fences or building, smaller branches and twigs for firewood. The cut underbrush is dried and later burned. Fences are made of wood or reeds, to separate pig-grazing areas from gardens. The fences may be wooden stakes, horizontal poles, or closely placed reeds.

This Chimbu garden has been completely cleared and tilled. The soil from the ditches becomes garden topsoil. In the background, a house and fence separate garden from bush fallow.

Most highlanders prepare the cleared ground by digging with a stick or spade to break up clods of earth, and often make ditches to drain the beds. In Chimbu and the Wahgi Valley rectangular ditches are cut in cleared grassland, and often also on cleared wooded slopes. In preparing ditches the earth that has been dug up is thrown on top of the bed, a ten- to twelve-foot square. In planting sweet potato vines a woman heaps this into about sixteen low mounds. In the eastern highlands such grids are uncommon, there are low ridges with small mounds, and drainage ditches run downhill. In preparing the land for a second crop, ditches are cleared and mounds are made, turning over and enriching the plant bed (Brookfield and Brown 1963).

To the west, especially in the higher altitude and cooler Enga area, a green compost mound of ten to twelve feet (3–3.7 m) across and one to three feet (0.3–1.0 m) high is made for sweet potatoes. Other types of gardens, and smaller mounds, are also made. The open fields of sweet potato are areas of large mounds in which, as the vegetable compost material decomposes, the mound temperature rises. This is valuable protection for sweet potatoes when air temperatures drop. In this system cultivation may be continuous; the Enga remake and plant a mound after harvest. The compost includes newly cut weeds that nourish the growing crop. This nearly permanent cultivation is developed in the most populous center of Mae Enga; other Enga use less intensive techniques. At high altitudes all crops grow more slowly and there is danger of frost.

Deep ditches are made in the southern highlands at Tari. Another ditching form for drainage, adapted to moist valley bottoms and resulting in nearly continuous replenishment of garden beds with mud from the drainage ditches, is practiced by the Wissel Lakes Kapauku and Dani of the Balim Valley (Heider 1970). Deep drainage and built-up garden beds allow intensive, permanent cultivation in these swampy valley areas. They control run-off and protect growing crops. The Dani replenish their raised beds with the mud from drainage channels and grow mostly sweet potatoes and some taro and yam. In compound gardens near settlements banana, sugarcane, gourd, and tobacco are grown. The slope gardens are long-fallow; valley floors are enriched with mud and rested in short fallow after several crops are grown in a continuous cultivation. Where the swampy Wahgi Basin is cultivated, some deep drains are made to divert major run-off and sometimes to keep pigs contained. The grid pattern is followed, with the depth of ditches adapted to local requirements.

Most of the garden preparation, fence construction, and ditch-digging work is done by men. Before European tools were introduced in the highlands the stone axe or adze was the main wood chopping tool; it has nearly everywhere been replaced with a steel axe which is harder, sharper, and more durable. The time formerly spent in clearing and fencing has been greatly reduced as the result of steel tools. The work of cutting or pulling grass and cane, carrying, burning, and fence building is done mostly by men; women often help in clearing grass. A work-group may be called by the main gardener to help. After clearing, the work of tillage and ditching is done mainly by men with wooden hoes and digging sticks, or, nowadays, steel spades. Enga men make large compost mounds. But sweet potato planting – which requires gathering vines from a garden, preparing the surface mound, often with a spade, and inserting the vine and covering it with loosely mounded earth – is generally done by women. In sweet potato and other planting the selection of varieties is done mostly by women. When a garden-owner has been helped by others, or a group has cooperated in preparing someone's area, some land is allocated to all those who have helped for their own use. Planting and weeding are done by individuals rather than collectively, and the crop belongs to the one who planted it.

Several forms of short fallow or nearly continuous sweet potato gardens are the most specialized and intensive agricultural land use forms in the highlands. All highlanders also cultivate other crops in an extensive fashion. For example, the Kapauku use an extensive or shifting cultivation technique of long fallow, eight to twenty years, on the slopes, with clearing, fencing, burning, and then planting in the cleared area. On the valley floor drainage ditches are dug, cleared with wooden spades, and the garden fence is simpler and takes less time to build than that constructed on mountain slopes. The Kapauku's valley-bottom gardens are cultivated in crop rotation for several years before fallowing in grass. A more intensive system with drainage ditches around rectangular beds and green fertilizer is used in the valleys for sweet potatoes and vegetables (Pospisil 1963). This is neither an annual nor multicropping land use system, but rather consists of permanent use for a variety of crops – sweet potato, manioc, white potatoes, green vegetables, and other foods, all of which grow at different rates. Planting materials for various crops include shoots, cuttings, seeds, and tubers. Some crops must be staked, weeded frequently, or protected from insects and larvae. They mature over a period of many months.

A form of mixed garden – with taro, yam, greens, beans, corn, bananas, sugar, cucumber, ginger, gourds, and other foods – is planted by the Raiapu Enga (Waddell 1972) mainly on the slopes where drainage ditches can be constructed. In the highlands as a result of the introduction of new crops, the mixed and occasional crops now include pawpaw, peanuts, pineapple, cabbage, corn, cucumbers, onions, pumpkin, beans, peas, lettuce, manioc, tomato, potatoes, carrots, and passion fruit. The more traditional fruits and vegetables include *Setaria palmaefolia*, *Saccharum edule* (pitpit), *Dolichos lablab* (hyacinth bean), cucurbits, gourds, and *Psophocarpus tetragonolobus* (winged bean). There are many varieties of these crops.

When several agricultural methods are used, different crops are grown and the subsidiary activities of fencing, tending, and preparing the crops also vary. The measurement of labor and assessment of intensity can only be piecemeal and approximate. There can be no doubt that permanent and intensive gardening requires much labor per acre of land, but it also produces more food for the area than extensive systems which use more land and require less preparation, weeding, and other crop care. The allocation of time and work done involves adjustment of activities to those of others in the household or neighborhood.

The Bomagai-Angoiang Maring of the Simbai River Valley, who garden extensively at a somewhat lower altitude, at about 1,000 meters or 3,300 feet, provide a contrast in land use and agricultural practice. Gardens are cleared in forest or long-fallow secondary growth and then cropped for eighteen to twenty-two months. The restoration of forest is stimulated by planting casuarina and Albizia, by being used as an area for defecation, and by the decomposition of plants. A clearing is fenced, and the main crops, taro and sweet potatoes, are planted. Other crops planted at the same time include yams, manioc, and a mixture of old and new plants: sugar, banana, pumpkin, and other vegetables which are allowed to intertwine and grow in clumps. During the productive period quick-maturing plants are harvested and exhausted as slower growing plants mature and are harvested. Toward the end of the cycle, weeds and jungle growth dominate, to become the fallow cover. Gardens are not re-planted. While most food is derived from these gardens, the Bomagai-Angoiang Maring also plant trees for oil, fruits, and leaves, and a few plants adjacent to houses for decoration, leaves, and tobacco; they also gather wild products and the produce of naturally occurring plants which have been protected or encouraged. This agricultural system has few permanent features, but the long-lived trees and decorative plants around settlements are preserved, and spontaneously-occurring plants valued for any domestic use in the forest or fallow will be remembered and collected as required. Maring gardening is less-intensive than central highlands agriculture: The clearing is not completely tilled, drainage not controlled, and a mixture of crops is planted.

Comparisons of the time and labor involved in cultivation pose many difficulties, but it is of interest to attempt a comparison when data are available. Clarke (1971) compared his observations of the Bomagai-Angoiang to those made of the Kapauku by Pospisil and concluded that in clearing Kapauku worked 200 man-days per acre whereas the Bomagai-Angoiang worked 165. However, the allocation of time differs: Kapauku spend more time in tilling, slashing, and fencing and less time in planting, weeding, and tending the growing crops, according to the figures presented. This considers only Pospisil's "extensive" system while the valley-bottom systems in Kapauku require a different allocation of time and labor.

The comparison of man-hours per acre does not demonstrate the yield of different systems. A partially cleared, irregularly planted, shifting field may produce large tubers, but the total harvest weight of a fully tilled and evenly planted permanent garden may be much greater. Pospisil's (1963: 444) yield figures for the intensively worked Kapauku gardens are 1.69 kilograms per square meter, or twice those of the hill slopes (81 kg/m^2) and higher than the valley (1.38 kg/m^2). This increased production, especially when population pressure is felt, justifies the higher labor input. Further, it promotes permanent settlement, improvement of housing, trees, and orchards, while reducing convenient supplies of wild products and animals. This process of intensification in the New Guinea highlands has stimulated concentration upon a single crop, sweet potato, and reduced variety. This has had some unfortunate dietary and nutritional results.

In those areas of the highlands where settlement and gardens are more permanent, specialized techniques for cultivating the staple crop of sweet potatoes have developed. Each technique is particularly adapted to the local requirements to provide water, erosion, temperature, and other controls and to grow larger, heavier, and more frequent crops of sweet potatoes. Chimbu, Enga, Dani, and Kapauku utilize the intensive forms and have the highest population density. Some intermediary forms – with varying fallow, clearing, and less laborious preparation, planting, and tending procedures – are found in highland areas with less-permanent land use and moderate population density. In the Chimbu, Wahgi, and Hagen areas the ground is prepared for gridiron ditching. In the Wahgi Valley and at Mt. Hagen, after clearing and fencing a large area, rectangular ditches are dug, and the area is divided among the families for mainly sweet potato growing. Some subsidiary crops are grown in parts of this area, but most are placed in small and scattered gardens and near houses. Large areas of grass lie in fallow. In the eastern highlands, the preparation of a cleared field consists of tillage and some small mounds, and there is less separation of sweet potatoes from other crops. In general, technical elaboration with such forms as are given in Table 5 increases with density in the highlands. Where sweet potato fields are large and separate, they are strongly fenced against pigs.

Except among the Huli at Tari, where men grow and cook their own food (Glasse 1968), most sweet potatoes are planted, tended, and harvested by women. Bananas and sugarcane, eaten as snacks and presented to guests and at ceremonies, are more often cared for by men. An unmarried young man may have some sugar and banana plants in his parents' garden. Taro and yam are grown by either sex, and often used for special feasts or prestations. There are only a few other food crops which supplement sweet potatoes, but manioc, pumpkin, maize, and some others may become more important as they are introduced and cooking practices change.

Trees, especially nut pandanus and oil pandanus, which occur as wild trees and whose seedlings are nurtured or transplanted, are valued for food and gifts. Wherever useful trees have been claimed or transplanted, they are tended and preserved even if land is being cleared for a garden. Small groves of trees are sometimes planted and tended. Recently coffee trees have become an important, permanent crop, occupying sometimes large areas of arable land. A few other new trees and bushes are also cultivated: orange, tree tomatoes, passion fruit, and pawpaw – all of which are primarily cultivated individually rather than in groves. Tea is a new crop grown on allotments in the Wahgi Valley, and pyrethrum has recently been grown at high altitudes. Since the highlands are only 4° to 8° from the equator, there is little seasonal temperature variation. The cold air descends into valleys producing morning mists and cold, but snow is only found on the highest peaks in Irian Jaya, and falls very rarely on Mt. Wilhelm near Chimbu.

The most pronounced climatic variation in the highlands is in rainfall rather than temperature. The main wind current in the southwest Pacific is southeasterly. Most of the highlands have maximum rainfall from January to March, and minimum rainfall from May to August. But the average annual rainfall measured in different highland stations varies greatly. The highest annual rainfall is on the southern slopes of the mountains where 150 inches per year (3.8 m/yr.) is common. The Eastern Highlands province is distinctly the driest area with most stations receiving 80 to 100 inches per year (2 – 2.5 m/yr.). In Chimbu, the Western Highlands, and Enga provinces, most stations average 100 to 125 inches per year (2.5–3.2 m/yr.). Records for highland stations in Irian Jaya fall into almost the same range, 80 to 140 inches (2–3.6 m/yr.). There are occasional periods of intense and prolonged rain, and some of extended dry, sunny periods. But some rain falls in every month. Very heavy rain and flooding may endanger crops, as may prolonged dry periods. The frosts which may occur at high altitudes, usually in times of low rainfall, do affect growing crops and may produce famine, as that which occurred in parts of the Enga and Southern Highlands provinces in 1972. Frost is fairly common in parts of the Enga province where compost is used to provide some protection against the cold weather.

Most highlanders consider the climatic variations in planning their agricultural work. The major crop, sweet potato, may be planted at any time, matures in five to nine months, and is lifted from the ground over a period of months to provide a continuous unstored supply of the staple food. In digging up sweet potatoes, a woman sits, uses a short stick, and throws the tubers in a heap to be carried in her net bag. Vines are replaced in the ground to be harvested again or eaten by pigs later. Most families begin new gardens and plant new sections several times a year, so that there will not be periods of scarcity. We did not find any regular patterns of fallow and cultivation, but rather individual decisions about what land to use.

Nevertheless, there seems to be more garden preparation begun at some seasons than others. The clearing and burning phases of garden preparation are easiest in dry weather. Cut vegetation is often allowed to dry for some days before burning. Some may be dug into the plant bed. The digging, tilling, and soil preparation are easiest when the soil is moist, so this may be left for a rainy period. Sweet potato vines used in planting may wither before they become rooted if planting is followed by a prolonged dry spell. Rain hastens the early development of the plants. Neither dry nor rain are exclusive to the seasons, however. We observed more clearing begun in the Chimbu "dry" season, April to August, and many of these gardens were finally planted between September and December, but no single period was wholly spent in any one gardening activity.

The people in different areas spend varying lengths of time in the several stages of preparation. In the east where it is drier, garden beds are long and narrow with low mounds and shallow drainage ditches. The eastern highlands have little wood and some gardens are fenced with light pitpit, while deep ditches at Tari take the place of fences.

Within the range of garden practices one can see local and individual adjustments to natural conditions and crop requirements. New varieties, techniques, and plants are tried, and when results can be evaluated, new adjustments may be made.

Many new crops have been introduced by missions and agricultural officers, for food and for sale. Seeds or shoots are tried out and growing requirements are quickly determined. We found that orange and grapefruit seeds were taken to start trees, but grafting was not possible so the resulting fruit was far from what had been expected. Other plants are begun with cuttings. Crops, such as tomatoes and corn, were improved by seed selection, and the moist highlands provide favorable conditions for onions and cabbage. New varieties of fruits and vegetables that were grown in the highlands were sold to Europeans when possible and only slowly became additions to the local diet.

Those highlanders who value wild fruits and nuts visit and watch areas where they grow and may base the movement of their settlements upon the maturation cycle of these foods. Pandanus nuts are everywhere a favorite, and produce a flush once in several years rather than annually. In some areas, as this flush is observed, a few men build temporary huts in the groves where they sleep to watch the ripening and prevent theft. They serve as guardians for their fellow clansmen and store nut clusters in the houses as they ripen. Often, a flush is the occasion for an interclan or intertribe distribution. In the Chimbu area, oil pandanus is planted near houses and in gardens at lower altitudes. It, too, is used for gifts.

Feasts and group presentations of cultivated food must be planned and coordinated for group participation and prestige. The earliest explorers were especially struck by the decorative use of flowers and shrubs by highlanders. Especially in the Wahgi Valley and Mt. Hagen area, gardens and ceremonial grounds are lined by rows and clumps of decorative plants and flowers.

Aside from the preference to clear land in dry weather and to begin gardens in moist weather, other activities may be adapted to seasonal activities. Feasts and displays are spoiled by rain, so there is a preference for the drier months for these activities. House building is often coordinated with new gardening if a residential move is involved. Thus planning includes the time needed for building before garden preparation. Fencing must also fit into the garden preparation period, if the new gardens are in land outside the existing fenced area.

PIGS

Pigs are the largest animals that are eaten in New Guinea. The evidence available indicates that they were introduced thousands of years ago as domestic animals from Asia and Indonesia. There was no native wild pig. In New Guinea, pigs inhabit forests, grasslands, and the areas around gardens. The earliest evidence suggests that some pigs may have become feral in New Guinea, wandering and breeding throughout the interior. The oldest pig bones found in archaeological sites may be those of hunted, feral pigs. Accounts from explorers and travelers in forest areas often mention hunting wild pigs. The same areas are sources for hunting other game. In the interior, pork is the most favored meat, and the largest animal eaten; cattle, horses, and goats have been introduced very recently and are only rarely available. But wild pigs are hunted in all forest areas, young pigs sometimes captured and reared or fattened for future use, and domestic pigs raised for feasts. Nowhere in New Guinea are pigs a common item of diet; everywhere the killing of a pig is a matter for feast and celebration. Only wild pigs are killed without a prior plan or purpose. Domestic pigs are part of the household valuable property; their raising and slaughter is purposeful. Pigs are of great interest to the highlanders, but they are not an exclusive concern as are the herds of pastoralists. Garden produce is the main source of food for men and livestock in the highlands.

In the marginal and fringe areas, where some feral pigs and other game may be hunted, few or no pigs may be kept. A captured pig may be killed for a celebration, or a small collection of pigs cooked for a feast. But pig breeding and raising is not a major activity, as it is in the densely settled central highlands area where there are no wild pigs and little game of any sort. Here there may be as many pigs as people. Elsewhere there are domestic pigs in the village area and grazing land, and wild pigs in the forest or grasslands. The wild may be hunted, or captured and domesticated. Since some or all male pigs are castrated before reaching maturity, domestic sows mate with feral boars in many areas; their young are taken in to add to the domestic stock. Wild and domestic pigs are constantly interbred. However, it appears that there is a low rate of pig reproduction and of survival of piglets.

In those highland areas where pigs are sometimes wild and domestic pigs interbreed with feral, the human population is smaller and on the whole the gardens are not so dominated by sweet potato. Often, this is at lower altitudes. The largest numbers of domestic pigs and largest feasts are found in the dense, central highlands where sweet potatoes are grown both for humans and pigs.

How shall we define the domestication of pigs in the highlands? In their food requirements, pigs are omnivorous. In any open area they browse and forage for a variety of herbs, grasses, and roots, tubers, fruit, insects, worms, reptiles, and any other edible materials. When they live in association with man, pigs enter gardens and inhabited areas to eat growing crops and any other plant and animal materials they find. Wild pigs can be lured by certain foods, especially sago and sweet potatoes which they seem to prefer, and pigs become attached to their feeders. As a consequence, pigs become domesticated. Many people hand-feed their pigs tubers and the discards from their own meals. Domestic pigs are given raw and cooked food and scraps. The amount of cultivated foods and discards given to pigs varies greatly. While the Auyana (Robbins 1969) of the eastern highlands are said to feed pigs one pound of sweet potatoes a day, irregularly, Kapauku feed them 8.8 pounds (4 kg) per day (Pospisil 1963). Pigs in densely settled areas obtain less of their food by foraging than do pigs who wander in extensive bush and forest. When the highlanders are preparing for a feast, they fatten the pigs by a great increase in hand-feeding.

Unless pigs are kept in pens, a rare and very new practice in New Guinea, domestic pigs forage by day and are fed by their owners in the afternoon; they usually sleep in a partitioned section of a house also used, regularly or at times, by a woman and her family. The domestic pig goes to a house provided by its owner at night for food and sleep, and leaves in the morning to forage in an open area. To discourage wandering, pigs may be blinded. Pigs are kept out of growing gardens; if a fence is broken or weak, they enter, move about, and eat the growing crops, sometimes causing great damage and destruction. But after the main food crop is harvested, they are led into a garden or fallow area, tethered, and allowed to browse and eat insects, herbage, leaves, vines, and tubers. This is beneficial to

This pig house is built along the fence, so that pigs may come and go into the browsing area without entering the garden and house area.

the productivity of the garden in that pig feces fertilize the soil, and the movement of the pigs themselves overturns and softens the soil and destroys some weeds before the garden is prepared for recultivation. However, if there are growing crops nearby, the pig must be kept away from them. This control of pig movement and feeding is an important element of domestication. The provision of food and shelter certainly binds the pigs to their owners, but pigs do often wander off for some time. By tying a rope to a pig's leg, the pig may be led about by his owners, kept in or near houses in different areas, or tethered. Since boars are inclined to ill temper and attack and also have little fat, a boar must be constrained more than a gelding or sow. If kept for breeding, a boar is often castrated at two to three years and then fattened before it is killed. Young male pigs are killed as needed, whereas females are kept for breeding when possible.

Pigs are trained and attach themselves to their owners somewhat as pets. The piglets are fondled and hand-fed, even occasionally nursed by the woman in whose care they are kept. At a later age they are housed, fed, tethered, led, and groomed. Most young males are castrated; females are allowed to mate with wild or selected boars. Breeding of domestic sows is encouraged. Now that some new varieties have been introduced, there may be differences in size, weight, health, fertility, and survival of young, but the increase in the total number of pigs is still small. In Chimbu, I found that pigs were named by their owners as they grew up; typical names are the names of locations, colors, physical characteristics, the place they came from, what was given for them, animals, or plants. Clearly, in Chimbu domestic pigs are recognized as having their own individual habits and peculiarities. Chimbu raise and keep large pigs for periodic festivals, but to the east and west smaller pigs are traded or consumed at festivals.

A highland family devotes much thought and planning to its pigs. The owners manage their domestic herd numbers and sizes by exchange, purchase, loan, donation, fattening, and restraining. They may have their pigs under the care of relatives in other areas for a time when disease threatens or the household is otherwise strained. When preparing for a large feast, much of the burden of feeding may be shifted to these relatives, who will later be rewarded with pork. A pig cared for by another may later be killed, cooked, and given to the person as a ceremonial prestation. If a sow has a litter, the caretaker may receive one or more of the offspring. Pig breeding may be controlled by keeping females away from boars, or encouraged by bringing them together. Highland pig husbandry does not result in many large, fat pigs. A lactating sow often becomes thin. Generally litters are small, only three to four piglets, survivors are few; pigs grow slowly and are not fattened quickly for slaughter. Pigs become sick, lost, or stolen by hostile neighbors and this upsets plans for feasts; many quarrels and accusations involve pig care and acquisition. When a pig has damaged a garden, an irate garden-owner may kill the pig, thus depriving the pig's owner of a valued property and provoking demand for recompense. Some compensation is usually asked by the garden-owner for such damage by pigs.

Ceremonies in which a community slaughters most of its grown pigs occur in Chimbu and the Wahgi Valley at intervals of several years – sometimes ten or more. This requires a major coordination of breeding and fattening efforts. Between major festivals, pigs that are sickly or troublesome may be killed, but usually some occasion prompts the killing: A birth, a girl's puberty, or illness calls for a small family feast, whereas initiation, marriage, and funerals require several pigs to be killed and distributed. At these occasions the pigs may be selected with long-term interests in mind.

A family can expect to contribute pigs to celebrations for family members, and plans its pig-raising accordingly. There may be unexpected needs for pork: a dispute or compensation, death, the needs of relatives, or the demands of creditors. Thus the planned allocation of animals for large festivals is never fully predictable: The best animals may be lost before the occasion. A herd may be increased by trade or loan, or depleted by theft or epidemic. There is a balance of land use for pigs and food crops so that each family attempts to accommodate its needs from its resources and each community, made up of many families, may experience different pressures or resources at different times. This is especially the case in terms of the relationship between the human and pig populations in the highlands.

The coordination of individual-family-land requirements must be adapted to resources and phases of the pig-ceremonial cycle. In attempting to assess land and crop needs, it is necessary to allow for the amount of food eaten by pigs at the different points of a cycle – when the pigs are small and few in number and when they are large and their population is also larger. The proportion of food crops eaten by pigs may vary from 10 percent to over 50 percent. Some of the cultivated sweet potatoes given to pigs are rejected by people as small, stringy, or unappetizing, but at the point when the food required by pigs is greatest they must eat some sweet potatoes of the same quality as those eaten by the family.

The production of a large pig which, in addition to grazing, eats as many sweet potatoes as are eaten by a person, requires much effort in gardening and feeding. Every family must raise pigs for certain social obligations, and full participation or increasing prestige in the community require an additional supply of pigs. In many areas, big men have two or more wives whose gardens and pigs are needed to maintain the husband's position in society. When festivals are planned, big men must lead in pig production and encourage their fellows to provide pigs; the reputation and standing of the whole group is involved. Preparing for a large feast requires coordinated effort by many families and may involve intensified gardening and increased acreage in sweet potatoes, thus putting some strain upon the community's arable land. However, this great increase is short-lived; when the feast is over, only the people and some small pigs need be fed from community gardens. There is also some sharing of the extra demand: Pigs are agisted on the land of relatives in other communities who are not at that time planning a feast. The heavy demand of food for pigs can be regarded as a temporary intensification of land use. We could project pig-feeding requirements as a range from maximum to minimum: shortly before a feast and shortly after, or as an average over the feast cycle. In close examination of pig-raising practices, Hide (personal communication, 1974) found in Sina Sina that after a pig feast the numbers of pigs are increased by breeding and trade for several years, although few of these pigs reach a large size. Then, when a feast is planned, breeding ceases and pigs are fattened for the feast. Many difficulties may delay a feast, so that a ceremonial cycle is usually longer than the minimum time to breed and raise pigs. Other peoples have different forms of feasts and exchange cycles, with different pressures on production. The ceremonial cycle among the Enga emphasizes the number of pigs rather than their size so that the alternation of breeding and fattening is not so marked. Live pigs may be passed from hand to hand; thus the *te* exchange system distributes and moves the demand for feeding pigs from area to area. Each group keeps some pigs and gives some of those received, and some they raised, to the next group in line. When the last group has received the pigs they begin to slaughter and cook pork. Each group consumes some, cooks some new meat, and passes cooked meat to those who gave them live pigs. A more even demand for pig food may be found in the eastern highlands where smaller numbers of pigs are consumed at more frequent festivals.

The pig feasts organized and held by New Guinea highlanders are part of a total ecological-economic-social-political-religious system in which domestic production, interpersonal and intergroup relations, trade, and success are interrelated. Many pig ceremonies are connected with rites of fertility, group solidarity, and individual achievement. In these ceremonies the quantity of pigs and other goods for display and consumption are both indicators of success in the production of vegetables and pigs and appeals to the spirits for continued fertility. Different festival patterns involve the coordination of different groups of people; the groups themselves may number from less than one hundred to several thousand.

Both intensive sweet potato gardening and large pig festivals are part of an economic complex with concentrated communities and group planning. To hold large pig feasts a group must manage its land, intensify agriculture, fence its gardens, breed and raise its pigs, and provide for visitors to attend the festival.

Among the Dani, pig killing is prohibited for many months before a pig feast. Each group holds a feast every four to six years; the pig prestations of a single feast may serve to commemorate initiations, marriages, and deaths. This, too, is a coordination of tribal efforts and a combination of payments to relatives and exchange partners in other groups (Heider 1972).

Among the Kapauku, pigs are raised for feasts and for market. Pigs are bred, traded, and sold. An owner may give a pig to a custodian for raising and breeding. Pigs reaching maturity may be killed, and the cooked meat sold by the owner, to obtain money when no major ceremony is imminent. A feast in Kapauku includes house construction, dancing, gifts, and trade in pork and other goods. This is a major, planned, group event.

Most highlanders have pig festivals, large or small, frequent or infrequent. There is much variation in the concern and intensity of agriculture and pig production. In the highlands, pork is a rare and most valued food, available only on ceremonial occasions or by exchange. When large festivals are celebrated a great quantity of pork may be eaten at one time, and little or none for many months before and after. When pig exchanges are smaller and more frequent, consumption may be spread more evenly over the months and years. The total amount consumed may also vary locally. The relation between food supplies, nutrition, and health is discussed in Chapter 1.

Some writers, principally Vayda and Rappaport, have suggested that in natural processes of growth pig herds will become a strain upon vegetable production unless pig-killing feasts occur periodically. Feasts are held to remove the pressure on resources, and allow the people to return to a more manageable level of production. Other writers would place more weight on the decisions of people to organize and carry out large feasts. According to Rappaport (1968), the Maring kill and eat pigs when people require more animal protein for warfare, or to overcome illness, or misfortune. Pig killing is combined with ritual for human welfare. Every ten to fifteen years a feast *(kaiko)* in ceremonial cycle requires slaughter of nearly all a Maring group's pigs.

Cattle have been introduced during the past ten to fifteen years and are becoming an important part of feast foods as well as items used for sale and exchange. Since they require much grazing land, they will also affect land use and economic values, but this cannot be assessed yet.

Calculations of carrying capacity and pressure on resources should consider both the people's perception of and activities in production capacity and demand, and an objective evaluation of land productivity, technology, manpower, and productivity. There are environmental, technological, and manpower limitations, and also individual and group factors of goals and performance. The result is a complex of adjustment to environment and circumstances, and direction of effort toward certain objectives.

THE POPULATION

So far, we have seen that there is an ecological and cultural base of mountain life in New Guinea; the environment, cultural adaptation, and development of society is one of general form. But this covers a wide range in some respects: from a mixed hunting, collecting, and gardening subsistence to a 90 percent dependence on sweet potatoes; from a density of less than one person per square mile to over 400 persons per square mile (from 1/km² to 160/km²); from small, scattered settlements to concentrations of over 2,000 people. In this section, we will examine population processes and the distribution of people in the highlands.

The East New Guinea Highlands Stock language groups are nearly all in the Papua New Guinea highlands, whose total 1973 population has been estimated at 992,077. The subpopulations of this group include: the Southern Highlands province – 207,391; the Western Highlands province (including Enga) – 350,804; the Eastern Highlands province – 239,751; and the Chimbu province – 194,131.

Some highlands people – the Simbai Valley Maring and Gende, for example, and some of the Karam – are counted in the Madang province. Highland New Guinea people around Telefomin – at least 15,000 people – are counted in the West Sepik province. There are over one million highlanders in Papua New Guinea, and perhaps 400,000 or 500,000 in Irian Jaya.

For Irian Jaya no up-to-date figures are available. Previous estimates of some important groups are that the Dani of the Balim Valley number about 50,000, and that the total Dani population numbers 200,000. Kapauku are estimated at 60,000 to 80,000.

We are, then, discussing a sizable, distinctive, cultural segment of the world's people and their distribution in the interior highland area of one of the world's largest islands. The mountain fringes are sparsely inhabited by more distantly related peoples. In the center, the Star Mountains of Irian Jaya and the Telefomin, Miyanmin, Baktaman, and related groups in Papua New Guinea, most of whom speak languages of the Ok family, are what I call fringe peoples (cf. Chapter 1). At the margin, are such groups as the Maring, Gadsup, Awa, South Fore, and Auyana, who speak languages of the East

New Guinea Highlands Phylum and live at somewhat lower altitudes.

The western highlands of New Guinea were first observed by the Dutch in 1910, whereas the eastern highlands, then under Australian administration, were explored during the 1920s and 1930s. Previous expeditions by ship up the Sepik and Fly Rivers had found few people in the upper reaches of these rivers, and walking parties had not penetrated the steep mountains surrounding the main, occupied, highland valleys. New Guinea was first crossed by Australian officers from south to north – from the Fly to the Sepik – traversing a sparsely occupied region near the west New Guinea border. In 1929 Lutheran missionaries visited the eastern valleys. In 1930 gold prospectors entered the highlands from the northeast, to discover many highland villages, each at war with its neighbors: The prospectors traveled with local people who would not penetrate the borders of the next territory. Throughout, in what is now the largest New Guinea population, white men were wholly unknown. The prospectors, Leahy and Dwyer, not knowing where they were, left the highlands by the Purari River to reach the Papuan Coast. Great interest in the area developed, and a prospecting and government exploration patrol into the central highlands followed in 1933–4. The party moved in stages, with air supplies landed at several prepared sites, and a preliminary reconnaissance flight over the area then to be explored. While the small villages of the eastern highlands were known from the first visit, the large villages, big groups, and intensive agriculture of the Chimbu, Wahgi Valley, and western highlands were first seen in 1933.

Both government and mission posts were established at several places in 1934 and 1935, with continuing exploration. The southern highlands were explored from Papua in 1934–5; the area west of Mt. Hagen was explored in 1934 and later. But it was thirty years before all the scattered peoples of the larger region were located, reached by government service, and enumerated by census.

The Balim Valley was discovered in 1921. It is seven miles wide and thirty miles long, at an altitude of about 5,000 feet, and surrounded by high limestone formations. This area was struck by earthquake and landslips in June and July 1976.

The Archbold Expeditions of 1938–9 made important geographic discoveries in the Balim Valley and mountain areas of Irian Jaya. We still lack detailed maps and population data for some areas in the New Guinea highlands, and will necessarily have most to say about the more well-known peoples. The highlands of Irian Jaya have two centers of dense population: the Wissel Lakes and the Dani of the Balim Valley (see maps).

The Kapauku people of the Wissel Lakes area live at an altitude of about 1,500 meters, between high mountains and tropical forests. Kapauku are densely settled and culturally distinct from surrounding peoples by the fact that they practice intensive agriculture, drain swamps, and engage in competitive individualism and headmanship (Pospisil 1963).

Between the Wissel Lakes area and the Balim Valley is an area scarcely known, and about which very little can be said here. The Dani people are more numerous, and perhaps also more varied, than the Kapauku. The largest Dani population is in the Balim Grand Valley region, supported by an intense form of permanent agriculture with drainage canals and mounds in swampy land for garden beds. Tribal organization consists of large confederacies and alliances bound together by powerful leaders. The victory or defeat of these leaders enlarges or divides alliances. Several important studies of the Dugum Dani of the Balim (Heider 1970, 1972a, 1972b), the Wanggulam at Bokondini (Ploeg 1969), the Konda Valley (O'Brien 1969), and the Jalé (Koch 1974) give us an impression of the range of variation between the large groups of the Balim and the smaller populations, with less competition and land pressure, of the western Dani and others.

Further east, toward the Papua New Guinea border, the country continues to be mountainous. The Star Mountains people of Irian Jaya and those of the Telefomin area of Papua New Guinea speak related languages. Overall, however, this is a region of fragmented groups which we have discussed as the highland fringe. Heavy rainfall, precipitous land forms, deep forest, and low population density – under ten persons per square kilometer – are characteristic of this central mountain region. The languages are of the Ok family, related to, but not included in, the East New Guinea Highlands Phylum. Other peoples of the Upper Sepik area are linguistically distinct. This further supports the idea that these fringe people occupy a cultural as well as geographic position between the highlanders and lowland groups.

The largest numbers of highlands people are in Papua New Guinea, which has become a well known field of anthropological study. Two groups, Enga and Chimbu, are expanding centers of dense population and intensive agriculture with large competitive clans and tribes, great festivals, trade, and warfare. Between the settlements of these two groups, and to the north and south, are smaller concentrations of related peoples who make up the remainder of two language families – the central and west central. Chimbu, Hagen, Jimi, and Wahgi peoples speak languages of the central family.

The Enga, Western Highlands, Southern Highlands, Eastern Highlands and Chimbu provinces are all mountainous, enclosed by the high mountain ranges on the north, with numerous peaks. Mt. Wilhelm, in the Bismarck Range, is New Guinea's highest mountain, 14,760 feet (4,500 m). Broad intermountain valleys and plateaux at 5,000 feet (1,500 m) and above are the centers of settlement, with houses and gardens extending up the slopes over 8,000 feet (2,400 m) in some places. The Kubor Range forms the southern rim of the huge Wahgi River Valley, which is joined by many rivers from east and west to flow southward into the Purari, emptying finally into Papua.

The land forms, rock base, and waterways vary. There are many swampy areas in the Wahgi and southwest of Enga, although Lake Kopiago in the Enga province and Lake Kutubu in the Southern Highlands province are the only significant lakes. The southern edge of the highlands is a limestone barrier, an area of porous and broken rock which cannot be settled or cultivated. Few trade routes have penetrated this area. To the east the mountains are not as high or as steep.

A high mountain range separates the Wahgi River from its main eastern tributaries, the Asaro and Mai, and this marks the division between Chimbu and the eastern highlands peoples. The difference is cultural and linguistic. East of Chimbu are two additional language families – the east-central and eastern. To the west of the divide, except for the Chuave and Sina Sina peoples in eastern Chimbu province, settlements and houses are dispersed; to the east, hamlets and villages are usual. Settlement in village communities creates discrete communal groups surrounded by garden and bushland; to the west, settlement is mostly continuous and groups intermingle. The eastern highlands is less wooded, and grassland stretches over formerly cultivated slopes; the communities lack the seclusion and protection of either natural forest or cultivated casuarina groves. Thus, in this area fortifications were often built around villages.

Population densities in the far eastern area are generally rather low – twenty-five to seventy-five people per square mile (10–30/km²) – with small villages and hamlets surrounded by considerable areas of land which is cultivated on a long-fallow system. With the sort of warfare that has prevailed in this area until recently, much of the land might be too exposed for safe settlement and cultivation. Density declines from west to east, and is lowest among the various groups of the eastern-language family.

DENSITY

The most intensive agriculture, with dense populations, was found in only four areas: Kapauku, Dani, Enga, and Chimbu. Each has less populous areas around a closely settled and continuously occupied core. A density of 125 people per square mile (50/km²) may be a limit for shifting, long-fallow cultivation or the beginning of a more permanent form of settlement and land use. Thus, only the best land within these four centers of concentration has passed into permanent cultivation; there is always some poor, rough, or steep land rarely used, and other land cultivated on a long cycle. At moderate densities, between fifty and 125 people per square mile (20–50/km²), there may be a community core area occupied with houses and gardens for a long time or permanently, and other land cultivated intermittently or on a long fallow.

Fighting, disturbance, and migration make communities break up and move. Families seek help and sanctuary from relatives, but land is rarely taken over completely by a victorious neighbor. There is rather an ebb and flow of people in and out of a disturbed area. Thus the village communities, or centers of settlement, might be occupied for many years or permanently, whereas garden land is shifted from one area to another in a cycle of cultivation and fallow. But there is also invasion, raiding, burning, fleeing, and dispersal of settled areas. The community, with some losses, may be reestablished at a new location some time later.

The unoccupied stretches of grass, bush, and forest between concentrations of population might be viewed as an indication of capacity of the land to serve a larger population. But the resources must be also evaluated in terms of the potential productivity of this land, its accessibility, and the intercommunity relations which render the land usable: Is the land arable, in the agricultural sense, and is it safe from enemy invasion? Are there other factors such as malaria that affect occupation or population growth? If the land is arable and the population grows to need it, then some accommodation between communities may be required to make it usable and safe.

Population distribution and settlement, then, are influenced by a variety of environmental, cultural, and social factors – including the terrain, the land quality, technology, agriculture, community organization, and intercommunity relations. Where people cooperate in large communities, they may also join together for defense of territories, whether cultivated or not. But a small group may be unable to protect itself and lose its land to stronger neighbors. One community's strength and self-defense is affected by illness, crop failure, quarrels, and other occasional disturbances while another may seize the opportunity to expand its territory. These fluctuations have always been present in the New Guinea highlands, alongside other population growth and recession processes.

Since the introduction of sweet potatoes within the last 300 to 400 years, settlement has been made in higher altitudes of New Guinea and has provided a basis for a new spurt of population growth in the highlands. The specialized agricultural techniques developed by Kapauku, Dani, Enga, and Chimbu in their localities supported the densest and most permanent populations. The agricultural techniques practiced in the southern, western, and eastern highlands, using longer fallow cycles with drainage ditches and mounds or ridges for planting, may become a basis for more intensive and permanent agriculture in these areas. The population in these zones has not reached high levels, but in some places the density is now increasing. In some regions population expansion is limited by environmental conditions. The earthquakes and landslides that destroyed the villages and crops of thousands of Dani in 1976 and the occasional volcanic eruptions and ash falls have no regular or predictable effects on population. The western and southern highlands include some areas where frost sometimes occurs and even the composted mounds do not fully protect growing sweet potatoes. Occasional crop failures have prevented much expansion here. Sweet potatoes grow more slowly at higher altitudes and this, in turn, inhibits population growth. Regions of cold and cloud are present in many highland areas and these environmental conditions also limit population growth. The eastern highlands have less rainfall; sometimes crops are killed or much delayed by drought. And again, the population potential is less. Had the highlanders continued in their more or less isolated way for another thousand years, the relationship between population and sweet potato production with stone tools might have been tested. People may have created more intensive techniques or new forms of nutrient and water conservation in other areas. While population is dense in four highland centers, these levels might have been reached or exceeded in others. Now the changes in tools, crops, and health services have so greatly influenced many aspects of the population-land system that the former conditions cannot be tested and evaluated. There is diversification of economic activities and settlement on what had been little-used land.

In Chimbu the apparent center of population, where it is most dense and also where tribal tradition places the origin, is in the central and upper Chimbu Valley, a region of steep slopes and high-altitude gardens. The limestone-based soil is rich and productive, and there is no evidence that frost, drought, malarial infestation, or other environmental and disease factors had a long-lasting adverse effect on the population. Sweet potatoes are grown in permanent fields with short terms of fallow. With this high density, all arable land is cultivated. Forest products are only available at higher altitudes, where pandanus nuts also grow. Few wild animals are found in the forests, but pigs are raised for feasts and exchanges. They graze on temporarily fallow fields and are given cultivated foods. Density reaches 350 to 450 persons per square mile (135–175/km^2) in the cultivated areas, except in high-altitude forest areas.

This core area of the Chimbu Valley is a zone of intense competition for land, and all Chimbu tell of fights and migrations. A few Chimbu migrated north and east, but land there was limited and already occupied by eastern highlanders; the greatest trend of movement was south and west into less-settled land where a few more distantly related Chimbu and central-Wahgi peoples had settled. The populations mingled and reallocated land, so that in time western and southern Chimbu densities approached those of the Chimbu Valley. Another center of high density is the Sina Sina area in eastern Chimbu, where large villages line the ridges, and cultivation is nearly continuous close to the settled area. Population growth in Chimbu province has increased density still further and stimulated many to move and settle in less-occupied areas with relatives and, nowadays, in official resettlement areas or with host groups.

Sweet potatoes, which grow better than other tropical crops at altitudes over 5,000 feet (1,500 m), provided the highlanders with an adequate staple food and allowed the population to increase to the present high levels. But disease, occasional crop failure due to frosts, drought, and famine may stimulate migration and dispersal and restrict population growth. There is an interaction: Population increase makes the people use land more intensively, cultivate more frequently with improved techniques, and also stimulates group expansion and migration into less-occupied areas. In these areas, formerly used agricultural techniques may not be appropriate. Other ways may be developed, or the population may remain sparse. The complex interrelationship between population size, permanence of occupation or mobility, cultivation techniques, and agricultural intensity, competition, and land conquest make a somewhat unstable land and population system. Nevertheless, there do seem to be overriding trends: Population increase, agricultural intensification, and expansion into new areas is the general pattern.

Population growth is never unrestricted. There are physical, physiological, environmental, and social restraints so that rates of reproduction and growth do not reach and continue at the maximum possible. To understand the rate of population growth in the highlands, we must consider sexual practices, prohibitions on sexual intercourse, and mortality. (Marriage and family behavior will be discussed in Chapter 4.)

POPULATION GROWTH

We may not know all the factors in the reproduction and population growth process, but we can determine its main characteristics. Highlanders' maturation ages, sexual restraints, and marriage patterns result in few births to women under twenty years old. A long lactation period and sexual prohibitions when infants are under three years of age serve to space births at intervals of several years. The mortality of infants, children, and adults, and perhaps low fertility, limit family size. These factors all control population growth. There are setbacks due to epidemics and food shortages. When modern medicine is used to treat illness, and sexual prohibitions are relaxed, the result is that more children survive, families are larger, and there are more aged persons – all increasing the population to the extent that real population pressure is experienced in some areas and migration and resettlement occur as new sources of income and food are sought. This is evident today. Before such change in population, the slow increase of population and higher proportion of adults – with expansion of garden land and agricultural advances – seemed capable of producing adequate subsistence in all but the densest areas, where the population adapted to increased pressure by conquering other lands and migrating. However, if the population continues to grow in the highlands, safe limits may soon be reached if no new areas of land are made available. The carrying capacity is being tested now in some places.

There has also been a change in the economy; land is planted with cash crops, including coffee and tea, and the income from these enterprises is used to purchase food. In this partial market economy a family may be able to manage its land and income so as to feed more people. Recent changes affect all aspects of the land and population balance, changing the age structure, work patterns, food supplies, and living conditions so that trends can no longer be based on the interrelations between subsistence, health, and technology as they formerly were.

Fifty years ago the processes of population expansion had several outlets: warfare and land conquest, pioneering in the group hinterland, migration, and agricultural intensification. The limits had been approached only in a few places where settlement and agriculture were nearly permanent and soil was improved. The four population centers had developed intensive agriculture in an area of increasing size. But the hinterland could not always be intensified in the same way – different soils, slopes, altitude, and weather limited the use of some techniques. Here again, we see the interaction of environment and culture – the altitudinal limits of composting, the need for drainage, stone removal, slope retention, and the invention of new techniques in different environments.

Where extensive unused lands lay between highland settlements, some large areas have been acquired for coffee plantations, removing these from subsistence, introducing wage work, European settlers, retail shops, and a new economy for those employed in or living near the plantation. Much of formerly open areas in the eastern highlands and Wahgi Valley have become plantations, so population growth cannot be accommodated by expansion of subsistence agriculture. In Chimbu and Enga the native population was so dense that no plantations were permitted. Furthermore, neither the Upper Chimbu Valley nor the high-altitude slopes of the Enga area are suitable for growing coffee. Population expansion here is without local economic opportunity. In Chimbu, gardens are made successfully at altitudes of 8,000 feet (2,500 m), but in Enga and the southern highlands frosts occasionally damage high-altitude gardens. The most successful sweet potato subsistence gardening in New Guinea is concentrated between 5,500 feet (1,700 m) and 7,000 feet (2,200 m), between the malarial and frost regions where the people and the crops are healthiest and catastrophic setbacks are rare.

Estimating the human carrying capacity of land, even in a given subsistence-crop economy, requires detailed information on terrain, soils, climate, and technology. We lack adequate information for an assessment and can at best compare the information available. The densities recorded in the New Guinea highlands are mostly low to medium and reflect settled core-areas of villages, hamlets, or house clusters, and swidden cultivation with a ten- to twenty-year fallow for the main gardens. The four centers – Kapauku, Dani, Enga, and Chimbu – have each, in slightly different ways, come to a kind of climax, approaching the limits of population expansion under their present technology and social structure. Some groups, the Huli, Hagen, and Asaro, have a medium population density and intensified agriculture with special drainage or other practices. The population and agricultural practices of the Irian Jaya highlands are less known, but some valleys between the Balim Valley and Wissel Lakes may be densely populated. Among the factors which account for differences in population density are some noncultural ones: disease patterns, of which the presence of malaria at lower altitudes may be the most important, terrain, climate, and soils which may limit agricultural production.

We wanted to apply statistical tests to ascertain whether there is any overall correlation among these several elements, and whether the societies of the highlands, as far as we know them, may be measured or scaled in any consistent way. Are these apparent facets of intensity and size consistently interrelated? Can we set out hypotheses of interrelation, measure or scale or classify the societies, and test the relationships? After we developed these questions, Aaron Podolefsky planned and carried out a number of statistical tests, some of which are reported here; others have been published separately (Brown and Podolefsky 1976).

As an exercise in the method of comparison, we separately read and evaluated ethnographic reports on a number of highland societies and included geographic and government demographic data as appropriate; then the information was used in an attempt to assign measures, ranks, and categories for statistical analysis (see Table 6). Many techniques were considered, and certain problems of evaluation, such as insufficient data, uncertainty concerning the author's procedures, use of different standards in the source materials, and differences in the time of the study which affected the author's use of census and geographic information, were encountered. We will avoid a tedious detailing of our methodological efforts and failures here and present only some of the procedures and results in which we have some confidence. We consulted many ethnographic reports on the highlands and included all those that contained the data required. However, some areas have not been reported on, or the reports do not adequately cover our questions. We feel that the seventeen communities or societies (see Map 2) provide adequate

Table 6. *Population and agricultural measures for highland societies*

Society	1973 PNG Census density /km²	/mi²	Field research density	Settlement type	Agricultural intensity							Land tenure	Local clan (mean pop.)	Largest political unit (mean pop.)
					Enclosure	Fallow	Ground preparation	Erosion control	Water control	Fertilization	Total			
Kapauku (Irian Jaya)	N.A.[a]	N.A.	104	v[b]	1	2	2	0	1	-1	7	A[e]	200	600
Dugum Dani (Irian Jaya)	N.A.	N.A.	414	h[c]	1	2	2	1	1	1	8	A	N.A.	4,200
Huli	43.5	112.7	19	d[d]	1	1	2	0	1	1	6	B[f]	N.A.	500
Mae Enga	61.9	160.4	120	d	1	2	2	0	1	1	7	A	350	2,290
Raiapu Enga	34.8	90.1	185	d	1	2	2	0	1	1	7	A	270	1,072
Kyaka Enga	12.5	32.3	140	d	1	1	1	0	1	0	4	B	200	780
Kakoli	25.1	67.7	N.A.	h	1	2	2	0	0	1	6	A	318	318
Mt. Hagen	37.7	97.7	68	d	1	1	2	0	1	1	6	B	280	820
Kuma	19	49	100	d	1	0	2	0	1	0	4	B	383	475
Maring	14.6	37.8	64	d	1	0	0	1	0	0	2	B	40	200
Chimbu	86.8	225.1	260	d	1	2	2	1	1	1	8	A	650	2,400
Gururumba	44	113	37	v	1	1	2	1	1	0	6	N.A.	375	2,300
Siane	28.5	73.8	80	v	1	0	2	0	0	0	3	B	200	840
Gahuku Gama	35.3	91.3	N.A.	v	1	1	2	0	1	0	5	B	100	750
Bena Bena	34	88.5	N.A.	v	1	1	1	0	1	0	4	B	188	750
South Fore	11.9	30.8	33	h	1	0	0	1	0	0	2	B	39	180
Gadsup	30.4	78.7	58	v	1	1	2	0	0	0	4	B	N.A.	293

[a]Information not available. [b]Village. [c]Hamlet. [d]Dispersed homesteads. [e]Individual inherited land rights. [f]Group land-tenure.

comparable data for this study. Where more than one study in the same or different community was done for a given society, we have usually made those into a single case – for example, for the Maring – but independent studies in separate areas of such a large group as the Enga have been delineated into separate categories, specifically the Mae, Raiapu, and Kyaka. Unfortunately the data are inadequate to do the same for the Dani, although we know that the Dugum Dani of the Balim are denser than the Jalé, Konda Valley, and Wanggulam and that central Chimbu, the case used, has lower density than the Upper Chimbu Valley, Sina Sina, and portions of the Gumine area of Chimbu province, but comparable information is not available on agriculture and group size. We used the following sources: Huli (Glasse 1968); Mae Enga (Meggitt 1960, 1965); Raiapu Enga (Waddell 1972); Kyaka Enga (R. Bulmer 1960a, 1960b, 1965); Kakoli (Bowers 1968); Mt. Hagen (A. Strathern 1971, 1972); Kuma (Reay 1959); Maring (Clarke 1971, Rappaport 1968); Chimbu (Brookfield and Brown 1963, Brown and Brookfield 1967); Gururumba (Newman 1965); Siane (Salisbury 1962); Gahuku Gama (Howlett 1973, Read 1952, 1965); Bena Bena (Langness 1964, 1971); South Fore (Glasse and Lindenbaum 1971, Sorenson 1972, Sorenson and Gajdusek 1969); Gadsup (Du Toit 1975). Brookfield 1962 is used as a supplement in several cases. In addition, Howlett 1971, Brookfield with Hart 1971, and Brookfield 1972 have also been helpful to our investigation.

Population density can be measured on an overall basis for a whole tract of land, including high mountain, forest, lakes, swamps, bare rock and other nonagricultural land, some of which may be arable if cleared and prepared or exploited for wild foods, hunting, fishing, manufacturing materials, pig forage, and other uses. The measure of people to land where a large proportion of the land is nonarable will show a much lower density than is effectively the case, yet overall it may provide a common standard. We measured density and ranked societies in Papua New Guinea using the 1973 data for census subdivisions (see Table 6). Each of the societies could usually be assigned to the government-census subdivision which includes the community in which the ethnographer concentrated his studies. For the Kapauku and Dugum Dani of Irian Jaya we have only ethnographer's statements from studies some years ago (Pospisil 1958, 1963; Heider 1970, 1972b).

These 1973 census figures delineate all the Papua New Guinea cases for a single year, whereas the ethnographic studies were made over a twenty-year period, sometimes using early census data and sometimes before any reliable census data were available beyond the ethnographer's own local study. Some authors measure or estimate population density from their own local study of gardens, land use, fallow, and settlement. Others used government population and land studies, or generalized the local data for a larger area. Quite different information or standards might have been used in these studies. The average, or the highest figure might be given for a locality or a region, and the density measured by current gardens, by arable land, or by all the territory. These cannot be placed on the same scale unless carefully adjusted. However, after elimination of very deviant estimates we found a substantial correspondence between the rank order of societies according to census subdivisions and ethnographer's figures, so that we are fairly confident of our classification and ranking of societies, if not of the absolute figures. We then placed Kapauku and Dani in the census series at points corresponding to their place in the ethnographer's statements and constructed a density ranking for the whole series (see Table 7).

For agricultural intensity we have used a complex, weighted measure based on enclosure, fallow period, ground preparation, water control, erosion control, and fertilizing. Each society was then scored on agricultural intensity, with these values: fallow period zero to six years = 2, six to ten years = 1, ten or more years = 0; ground preparation including grids, trenches, or mounds = 2, complete tillage = 1, simple slash and burn clearing = 0; for water control, (usually by ditches), enclosure of gardens by fences, erosion control (such as walls), and fertilizing (with compost or enriched soil) the score was 1 if present, 0 if absent (see Table 6.). All of the highland societies enclose gardens to keep out domestic pigs. The results, translated to ranking, show a number of tied scores which have been so assessed (see Table 7).

Table 6 includes data on two other characteristics: settlement type and land tenure, which cannot be expressed in series. Settlement type in the highlands is noted as: v – village, d – dispersed homesteads, or h – hamlet. The presence of a men's house in the settlement where all males of the locality sleep and center their social and political activities after weaning or during childhood is characteristic

Table 7. *Ranking of highland societies*

	Population density	Agricultural intensity	exogamous local clan population	Largest political unit
Dani	1	1.5	N.A.	1
Chimbu	2	1.5	1	2
Mae Enga	3	4	4	3.5
Gururumba	4.5	7.5	3	3.5
Huli	4.5	7.5	N.A.	12
Kapauku	6	4	9	11
Hagen	7	7.5	6	7
Raiapu Enga	9	4	7	5
Gahuku Gama	9	10	12	9.5
Bena Bena	9	12.5	11	9.5
Gadsup	11	12.5	N.A.	15
Siane	12	15	9	6
Kakoli	13	7.5	5	14
Kuma	14	12.5	2	13
Maring	15	16.5	13	16
Kyaka Enga	16.5	12.5	9	8
South Fore	16.5	16.5	14	17

of New Guinea settlements. It may be on the village or hamlet plaza or on a ridge-top or slope, with other houses clustered or lined nearby. Where homesteads are dispersed among gardens and pig-foraging areas, the men's house, in a clearing, is a social center for the local group. Men's ritual and other affairs are planned in the men's houses and conducted there or in a secluded place away from the uninitiated. Settlement form has no apparent relation to population or agriculture; village forms predominate in the eastern highlands whereas dispersed-homestead or hamlet clusters are more general elsewhere. Village clusters and long-house structures are found in central New Guinea near Telefomin and in some highland fringe societies.

Land tenure, further discussed in Chapter 3, was assessed from the highland literature with two categories: A – predominantly individual, inherited rights to specific marked plots; and B – predominantly rights to use land in group territory when it is taken out of fallow. Whereas group territory is recognized nearly everywhere, individual plots are held and inherited mainly where the fallow period is short, and trees and shrubs are planted.

The next important question concerned the size of groups – exogamous local clan-groups, and the largest political unit whether that be the tribe, alliance, parish, phratry, or clan cluster. Some ethnographers concentrated their studies and presented detailed information on a village or locality. Others provided some information on all clans and tribes of the language and cultural group, often using government census figures for clans, tribes, and regional grouping. We attempted to derive an average size of the groups for ranking, classifying, and comparing. This was possible for all but a few peoples, such as the Huli and Dani, who have no localized exogamous group, or for those people for whom the author has not presented the required information. Wherever possible we calculated a mean population size of the exogamous, local clan-group and the largest political group and ranked these. The further analysis of this material will be discussed in Chapter 5, where the implications of the relation among population density, territory, and the size of clan and tribe will be considered.

In our correlations we employed population density as an independent variable, measuring its association with agricultural intensity, the population of the exogamous local clan, and the population of the largest political group. Spearman rank order correlation (rho) measures agreement in ranks assigned to the societies. The value of r_s^2 is the percentage reduction in error in predicting one variable from the other. We found density and agricultural intensity to be:

$$r_s = .845$$
$$r_s^2 = .714$$
$$p < .0005 \quad \text{one tail}$$

The descriptive and non-parametric statistics show that population density is directly associated with agricultural intensity. Agricultural intensity is a measure composed of six variables, as shown in Table 6.

We also followed two other procedures: classifying the societies into three groups of high, medium, and low for all the variables, and dividing them into two groups of high and low for each of the variables. We used gamma (γ) for the classifications of the three levels and Yule's Q, a special case of gamma, for the dichotomizations into high and low. Gamma (γ) and Q are the percentage of guessing errors eliminated by knowing the second variable. On population density and agricultural intensity, we found:

$$\gamma = .861$$
$$Q = .964$$

This duplicates, in terms of categories, the findings according to rank order correlations. The association between the population density and agricultural intensity is very strong.

Land tenure in relation to population density and agricultural intensity were examined, using a dichotomous division. The findings are:

on population density and land tenure $\quad Q = .72$
on agricultural intensity and land tenure $\quad Q = 1.0$

All three of the variables – agricultural intensity, population density, and land tenure – are associated. We then attempted to discover the reasons for this. When controlling for population density, the relation between agricultural intensity and land tenure remained; however, when controlling for agricultural intensity, we found no direct association between population density and land tenure. Because the components of agricultural intensity are many and varied, and combine in different ways to make the correlation with population density, we believe that there is an intricate, complex interaction between population density and agricultural intensity, rather than any unidirectional cause.

Further examination of the relation between agricultural intensity and land tenure reveals that the closest relation is between the length of the fallow period and land tenure: Individual land tenure is a product of short fallow and frequent land use. The recollection of use and marks of ownership in plants and shrubs provide the basis of individual land claims and inheritance rights.

The techniques and varied forms of agriculture, when placed on a scale of intensity, are closely associated with population density. Agricultural intensity, and especially the length of the fallow period, is associated with land ownership, so that the relationship may be depicted as:

population   agricultural   land tenure
density   intensity

No single element in agricultural intensity is closely correlated with population density. Adaptation to local conditions has produced many kinds of technological developments by highland peoples, and many varieties of agricultural intensity. The most densely populated peoples have the greatest number of intensifying agricultural practices, the least populated have the fewest, and between are medium density populations with intermediate agricultural intensity.

3
Land and locality

New Guinea highlanders know and appreciate the resources of their locality. Forest and bush is never wasted or destroyed. When land is prepared for gardens, wood and materials used for fences, building, tools, ropes, clothing, and so forth are set aside, and little of value is burnt. Both communal and individual property rights are recognized. Unimproved or uncultivated land and its products belong to the people of the locality; a garden plot cut from forest belongs to the individual or group who made the clearing, and the person who plants owns the crops. Similarly, a house is the property of builders and residents, to be used by their families and guests. Household goods, pigs, clothing, ornaments, and tools are individually owned even if they are shared in a family. Everywhere, the land of the ancestors is traditionally considered group territory; the products of one's labor are private or family property. Taking of property of any kind without permission of the owner may be considered theft, but the relations between the parties can make one instance a tolerated assumption of sharing among close relatives, and another an act of provocation to warfare.

In this chapter the environmental and technological aspects of highlands life will be discussed in relation to the land and to the rights of individuals and groups to territory and property. We will see how territory is a group resource, whereas occupied or improved land, used for gardens, houses, and other individual or group purposes, is property. The differences in land tenure are closely associated with the regularity of use: Long-fallow land and long-abandoned house sites may become available to any member of the community, but planted trees and occupied sites are individually or family owned. The relation between land rights and population density will be empirically demonstrated, with examples from several highland peoples. The meaning of locality, and importance of relations between people and places within the local area, will also be examined. Finally, settlement types will be discussed in relation to the distribution of land and territory.

TERRITORY

The group – a tribe or clan, often with a name distinguishing it from others of the same language and culture – has a general attachment to a local territory, that is, an area of land with all its resources. Territories may be subdivided into land of subgroups – clans, subclans, men's house groups, and families – who by tradition maintain rights to use resources and to make gardens in defined tracts of land. The crucial distinction is the present and past use of the land and its value to the community or individual. Any land with standing improvements – house, fence, planted trees, crops, land prepared for or in cultivation, and land which has recently been used as a burial ground, house site, garden, or ceremonial site – is known as personal or group property. All of the personal and group property, taken together, plus the intervening streams, forest, grassland, and arable land in long fallow in the locality are considered group territory.

Where land, forest, and resources are plentiful for the population, there may be little intergroup competition or concern for land claims. But some resources, especially trees which produce fruit or nuts, are of greater value and may become a source of conflicting claims while the settled areas and garden land are not attacked.

Everywhere, one important source of group solidarity is the need to defend property and territory against outsiders. The group with a territorial interest is larger than the family, smaller than the language-cultural group, and its territory comprises the area used for hunting, gathering of food and other domestic needs, gardens, and house sites. In the low-density highland fringe, group territory may be a vast tract, with valued sites for collecting and cultivation widely dispersed in the forest. Coordinated group activity is infrequent, but each family has a right to the resources of this territory. In the highlands, villages and homestead sites are used for long periods and rebuilt. Houses and gardens are private and family property. New gardens are made in forest or long fallow where the local group has a territorial claim. The exact boundaries of current gardens are clear. Planted trees and useful shrubs in fallow are individual property, marking former occupation and use, but overgrown fallow with no special tree planting loses its identifying marks and becomes available to the next generation of group members.

LAND TENURE

LOW-DENSITY AND SHIFTING AGRICULTURE WITH GROUP LAND-TENURE

The Baktaman of the highland fringe serve as an example of a group of very low density, shifting cultivation, and group tenure with no individual rights in fallow. Baktaman territory, in the Upper Murray and Palmer River region, covers 250 square kilometers of mountain and valley, most of which is utilized for hunting and gathering. The community of 183 people dwell in a close group of ridge-top hamlets, clearing the slopes around the settlement for defense. Taro is the most important food crop, maturing in six to eight months. Adjoining clearings in an area of fifteen- to twenty-year-old fallow land are made from time to time by a large number of families. The useful material cut down is taken for firewood or fences, large trees are ring-barked, debris is burnt, and each woman plants for her family. Individual trees and groves of sago, breadfruit, and pandanus are individually owned, whether discovered in the forest, planted, or transplanted in fallow land.

Parts of the eastern highlands have been cleared, cultivated, burnt, and then become stable abandoned grasslands no longer valued because the former garden area has not regenerated to arable land. Other garden techniques, planted grasses or trees, cattle raising, or other land uses may make these grasslands valuable in the future. But the slash and burn technique of clearing and cultivation, unimproved fallow, and further damage in warfare and successive burning has created these abandoned grasslands. Among the Fore of the eastern highlands (Sorenson 1972), where small hamlets are the usual settlement form, the land around the settlement is generally adequate for community garden needs on a long-fallow cycle. Pig-grazing land may be farther afield, with forest and grassland between settlements. The hamlets in Fore are impermanent settlements consisting of a group of kinsmen and sometimes nonrelatives. As a garden area is used up, new incursions are made into the forest, a hamlet established with a house for men and boys and two to three women's houses. This hamlet group is often an offshoot of a small village group. Several villages and their attached hamlets make up a local territorial group. Hamlets may include members of several sections of the larger local group. There has been little competition over residence and garden land and land claims mostly concern present and recently used land. The grasslands carry no marks of ownership. The accessible rain forest in the group's territory is considered desirable land for new gardens and houses. With population growth, increased garden land is required to feed people and pigs. In some areas competition for new land has led to warfare and alliances of villages, with hamlets and villages larger than the former settlements. If more of the forest area is cleared, a more intensive land use system may be developed with permanent territories and property rights in fallow.

Contemporary Fore hamlets are local sections of a territorial unit, a local group that is united to maintain and defend its boundaries. The local group is the domicile of several component kin groups, and these kin groups traditionally own sections of the territory. But this does not make for rigid membership segregation in localities or exclusive use of land by descendants of the founders: Immigrants, kinsmen, and refugees become established residents; they build houses, settle in localities, make gardens and participate fully in community life. Local and parish groups cannot be equated with kin or descent groups. Nevertheless, among Fore as among the more densely populated highland areas, there is a strong relationship between patrilineal kinship and land. As boys become men, they marry and raise families, remaining in the locality of their fathers. A patrilineal local group develops and persists through the generations, although individuals may enter or leave.

As an example of another highland group, of low to medium density and shifting agriculture, we take the Bomagai-Angoiang Maring (Clarke 1971), whose land, on steep slopes with numerous streams, is almost surrounded by forested mountain crests. In 1965 the whole group contained 154 people in two clans, each holding specific territories, sacred groves, and forest resources. On slopes in the settled, central area, garden land, house sites, and many wild products are found. The mountain forest is not inhabited, but some foods and materials are gathered, wild pandanus grows, animals are hunted, and some outlying gardens are prepared.

Gardens are cut from forest or long fallow. Crop growing and harvesting takes eighteen to twenty-two months. A great variety of crops is grown here at altitudes around 3,000 feet (914 m), which is lower than most of the central highlands. Clarke estimates that the present population could continue in the basin, with about a forty-year fallow period, cultivating at all times about one-fourth of an acre per person for subsistence needs. Garden and fallow land in reserve would allow eight acres per person without affecting the virgin forest. However, virgin forest is often considered good for a garden. Since land is abundant, and long-fallow land does not carry marks of ownership, there is little sense of land shortage. The preferred garden sites are chosen for their soil types, fallow cover, or convenience to a family. A man, alone or with some of his close kinsmen, selects a site and proceeds to clear and fence it for the family or families. Each wife of a man who clears has a garden section to plant and harvest; often friends do also.

Tsembaga Maring (Rappaport 1968), a nearby territorial unit of 200 people, is divided into three separate territories, and each small group has several scattered tracts, giving everyone access to the valued types of land. A house site or garden is inherited, but transfers between clansmen are readily granted. If a man of the group notices land which has been fallow for a sufficient period as especially convenient, he may ask the previous user for permission to use it. Land for gardens is also freely granted to other clans in the larger territorial group. Relatives from other Maring groups, affines, and friends receive land as loan and as permanent gift from the owners. The shifting attachments of men and their families make some gifts temporary; other gifts of land may be reclaimed for another garden cycle. Thus temporary needs can be accommodated in the relatively abundant land resources of the Maring. Movement and relocation of residence and garden take place within the group territory.

LONG-OCCUPIED SITES

This lack of exclusive, permanent, individual possession of land is found widely in the highlands, but land tenure shows many variations. Central highlands people, the Melpa of Mt. Hagen (A. Strathern 1972) are more numerous and have larger territorial groups or tribes of about 800 to 1,000 people. The density varies from about 68 to 118 persons per square mile. Near Mt. Hagen, settlement is more dense and tribal size is larger.

Settlements have as a permanent center a men's house and a cere-monial ground, with women's houses – where pigs are fed and sleep – nearby. These are often placed at a land use boundary, where a fence separates the inner garden land from the pig-forage area out-side and pigs enter from the outer area. A settlement usually consists of the families of two or more men, often a father with married sons, or a group of brothers; men not so closely related may join such a family group if it has a strong and active leader, or big man. A separate homestead of a man and his family may be established before the family grows or others join the group, and may remain after some residents have departed. Land needs for shifting cultiva-tion and pig-grazing areas, with retention of rights in fallow land by previous users and their descendants, make homesteads and settle-ments core areas. Although people may move, visit, and share with kinsmen and affines, they retain claims to settlements and land in localities where they have resided and gardened. Sometimes these are many miles apart and provide for diverse agricultural or social interests, with intensified pig raising at one site and some gardens at another. Modern roads make this type of divided residence possible.

Clan and tribe territories are made up of the settlement territories of their members and some bush or forest land. But land holdings are not static. Expansion and pioneering, conflict and competition change and redistribute land claims. Immigrants and refugees are given land, and the hosts expand their territory. An expanding group makes incursions into the outlying territory of neighbors and initiates a general movement into the area. Because of personal needs, a man and his dependents may make a temporary or perma-nent move to join affines or kin; thus, they may become personally attached to a landowner outside the man's own locality. If they remain, they are allocated additional land over time. Later, sons inherit this land and use it as long as they live in the locality. War refugees become dependent on their hosts and may be incorporated into the host's group.

Mt. Hagen is a moderately populated area; there are some continuously occupied and gardened areas interspersed with short-term gardens, land in fallow, and grazing land. The settlement areas are marked with planted trees and shrubs and defended against encroachment. Home sites and gardens are not relinquished, but the interests and alignments of people over time may shift, the former sites abandoned or lost in another group's expansion, and much of the land between settlements unused for years. The need for more garden land acts as the impetus to occupy or reoccupy bush and fallow land. Throughout, the group and tribal territory is recognized, and only warfare or large-scale migration changes these general boundaries. Yet without land pressure there have been substantial population movements between territories of different types and resources, for example, between hills and swamps that require complex drainage techniques.

LAND SHARING IN GROUPS

All of these land-tenure and property rights suggest an open group recruitment, land sharing, and especially a willingness or desire to have relatives as neighbors sharing resources. Property rights and sharing are the land and territorial aspect of interpersonal ties between kinsmen. In the eastern highland village communities, as well as the western highlands homestead settlements, individuals, married couples, families, and sometimes larger groups may, by inclination or as refugees, use unclaimed or long-fallow land in their own territory or in the territory of a relative of one of the group. If this land is in the residential locality, it may require no new building, but if it is too far away for daily walking convenience, a temporary or long-term move, and new houses, may be involved. The move may be instigated by a need or desire of the host, perhaps for the company and assistance of his daughter and her husband, or it may be the wish of a man to live near his sister and her husband. Good relations between host and immigrant are essential when the move is made, and the arrangement does not outlive the mutual satisfaction. But the relationship may outlive the host, as when the couple become active participants in the locality of a wife's father and stay on when he dies. We have found no significant differences in frequency of intergroup movement related to the villages or homestead settlement patterns. Although a family may use the land in two territories when they are adjacent and convenient to border area homesteads, land in two group territories is rarely convenient to two villages. Villages and their territories are certainly more discrete than scattered settlement in clan or tribe territories. Even when land is plentiful, some land is especially desirable because it is more convenient or productive for some purpose. Settlement and gardens may cluster in certain land forms, types, soils, altitudes, and so forth. The continuously used sites are planted with trees, shrubs, and flowers, individually owned and inherited patrilineally.

Modern facilities for movement in trucks and cars and economic diversification have increased the use of separate locations, and now families may have houses, gardens, and other interests in places separated by many miles. Those who have settled in economic development areas keep their interests and often keep land in their home territories. Older migrant groups have intensified their participation in activities at their ancestral homes.

Some groups, regularly or occasionally, clear, fence, and prepare for planting large tracts of fallow land in which no individual marks of ownership and former use remain. Such a garden tract is made by the Siane (Salisbury 1962) for special clan or local group distributions. Wahgi Valley Kuma, Melpa, and Chimbu may also organize large communal work-groups to clear and fence a broad garden area. This is done in grassland more often than where casuarina trees have been planted individually by owners of fallow land. The area is subdivided into sections for smaller groups, and within these, plots are individually owned by one person, but often shared with helpers. Plots may be designated for a special group use or ceremonial distribution; afterwards, when these plots are left to fallow, they may be reused by members of these groups, unless the entire area is in territory clearly held by one smaller group that asserts the claim later. Such land tracts have become communal cattle yards, coffee groves to be subdivided into individual sections, and other cash-crop fields communally initiated. Individual rights to trees, crops, and livestock are usual, even if the initial investment was communal.

Where group territories are discrete, as perhaps in Enga and Kakoli as well as most village areas, it may be rare or impossible for one person to maintain active participation in two territorial groups.

But many highland people do use land in their inherited and other territories and also are actively involved in exchanges and social activities in more than one group. The Huli often maintain houses in two or more territories. It is only when great distance prevents such multiple participation that membership is exclusive. In times of hostility and warfare, it might be necessary to take one side against another; this would be the ultimate test of loyalty, participation, and membership.

The warfare test may disappear with political unification in self-government. However, present development requires more land because population has grown and land is used for cash crops, coffee, and cattle as well as subsistence needs. Thus, the demand for land by members of territorial groups increases, and land is permanently in private or group use for subsistence and income production. There may then be an increase in permanent forms of land use and competition between individuals and groups for land as a basic resource in economic development.

PERMANENT SETTLEMENT AND GARDEN SITES

The formerly sparsely populated areas have a higher proportion of virgin and long-fallow unimproved land than do the higher density areas. Although one might expect that the main distinctions in ownership might follow the same principles in the lower as well as the higher density areas, the shorter fallow and core-settlement locations in the denser areas permanently retain marks of previous use and ownership – in planted trees, shrubs, fences, and other features – whereas the lower density areas do not. A long-established village, and its immediate surroundings, even in a region sparsely occupied, forms the center for a group of individual land-users and heirs. The Siane plant decorative cordyline plants in fallow land to mark the plot of a former owner; this is the basis of ownership claims by a landowner and his descendants. When fallow land is prepared for cultivation, the plot or strip is cleared by a group within the village, fenced by the men of the village, and then planted individually. A homestead site, ceremonial ground, grove of pandanus trees, and individual plants, or other resources are property with a permanent value. When land, whether in a garden or fallow, contains some perennial crops, trees, boundary marks, drains, mounds, fences, or other improvements from former use, the user or his successor or heir can point to these as property marks, validating ownership claims. The shorter-fallow garden lands, surroundings of settlement sites, and densely occupied areas carry such indicators in most or all of the group territory. Proportionately more of the group's land is claimed as private rather than communal property.

When land within such closely claimed territory is not used by its recognized owner, the owner may grant use rights to a visiting kinsman, or to a member of the group with need or desire for it at the time; such a grant may be specified as a limited loan, not a gift. However, when a fallow cycle follows such use, several marks of ownership may be present, and the rights of the original owner may be forgotten. Thus, land not in current use may be considered to be owned by more than one previous user or owner or to be group property. Still later, when the land is again prepared for gardening by one of the claimants, he may be stopped by a rival claimant, and a fight, mediation, or relinquishment of claim may resolve the conflict. But even in the densest areas, where there may be competition for valued land, the cultivator frequently allocates sections of a garden to friends, neighbors, and relatives to plant and harvest for themselves and sharing. Thus inherited or otherwise individually claimed land is often shared with others. Within the local group, among close kinsmen and cooperative neighbors, mutual aid, sharing, and sociable interchange prevail.

The marks and claims to property in land announce to all that a man and his family hold legitimate and demonstrable rights. But they are not bound to use these exclusively. Among the group that holds the territory as a whole and their kinsmen, actual land use does not strictly follow these rights at all. Convenience, preference, friendship, and other factors of personal choice are active forces which bring about individual and family movements, cooperation, visiting, and sharing. From the clearing of the land to the consumption of the crop, kinship and friendship operate in the sharing of work, subdividing of plots, and helping in collecting, carrying, and preparing the crop.

We have seen that population densities reach medium to high levels in some parts of the highlands, and that these areas have developed more intensive forms of agriculture: shorter fallow, permanent settlements, complete tillage, compost mounds, drainage and erosion control, more permanent fences, and longer cultivation periods with replanting. The person who has improved land defends his property; this also applies when a group has cooperated in improving a specific area. Arable land is allocated to group members who regularly use it and is not openly available to migrants or pioneers unless they are kinsmen or accepted guests. Territorial claims of groups are defended against intruders, if the land is rot in regular use by individual owners.

But the attitudes, territorial rights of groups, and individual practices of land tenure are not the same throughout the highlands. We may consider the Enga, whose density is medium to high, but whose cooler temperatures and liability to frost restrict crop growth. Enga prefer river valley gardening and construct large compost-filled mounds for sweet potato beds. Enga territories are clearly delimited; each clan, and within it each subclan, has a strip of land that runs through valley, river terrace to ridge-top, with a share of every available land type. Each family or lineage group occupies a number of homesteads and land plots in cultivation or short fallow. Planting casuarina seedlings in old gardens is the usual way to mark ownership.

Meggitt (1965: 223ff) explains the rights to land among the Mae Enga. A district about fifteen by fifteen miles is claimed by the Mae, but almost all the land, except mountain ridges and swamps, is claimed by smaller groups. Each phratry has a distinct territory, usually in one block. But within the phratry, clan territories are separate. The only common land might be ceremonial dance ground, the ancestor cult house, and drinking water springs. Clan land includes forest, swamp, bush resources used by all, streams, and pig-forage areas used by members and sometimes granted to other relatives or affines. The arable land is owned by individuals; if a permanent grant to outsiders is made, the clan members may object. Invasion of any part of clan land is resisted by clan warriors. The land of lineages, and usually of subclans, is scattered and intermingled within the clan territory. Any alienation or loss to outsiders obviously reduces the clan territory. Each small locality and garden area is divided into small plots belonging to individual men and families. When cultivated, the family plot is fenced, and its boundaries are recognized in fallow. Family heads with several sons allocate their garden land among their sons. Brothers keep a common interest; they or their sons take over land of a childless brother or guard the land of young sons of a deceased brother. The only assured land rights are those of patrimonial inheritance. Family surveillance of land rights protects patrilineage and subclan territories by group defense against invasions. The Enga have more fixed territories and firmer agnatic land rights than other highlanders. This is consistent with their recognition of land limitation, but it is not the prevailing rule among the more densely settled Chimbu and Dani.

CHIMBU LAND RIGHTS

Both the Chimbu and Dani peoples are spread over a large area, in different zones and at different population densities. Available land resources range from adequate or surplus to inadequate for the needs of the population. The traditions of the Chimbu tell of an original core population at Womkama in the Upper Chimbu Valley, then of fights, migrations, dispersal, and resettlement of groups in unoccupied or sparsely occupied territories in all directions outside the valley. From these traditions it is possible to understand the process of occupation, settlement and land tenure, adaptation of cultural patterns to local conditions, and individual initiative. The development of land tenure processes (Brookfield and Brown 1963) and population changes in the Naregu tribe can serve as an example.

According to the tradition, the Naregu were formerly a Chimbu Valley tribe, with land north and east of their present concentration. At that time, about one hundred years ago, the Gamgani group and the Numambugu clan of Naregu had a large holding of most of the southern and western land, with the Pentagu branch of the Numambugu in the eastern part of it. The Kombaku clan of Naregu, living in the Chimbu Valley, was defeated and driven out of the valley by the Kamanegu, a strong tribe then expanding. Individual families and subgroups settled in unused portions of the Naregu area and were invited to do so by the Numambugu who had no immediate need for such a large area. Gamgani had previously been an independent tribal group; some migrated westward while the dwindling remnant became closely allied to the Numambugu. They have now come to be in some ways like a small division of this group. Meanwhile the Pentagu grew and were established as a separate clan, with a broad strip of territory of the Kombaku separating them from the Numambugu. By 1930, the Naregu had four more or less distinct clan territories: the Gamgani in the southwest, and the Numambugu, Kombaku, and Pentagu rather like parallel strips each including lower southern grasslands, the middle slope of garden land, forest slope, ridge top, and some land into the valley to the north. The favored settlement location in this area is in the middle range of gardens, where men's houses and women's houses are more concentrated among gardens in various stages of growth and land is rested for a short time before replanting. Land claims are individual and permanent.

In Naregu territory the best land on the slope, about 12 percent of the total, is limestone soil which only rests briefly in fallow between harvest and recultivation. Families who have used these plots retain their interests with numerous planted trees, shrubs, and boundary markers. Plots are divided among brothers, and the groves of pandanus nuts are guarded at harvest time. These permanently enclosed garden and settlement sites are defended against any intrusion. Every part of the area is well known, its history of use is remembered, sites are named for past events, and ownership is fully recognized. The present center of settlement, close to the highway, is also clearly divided into individual property and frequently recultivated even though some of the soil is unproductive and crops may be poor. Other good and accessible garden land, also in the main gardening area but with soils or other conditions that do not allow or require such nearly permanent cultivation, is owned by individuals or sets of brothers. Precise boundary marks may not be maintained in fallow. The location of a garden is recalled by the gardening family and its neighbors, but when preparing for the next cultivation cycle, some years later, those with claims in the area subdivide according to mutual agreement. A newly married son or brother is allocated several plots, and the land formerly used by a family not now present may be used by another. There is flexibility in the size, location, and fallow of good land, which constitutes 44 percent of the area. Ninety percent of the people live in areas considered to be on the good and best land. In Naregu, poor soils, less accessible locations, swamps, and difficult terrain are less frequently used for gardens or houses than the best and good land. After cultivation a long fallow follows in which individual plot marks disappear. Today, some has been allocated to a group's cattle. The land is recognized as territory of a subclan; personal claims to ownership are made only when the land includes a garden, house, pighouse or bears other signs of individual use. Pigs may forage on all sides of the individual plots. The Naregu, we found, is a tribe with medium density as compared with other Chimbu tribes. Density is higher in the Chimbu Valley where people have less long-fallowed land, and most land is used more intensively.

The general rule is that individual ownership – of gardens, houses, groves of pandanus nuts, planted trees and shrubs – prevails in the best land. Sons garden with their fathers and take over the land as they marry and need it. Collectively, individual claims combine to make up subclan territories. Recently cultivated, long-fallow, grasslands, and pig-forage land of individuals and subclans also are considered subclan territory. The territory of a subclan is scattered in parcels, interspersed with the land of other subclans in the clan, so that each subclan, and each family within it, has access to land of every available type. The best land is minutely subdivided, while land cultivated on long fallow, perhaps once in twenty-five years, carries few individual marks of ownership. The combined subclan territories form clan territories, which on the whole lie as strips that traverse several land types. A few outlying gardens, in rare land types or pandanus groves, are exceptions to this strip principle and demonstrate the importance of individual access to these special resources. Forest resources, wild plants used for food or in manufacturing rope, twine, or other products are shared by groups.

The present pattern of individual land rights developed through pioneering, inheritance, and gifts from kinsmen and affines. Except on the boundary between clans or tribes, individual plots of land do not pass from the territory of one group to that of another. Rather, a guest is allocated temporary garden rights which revert to the owner after harvest. But if the guest becomes a permanent resident, he and his children become incorporated in the group and will gradually acquire permanent rights to land which they are invited to use. If new fallow land is prepared for a group of gardens, this guest family is allocated a section by the host or local leader. They may be given some very good land or trees that belonged to their host or to a local man who died without heirs. Such reallocation of highly valued resources is managed by the leading men who have control over their own holdings and act as trustees of land and resources for the group, guarding the interests of orphans, migrants, members, and guests. In return, a guest provides the host and leaders with garden produce and pigs, supports group endeavors, and joins his other followers. While some war refugees have no other home or land many migrants have land in two territories. All migrants have joined their kinsmen, or their wife's kinsmen, and are immediately linked to hosts. Today, access to cash-crop land is a stimulus to resettling with relatives or in blocks.

In defeat and forced migrations of larger groups, as happened to the Kombaku several generations ago, the displaced group may receive a sizable tract in a grant from another subclan or section – often a gift to a daughter's husband's group, or to another section of one's own clan. This transaction nearly always occurs within the tribe. Only a few refugee gifts to small groups of kinsmen or affines of other tribal origin are recounted, and these are usually gifts of infrequently used borderlands. The boundaries of subclans, clans, and tribes change with these border loans and gifts and are sometimes disputed later. At the time, the land may be regarded as of little value and not needed. The donor may welcome friendly neighbors, who provide a bulwark against enemy tribes. But with intensive use or if trees are planted by the new owners, the land may gain in value and productivity; fallow planting of casuarina, tillage, and trenching improve soil fertility.

The settlement core of the tribe is in the central area, often on the best land available. A tribe has a block of territory that it defends as much as possible. Where good land is on the boundary of two tribes, competition for this area is a constant source of friction, attacks, fighting, looting, and reoccupation. When the highlands were under Australian administration, and since independence, some of these most valued locations have been the site of ceaseless litigation and continued warfare. Only where a relatively undesirable no-man's land separates Chimbu tribes is there little competition and fighting over land by neighboring tribes.

As we have mentioned, the Naregu's population density and land resources are about average among the Chimbu. In the Middle and Upper Chimbu Valley, the traditional origin of all Chimbu, densities are higher, most land is permanently fenced and fallowed for shorter periods, and individual claims are kept in fields with permanent boundary marks. The holdings of individuals and clans are tightly interdigitated. There is no long-fallow land or large area for pig forage. The Naregu's pigs forage in forest, grassland, and fallow fields, whereas pigs in the Upper Chimbu Valley forage in limited areas, are tethered in old gardens, and receive more of their sustenance through hand-feeding than do Naregu's pigs.

The system of kinship and marriage, and the prevailing good relations between kinsmen and affines, allow a Chimbu to obtain short-term, long-term, or permanent land gifts from relatives within the local group of his own subclan and clan, or from his mother's or wife's clan, which is usually nearby. Thus the gift of land does not necessitate changing residence. A move to another tribal territory for access to land may lead to the permanent migration of a family. Cumulatively, this redistributes population among tribal territories. Group migration into sparsely occupied land has occurred in periods of crisis, for example epidemic, acute crop failure, or large-scale defeat. Outlying groups of Chimbu tell of past migrations and of establishing settlements and gardens at their new locations. Often they obtained their first land as guests of host kinsmen, and other members of this group followed these leaders. A migration into unoccupied land might also be pioneered by a few who were later joined by their fellow clansmen. When a migrating group has a large area available, this becomes their group territory and the group may work together to clear and fence a tract for gardens and allocate plots to individual men and their families. During and after cultivation the man is considered owner of the land, although the crop owner is the one who has planted, usually the owner's wife or a guest. Boundaries may be marked with cordyline shrubs. If the man dies before recultivation, his sons assume his ownership rights. When it is time to prepare the land for cultivation again, the sons decide how to allocate it and may keep it jointly or as separate holdings. Individual preferences, cooperation, and agreement guide their actions. No sons are deprived of claims to sufficient land, and none are forced to garden against their wishes. Outsiders, friends, kinsmen, or guests are also accommodated by general agreement.

The Chimbu system is adaptable to population changes and needs resulting from personal or group movements. Expansion from the central valley into outlying areas has accommodated some land needs, but the current population distribution continues the original pattern of great density at the center and less density at the western edge of expansion. To the north, high mountains form a population boundary. To the east and southeast other dense populations of Chimbu, Sina Sina, and eastern highlands peoples are encountered. The southern boundary at the Wahgi River is of less desirable land, but the Marigl Valley is very densely settled. Little expansion to the south of this has occurred, for reasons not yet understood. Thus, the westward expansion has been greatest. The Chimbu now inter-mingle with people of the Wahgi Valley, which is a moderately settled area.

High density in the central core is also found among the Balim Valley Dani (Heider 1970) and the Wissel Lakes Kapauku (Pospisil 1963). At Dani settlement sites the land is intensively used and individually owned; in the flat valley with its ditches and channels, land is cultivated very frequently. Kinsmen and affines often move and share in settlement compounds and gardens within the larger territorial group.

Kapauku agricultural land is owned individually. A village is a center for a patrilineal group, with some attached kinsmen and af-fines also resident. A landowner plans garden development for his family and dependents. A man inherits land from his father. During the father's lifetime a son who is allowed plots for cultivation may later claim these as his own. Sons divide their father's land after his death, the eldest having more choice than others. If a man has no sons, then brothers, brothers' sons, or father's brother's descendants inherit his land. The Kapauku big men have no authority over land. Some land is transferred by sale, lease, gift, or other arrangements. The land tenure practices of these peoples, densely populated inten-sive agriculturalists, confirm their concern with having sufficient land for family and group needs.

Permanently and densely settled groups in the highlands practice the more intensive forms of agriculture, including recultivation and short-fallow of good garden land, fertilizing, maintaining rights to land with boundary marks, and planting trees and shrubs during fallow periods. The rights of sons and brothers to inherit land are defended. Where the overall density is moderate or high, especially productive or protected sites with the best soil are closely guarded, individually owned, and inherited.

LOCALITY

Until recently the Papua New Guinean's world was very limited. Travel outside a clan or tribe territory was uncommon. Trade friends and distant relatives acted as hosts and protectors outside the home territory. But within this territory, all resources, streams, hills, slopes, flats, pools, trees, plants, animals, and people were closely known. Since Australian colonial control, road and air travel for migrant laborers has been common. Yet few workers migrate permanently and most highlanders rarely leave their home regions for long. Most relatives or affines are in one's own or neighboring group territories.

Living his whole life in this area of a few square miles, at most a few dozen, and living in and with its land and vegetation, a highlander learns its every feature – every rock, pool, bend in a stream, diverted path, fallen tree, and growing bush is recognized. Its present and previous condition might be compared. Events that occurred at each spot are recalled; people who lived, sickened, quarreled, made gardens, or saw ghosts at these places are remembered, their experiences recounted. Every knoll, house site, brook, and any spot where some memorable event occurred bears a name. Names call up physical features, past events, and stories. Within the territory, the distribution of useful plants is known; this information – the nearest source of a certain tree, medicinal plant, roofing material, fruit, bark, and so forth – is shared and passed on to children and immigrant wives or other relatives. At the same time, a scarce good may be very hard to find in unfamiliar territory, and, in fact, the presence of variants, substitutes, or alternatives may be a basis of differentiation among tribes of the region. The lifelong association with a territory makes every part of the locale a reminder of the past, a force for continuity. Tales of the past are repeated to the young, become a part of their tradition, and tie them to the area and to identity with the group.

The names and stories of the territory, even more than the evident physical features, are a special possession of its people. They are a body of knowledge, the cultural tradition of the place and its residents. When strangers come, their strangeness is reinforced by their ignorance of these traditions; they do not know the place names, the group names, or the stories of important events. Pioneers must create the names and stories of their new homeland. Newcomers or conquerors may not know the dangers, spirits, or significance of places and their names. Locality associations are retained: A displaced group carries its tradition of abandoned sites and lost ties to the past. They may hope to recapture the land and reestablish the ties to locality.

A people's tradition includes sites where the group's identity and history is especially meaningful. In New Guinea, among shifting cultivators, forest features may be distinctive – peaks, valleys, exceptional trees, pools, and sites favored by game animals. Garden sites may be chosen for their physical characteristics or for traditional reasons. Places associated with people are most important; the lands, trees, burial grounds, ceremonial grounds, and house sites have a particular meaning if they are remembered as being associated with enemies, relatives, spirits, occasions of success or failure, or group pride or disappointment. When ceremonial grounds are the arena for group display, exchange, or expressions of solidarity, the ground and its name signify the group's prestige.

These places become the dwelling places of spirits whose support makes achievement possible. A group symbolizes its unity and existence by the place names of its territory; its migrations by its lost sites, sites traversed, and occupied. The home territory and settlement place of a highlander is the source of his livelihood, his security, and his welfare. The place where he has lived is also the home of his nearest relatives, the people upon whom he depends and with whom he defends his property rights. The most important ties between people are those of coresidence.

THE MEN'S HOUSE GROUP

Traditionally in the highlands, giving birth took place in or close to the mother's main dwelling house, but today many births occur in medical facilities. Some highlanders construct a separate birth hut as a woman nears parturition. The infant spends most of his time with his mother, and the family gathering place is the woman's house. A child is carried to gardens and neighboring houses in the hamlet or homestead area: The child's acquaintance with all members of a village or dispersed clan develops gradually. There may be some restrictions on exploration; often girls and women are barred from sacred sites. Boys may be initiated into certain secret cults and shown the objects in a group ritual. However, even before initiation takes place, the existence of secret rites and places is known by the children.

A hamlet or neighborhood, consisting of a number of houses clustered together on a ridge, hill top, or gentle slope in a clearing with some shade trees and garden plots nearby is perhaps the most typical basic settlement form. A number of small, separate women's houses, round or oval, are clustered near a larger men's house where married men and youths gather and usually sleep. Other houses, gardens, and livestock belonging to the settlement group may be dispersed and intermingled with those of other local groups, but this hamlet-neighborhood group is a cohesive unit of kinsmen and mutual aid. The typical hamlet group consists of a small patrilineage or extended family – a few men (less than ten), and their wives and children. For the most part the men are related; they may be the sons and grandsons of one man, or a group of two to three brothers, or several men of the same subclan who hold adjacent land plots and cooperate in building and gathering. Any male guests – son-in-law, wife's brother, or matrilateral cousin, for example – of men of the group will sleep in the men's house. If these guests settle among the group, their wives and children will have a house in the cluster. In the Chimbu's territory, there is much mobility and regrouping within the subclan, and even with other subclans or clans.

The men of a local kin or family group have a lifelong association; they may visit kinsmen elsewhere, or choose to live in another part of the community land for extended periods, but from birth they are interdependently linked in common interests. Any threats to safety and security, loss, or need of an individual or family affects the others. Their welfare depends on one another; success in gardening or in competition with outside groups is due to cooperation and the work of all. This interdependence is the basis of mutual aid and social control. A man, with his wife and children, can satisfy subsistence needs alone while in good health, but any disability or attack endangers this independence and requires assistance from others. This basic, local cooperative group of the families of kinsmen is almost a worldwide phenomenon among rural peoples. In the New Guinea highlands, it varies in size, composition, and permanence – both among areas and within a tribe. The hamlets and villages of the highland fringe may be isolated and independent, but in the central highlands they are usually part of a larger clan and tribe.

The men's house, which serves as a focus of men's activity and the social center of the settlement is, traditionally, almost universal throughout New Guinea. Valuables and sacred paraphernalia may be kept there, where women and uninitiated children may not see them. While men and older boys do usually sleep in the house, some men have small private houses which they sometimes share with their sons or visitors. But the men's house and its foreground clearing is the local group's gathering place, where men and youths spend much of their leisure time, make and discuss plans, prepare for ceremonies, rituals, exchanges, and warfare. The wives and children of these men are drawn into their activities, but may not take much part in making plans.

The men's house is larger and often more prominently located than other houses. Numerous paths connect gardens and other houses, and visitors are naturally led to the men's house clearing. When there are intergroup hostilities, the men's house is the center for mobilizing the group for attack and defense. In the past, a common form of attack was a predawn raid to set fire to a men's house. Thus escape tunnels were sometimes built and thickets or fortifications used for protection. Individually and in group discussion, men decide about and plan execution of economic, social, political, and ritual activities – for example livestock allocation, garden clearing and development, building, fencing, initiation of youths, display and exchange ceremonies, warfare and revenge, marriage exchanges, death payments, and birth payments. The daily gathering of the men's house group, where such matters are first discussed, provides a forum for suggestions, the airing of disputes and problems, teaching and practice sessions for songs, and the recounting of myths, stories, and experiences. As boys are integrated into their father's house group, they join a group of men and boys with strong common interests in the locality and welfare of the group. The men often jointly clear and fence a garden area for the other family plots.

The wives and daughters of these men have a more separate and independent life in scattered houses. Women's house locations and distributions are integrated with gardening and pig-raising requirements. When village or hamlet settlement form is general, a group of women's houses are clustered or in the clearing near each men's house. Among the Dani a fenced hamlet contains men's houses, family houses, pig houses, and kitchens. Some eastern highlands people build large villages with a men's house at one end and a large open space with women's houses on each side. Other settlement forms include clusters, streets, and irregular groupings. Whatever the form of the settlement, the men's house is a central place for the inhabitants and a focus of communal life; it is usually prominently sited. A woman's house, in contrast, is more often sited for convenience to her domestic activities, especially gardening and food preparation. If the garden and food preparation areas are not convenient to the pig-forage and sleeping areas, another house may have to be constructed. Where villages are large, in the eastern highlands and eastern Chimbu, most women have a village house, used during group activities and for some food preparation, but also regularly visit and often sleep in a distant house, near gardens which must be tended and harvested to feed the family and the pigs. In dispersed homestead forms, where gardens are widely scattered, women often move among several locations of old and new gardens and houses. A woman's neighbors in these several locations may be of different local groups. Each woman moves in an independent round of activities. In their daily life, women work more independently than men; they have separate garden plots, separate houses, and spend much of their time alone or with their small children. A woman is rarely far from neighbors whether she is in her garden or house. She joins with other women often to cooperate in gardening and to prepare food for men and visitors to the men's house, and for social gathering. But her primary responsibility is for her husband, children, and livestock. A woman, more than a man, is likely to be berated and accused of neglecting her family for other activities.

A men's house population is augmented and decreased as men move into or out of the locality. Several studies show that while a father is alive, his sons, married and unmarried, usually stay in the same house as he does. However, when the father is dead, adult brothers often live in different men's houses. They plan and move independently, using their inherited land plots in different cycles, and cooperating with age mates and friends in the subclan. A man's work in gardening consists mainly of preparing the land and fencing: After that he may plant some sugar and bananas, but most planting, tending, and harvesting are done by women. Thus the man need not reside near an established garden, but may prefer to stay in a location that is nearer to the center of the settlement. Men's activities and interests in exchanges and intergroup relations take them out of the locality to visit and plan with other men. A prominent or big man spends proportionately more time in traveling, visiting, and arranging exchanges or intergroup meetings than do other men of the group. He often has dependents who carry out domestic and subsistence work.

The men's house must be replaced from time to time: In Siane, men's houses are replaced every three years, whereas we found the average houselife in Chimbu was four years. The houses, as we have seen, are built of wood, reeds, and grass, not of permanent materials, and in time they deteriorate, leak, and rot. The interior of the house becomes smoke-charred and infested with bugs and vermin. A few timbers may be reused, but new wood, vines, bamboo, reeds, and grass are required. Besides the need for fresh materials, a change in site may be required because of garden area shifts, ceremonial plans, population expansion, or dispersal to different locations in the territory. Even during the lifetime of a house, the inhabitants may use it intermittently, or abandon it, because of interests elsewhere. Some men may quarrel, build a separate house, or visit or migrate to other houses within the clan or subclan group or join relatives in other areas. Choices and needs may direct activities elsewhere, so residence is changed.

House construction is a major, group task of men. The responsibility is with the family to replace or establish a new women's house. The husband, usually with the help of some men of his men's house, or others, gathers materials and, in the course of some weeks of intermittent activity and with help from time to time, builds the house. An old widow's house is built by her sons or other men of the group. The men's houses are bigger than those of women, and a coordinated group effort is made when a men's house has to be replaced or established at a new location. The men who intend to reside there, plus some helpers who may be members of the local group although currently residing elsewhere, plan and work together. Often a leading man of the subclan takes the initiative, which includes plans for gardening and exchange ceremonies. Men work intermittently. Framework, wall, and roofwork require several men working together, while one or two men may carry on between spurts of group effort. In Chimbu, the women's main contribution to house building is cutting and carrying the grass for thatching the roof. This ordinarily is called for, and done by several wives of the men workers after the walls and roof supports are finished. On days when many men work together, some of their wives may cook food and provide the workers with an afternoon meal.

Clearing of forest or long-fallow land, preparing ridges, ditches, or mounds, and fencing tracts of garden land, are also often, but not always, cooperative efforts of a men's house group. Men who have land interests together plan and organize building and garden preparation for their families. A man may choose to live and work apart from others, or he may vary his participation by visiting and sharing with relatives elsewhere. Another cause of dispersal may be the frictions of communal life – conflicts over property, unwillingness to participate in group enterprises, and a feeling on the part of one man or family that the demands that have been placed upon them are excessive. Nevertheless, joint interests and the satisfaction of cooperative work bring men together more often than not.

There is everywhere a group of men, with one or more who usually initiate activities, that takes an active part in planning and carrying out group enterprises. They join with other men's house groups in the neighborhood, the village, and the clan territory for larger scale action such as preparing a large garden for a food display and distribution to another clan. They also cooperate for defense of local territory. Some married men with little ambition, the old, widowers, bachelors, and others so inclined, keep more apart, often having smaller gardens, fewer pigs, and a retiring life. They join in some group enterprises, but not all.

Leading men, or big men, often have dependents who work at their direction. A big man may have several wives and a group of followers which includes his wives' brothers, wives' fathers, and sisters' husbands – that is, affinal relatives who have moved from their home area and use land belonging to the big man. A big man often adopts young kinsmen and helps them establish a family. These affines and kinsmen are so indebted to him that they consider their food production and livestock to be at the disposal of the leading man. When a cooperative group land-clearing or other task is done, the wives of the big man and his dependents prepare a meal for all. Or when the men's house group has visitors from other groups, for example to plan a marriage or a feast, the women provide food for visitors. Big men usually have several wives, who can provide food for such gatherings and pigs for exchange. The wives of dependents, often including sisters of the big man, also bring food from their gardens and cook at the gatherings. Thus the big man, with his dependents, is the center of a men's house group which makes local decisions about activities. Some dependents may later move out on their own, so that the big man cannot indefinitely rely upon their contribution. If they are birth members of other groups, they may return home with their family. If no big man dominates, several men form a men's house core group, a flexible and variable unit. However, men may be drawn away from alliance with such groups by a big man whose plans and energy attract followers.

Women have a very important contribution in food and pig production, which is essential to subsistence and prestige. Their needs for land and houses, and decisions about locations, scheduling of ceremonies, and organization of group activities are the responsibility of men. Women take little part in men's group discussions: They are rarely present when decisions are made, and are not often consulted. A man should know the condition of his livestock, crops, and valuables so that he can decide when and how to participate in payments and exchanges. Only an occasional woman, a widow or dominant wife, makes payments or receives valuable gifts in her own name. Some vegetable gifts are made to or by women in Chimbu.

The men's house group is a primary affiliation. In past times the danger of attack and need for joint defense made coresidence of men in groups necessary. Men's ceremonies were planned in the house and performed in seclusion from women and children. Garden lands and other activities were sited together for protection. Thus the needs of security for individuals and mutual assistance combined to favor local group solidarity. However, at present the size, level of joint activity, and permanence of these local groups is highly variable both within and among communities. With the enforced truce of recent administration, and decline of men's ritual activities, men's house groupings are of less importance. In many areas small houses or family dwellings are increasing, and the men's house has become an occasional leisure gathering place and dwelling of a few men. Nevertheless, the communal gathering, planning, and small-scale ceremonial functions of the men's house and its clearing do continue.

Highland peoples vary in their eating and visiting patterns. Often, men have afternoon family meals at their wife's house and then return to the men's houses for the night. Thus in villages, hamlets, and neighborhoods a convenient distance between eating and visiting areas is usually achieved. But when a woman feeds pigs and sleeps far from the men's house, she may have to arrange for someone else to bring or prepare food for her husband, especially during the rainy season. Because it is reported for some highland peoples that women are prohibited from entering a men's house, the woman might send a child to the men's house with food for her husband.

Huli men maintain land interests in several areas and often have houses at two or more localities. They harvest and cook their own food, independent of their wives. The men's house in Huli is small, built by one or more men, and used by the owner, his sons, kinsmen, and tenants with an average of 2.7 persons per household. Women's houses are used by a woman and her children, with often a kinswoman of the woman or her husband. The Huli's use of garden and house land in different territories and the separation of man and woman in food preparation is unusual in the highlands. Cognatic descent is another facet of this social system: Rights to land and residence are inherited by men and women, and men get these rights from mother and father, so each husband and wife pair is affiliated with several territories. The Huli may live and garden in several territories (Glasse 1968).

The dispersed settlement pattern in the Mt. Hagen area takes a somewhat different form. There are ceremonial grounds where a big man and some of his followers have a house which is the main ceremonial meeting place of a subclan group. The settlement may center around this house, or garden interests may disperse the group. The settlements may consist of the dwelling of one family, or of hamlets, where up to sixty people may live in a cluster of men's and women's houses. The settlement may consist of one senior man, plus his sons, their wives, children, and others, or two or more men and their dependents. Pioneer homesteads are built to exploit new garden areas, and the population in these areas declines when the land is depleted. Most moves are within clan territory, but moves to join kin in other territories are frequent (A. Strathern 1972). The settlement group, rather than the men's house, would seem to be the basic local unit in this area.

Mae Enga men's houses average 5.4 men and boys (Meggitt 1965); women's houses average 3.3 persons. Family land interests are distinct, and people live where they have rights to land. But the land of a man is scattered throughout the subclan and clan territory, so that garden neighbors need not be lineage mates. The men who share a men's house are frequently members of one subclan, but as in other highland societies, men join other groups near their own land or move in temporarily or permanently with relatives and receive a share of garden land. Among Enga groups, there are different styles and sizes of men's houses.

A distinctive, fenced compound is built by the Dani in Irian Jaya (Heider 1970). Inside, a large round men's house and two or more smaller women's houses are clustered, along with pig sties and a communal cook house. Pigs run in a fenced area and may be led into foraging land outside the compound. Sacred objects are stored in the men's house, from which women are excluded. The courtyard is a pathway and gathering place for inhabitants and visitors. Banana, tobacco, and some other crops are grown in a small area within the compound, but the most important garden beds, which are in the valley floor and on slopes, are used on a short- or long-fallow cycle.

Compounds cluster in groups. The many small compounds are not distinctive territorial or social units, but members have close ties, neighboring land, and fluctuating residence among the compounds in the neighborhood; in one area of about two square kilometers, there were thirty-nine compounds and 361 people. Territorial protection against enemy raids, land use, garden preparation, and ceremony bring together men of different compounds. The individual members of the Dani compound are very mobile.

SETTLEMENTS

The sites of village settlements in the eastern highlands are often permanent, with replacement of houses on the same site as required. A village may be an expanded locality group, consisting of a large men's house and associated women's houses. Susuroka (Read 1965), for example, contains a men's house and thirteen women's houses on a street, with forty-five people. The occupants are mainly of one clan, but the big man had also attracted some members of a second clan in the tribe. Land here is plentiful, and the two clan-villages together make up one tribe. Other tribes, with two or more villages, have territories in the surrounding region. Besides the village houses, outlying dwellings are used by people and pigs. Where village settlements are larger, garden and pig houses are more important. The pattern of outlying houses in the eastern highlands is quite similar to that of outlying pig houses in Chimbu and the western highlands. The Bena Bena villages are surrounded by their gardens, and form together a discrete territory with a population of 750.

Yet villages among Siane (Salisbury 1962) have a discreteness that homestead settlements of the Chimbu and Enga lack. Each village of about 200 people is at a permanent site, the location of a clan, which is a separate unit in politics and ritual. The village is divided into wards, each of which centers around a men's house in a clearing with twelve to fifteen women's houses on a street. The ward has about thirty men and young males in the men's house, whereas twenty-three married women and eighteen unmarried girls and young boys live in the women's houses. A village is composed of a group of wards, the subdivisions of the clan-village. Among Siane, as among most eastern highlanders, land is relatively plentiful, and pigs forage in the outlying bush. Although many outlying houses for pigs are built, pig care does not take as much work as in the more densely populated areas with less forage land.

Larger communities are built by the Gururumba and Sina Sina. But the present, continuous village form seems to be a new type. Formerly, hamlets of a men's house and groups of women's houses were more common. Each held a ridge-top, for defense, and used land surrounding it. As many as twenty hamlets have combined into one large village today. The present village form was encouraged by missionaries in the 1940s and 1950s. Observing the convenience of large groupings for communication and large-scale work projects, native leaders have also promoted the larger settlement form. The Sina Sina have combined into large villages, although this type of settlement often requires long absences and carrying of supplies to gardens and pig houses. Much more time is spent in daily commuting and carrying, especially by women, than among peoples with other settlement forms (Hide, personal communication, 1974). Central Chimbu have not followed their leaders' urging to gather in villages, although settlement has been increasingly concentrated near the roads.

People may be caught by conflicting interests: On the one hand, communal activities, planning, and social occasions draw them into larger settlements, but on the other hand the wide scatter of land for different uses disperses their interests throughout their land holdings in all parts of the group territory. Although there are several possible settlement forms which might be adopted, perhaps the type best suited to a rather sparse population is found among the Fore: a small village of about fifty persons, with gardens and forage land within easy walking distance. Social ties, exogamy rules, major ceremonies, trade, and other external relations require some connections with other communities. A major expansion of a large group, or some other crisis, can wipe out such a small village. Where the population is denser, in other highland regions, the need for resources and land of all types has necessitated different forms of settlements. Two distinct types of settlements have developed. The first of these consists of a village with a close group of houses in a street or around a square. A large village is segmented into several wards of hamlets, each with a territory but coordinated for some purposes, as in Siane,

Sina Sina, and some other eastern highlands groups. In some areas the village is a cluster of several hamlets, each with a men's house and women's houses. The second and more common type of settlement in the highlands consists of clusters of houses centering around a men's house, but with some dispersed associated women's and other houses. Other gardens and pig houses are farther away, as land use varies with ceremonial sites, fallow cycles, and needs. This type of settlement is found in Chimbu, western highlands, southern highlands, Enga, and in West Irian. The people of Mt. Hagen have more or less permanent ceremonial grounds that bind a group of men to a site, whereas Chimbu and Kuma come together only for rare (once every seven to fifteen years) pig festivals at large ceremonial grounds where houses are built for the occasion. Territories of clans may be discrete, or may have some outliers on rare land types.

Our statistical analysis of population density, agricultural intensity, and land tenure seems to indicate that settlement type is not associated with these factors. Nor is it associated with the size of groups. Villages, hamlets, and dispersed homesteads appear to be regional types. See Table 6 and Map 2.

In both settlement types the individuals and families have rights to land and resources throughout community territory, with a common interest in security and maintaining these resources. An individual may shift his residence to another site within the territory to use certain local resources. The whole territory available is within walking range and members living in any part can come to group gatherings. This distinguishes highland territory use from that of the fringe, where a territory is very much larger and areas are exploited at different seasons or periods.

The differences in settlement form are between eastern highlanders, especially the development of large ridge-top, street, or rectangular villages in the area around Goroka, and the small clusters or dispersed homesteads further west. In some places villages have been established since contact with the Australian government and encouraged by the missionaries or administration. But there were villages in the eastern highlands at the time of discovery. Perhaps an ecological-social explanation is appropriate: The concentration of people and gardens in villages is best adapted to or required by the open grassland terrain, the shortage of trees for concealment, and the limited amount of wood available. In such terrain, enemies can be seen approaching at a great distance and resisted by a unified community force.

Village sites are probably more permanent than homesteads, and suitable where adequate land is available for shifting cultivation in perpetuity. Homesteads can be shifted to different sections of a territory as land activities change. The homestead form is a more flexible settlement system which can include permanent use of some sites and intermittent use of others.

In this chapter we have explored the connections among population density, settlement type, and land use in the highlands. Where the population is dense, good garden land is scarce, individual land rights are maintained, and group territory is defended against intrusion or invasion. Common interests in the locality and land are a binding force. In the New Guinea highlands these focus upon a group of men sharing a men's house; the men's house group consists mostly of members of a patrilineal kin group that has traditional rights to the territory and its land. A men's house group – with its associated neighborhood of family dwellings, which may be clustered in a village or dispersed as scattered homesteads – and its garden land is the most important group of cooperation, mutual aid, and defense. The families of the men are united by these local interests.

4

Family and kinship

The core of small and large units in the highlands is, ideologically, patrilineal: Membership, group continuity, rights, obligations, and solidarity all derive from the patrilineal descent-system. This idea unites men through the generations and across localities. The largest social groups may be acknowledged as two or more allied clans or subtribes of separate origin, as in Dani and Chimbu. However, among most highland peoples the largest units in local relations, ritual, and warfare base their solidarity on the patrilineal descent-groups of a clan or several clans of common origin. Male solidarity and clan unity are reinforced by beliefs concerning sex differences, male initiation, and cults.

In this chapter we will discuss social life, activities, and obligations of children, youths, and adults. Courtship and marriage practices will also be described, as they are the foundation of the family and kin groups. Rules of marriage and exogamy separate the units of support and solidarity, clans, or sometimes great-clans, from alliances and tribes that include more than two clans which often intermarry. Where population is sparse, there may be units of less than 100 people, whereas clans of 500 or over are common among densely settled peoples. The territorial range of a clan or tribe, whatever the population, seems to be an area that permits visiting and cooperation in ceremonies and warfare. Affinal and kinship ties are mostly concentrated within a convenient visiting range, but some distant relations are also favored, as they allow exchange of goods and movement of people into areas with some different resources.

Highlanders have families, but their daily life is not centered on the nuclear family unit in the same way as in Western societies. The mother, daughters, and young sons who sleep in one woman's house at night are a close family group. The father and older boys of the nuclear family usually sleep with other males in a men's house. Men and women also often work at separate domestic activities. The

144

daytime pattern of activities and groups brings together the people of the settlement, and many occasions include residents of different settlement groups. Highlanders, whether they live in hamlets, villages, or homesteads, are associated with larger numbers of people than the very small and scattered communities of Hewa, Miyanmin, and other fringe peoples. There is little privacy or isolation for anyone; to obtain privacy for sexual intercourse, husband and wife usually seek a secluded place in the bush. The family unit of parents and children are a household, a productive unit, a land-using group, an important element in society. But they are rarely together as a separate, discrete group. Family occasions are – except, apparently, for Huli – most often afternoon mealtimes, frequently at the house of a woman, with her husband and children. Discussions about domestic activities – the land, gardens, houses, pigs, children, relatives, and obligations – take place here. In Chimbu, I thought some families were very close, whereas others were either quarrelsome or distant. Many older children were more often with their age mates than at home. This might be thought hardly surprising of families almost anywhere. Although the highland family is not always together as a distinct, exclusive unit, it is rarely far apart or long separated. Ordinarily, the whereabouts and activities of family members are known to one another; the alternatives are not many, and the distances short. A man, alone or with other men, may take a long trading trip, or go to nearby groups for ceremony or exchange; he may be away for days or weeks. The increase in roads, schools, and jobs has augmented individual mobility. Marriage and residence at a distance is now becoming common.

YOUTH

A mother and her young children are seldom apart. Babies are born in a temporary shelter or house and are often kept away from other people for some days. Infants are nearly constantly held or carried by, or are resting near, their mother. They are not left alone or with others for long. One may be placed on the ground, or in a net bag hanging from a branch, while the mother works in a garden. The infant's net bag is carried, suspended from the mother's brow and resting on her back along with bags of food, firewood, or other goods, as she goes from gardens to houses and settlements. Where little preventive medicine is known, children are considered delicate, subject to illness and magic, and they are protected from strangers. An older baby may be left in the care of a relative or an older sibling for a short time. But the infant depends upon its mother for milk and other food. Fathers, and sometimes uncles or other men, may fondle and carry babies, although rarely far from their mothers. Boys especially are often with their fathers, carried or held on the shoulders, playing, or resting. When a mother dies, her baby is sometimes fostered by another woman; however, cases of successfully raising orphans from infancy are rare. Infant mortality is common in the highlands; babies are mourned by their parents, and neighbors and relatives console the bereaved family.

Nevertheless, large families are not encouraged in the highlands. Knowing that a baby is heavy to carry and hard to raise, a woman who is not satisfied with her married life may attempt abortion or kill her infant at birth and then say it was stillborn. At a divorce the future home of the children becomes a matter for argument. Thus a dissatisfied wife may run away before the presence of children makes separation difficult. If one baby is hard to carry everywhere, two are almost impossible. In the past, one or both of twin births might be suffocated in the birth hut. Traditionally, while carrying and feeding an infant, sexual intercourse is prohibited or refused. The long period of lactation and sexual prohibition serve to space babies several years apart, so that the last child is a toddler or older when the next baby is born. There are many times when sexual intercourse is prohibited to men for ritual or other reasons. This affects the frequency of intercourse and thus of conception. Although some peoples may consciously limit reproduction in order to reduce the strain on land and food resources, the prohibitions on sexual relations in the highlands are mainly phrased as protecting the living against mystical dangers. However, these practices and prohibitions seem to be decreasing now, as many families now share a house and babies are spaced more closely. I knew several sets of twins and siblings one to two years apart in 1976, when supplementary baby foods were becoming common.

Girls enter into the realm of women and children, centered in the woman's house, and take part in gardening and pig care, preparing food, and the carrying of food, firewood, and water. Girls join women in carrying food to group festivities. There are few organized, separate children's activities or games. Rather, small girls are usually with their mothers, or in a small group together nearby. They join in some of the work, but have no great responsibilities during childhood. Children who are attending school make little or no contribution to the family domestic production. The increase of schools in the highlands may change the traditional allocation of household tasks in the family.

At puberty, in some highland societies such as Chimbu, Kapauku, and Bena Bena, a girl is secluded for two to three weeks at her first menstruation, and new clothes, sometimes special foods, songs, some instruction or lecturing, and a small feast are prepared for her. It is mainly a private matter except, perhaps, for the killing and distribution of a pig by the girl's father or guardian. No special celebration is reported in many places.

At adolescence, Chimbu girls from the same settlement go about in groups of two or more in a brief period of freedom, and in some highland societies but not all, they are allowed considerable sexual freedom. They wear ornaments of fur and shell, or nowadays clothes and jewelry purchased in local stores. They invite young men to visit them, or go on interclan visits for courtship. Often, they sleep in a group together in an unused house or with an older woman without young children, and with young men. All-night courting and singing parties are frequent, and they spend more day time resting than working. The next major event for every girl is marriage. This is when she leaves her family and settlement group.

Boys begin to spend time with other boys and men of their settlement group from the age when they are toddlers and weaned. Small groups of boys under ten years old are more common and more separate than those of girls. Boys sometimes accompany older boys or men at work, but their contribution to the work is slight. They catch and gather insects, lizards, and other foods. When boys go to school, they have little opportunity to collect food; if the school does not provide nutritious meals, they may suffer. During boyhood, they associate in groups mainly of a settlement, sometimes visiting relatives or making friends in other settlements. A boy's break with his mother's house comes gradually as he joins male groups and activities. It is marked by some stages. He sometimes accompanies his father, and others in the men's house, sleeps there, and spends little time at his mother's house except perhaps for meals. The group of boys of a settlement – sons of the men's house and hamlets – form life-long associations in boyhood. Many highland societies have periodic initiation rituals. These ties may later be changed by migration or disrupted by other interests or activities, but they are the basis of affiliation and group cohesion throughout the highlands of New Guinea. In Chimbu the age mates of a subclan are very close, and often join with others of their clan: These *yaglkuna* have a special bond in youth activities, courtship parties, and formerly in war parties which may persist at group ceremonies, in adult friendship, and cooperation.

PATRILINY

Much has been written about descent, lineage, and clan ties in the New Guinea highlands; the interplay of kinship theory and documentation is as complex here as anywhere. Male activities, boyhood ties, initiation, inheritance, and community pride help to establish and maintain the interdependence of men and families in local and kinship groups. An ideology of patrilineal descent dominates highland group concepts: A group is said to be descended from a founding male ancestor through generations of their male, agnatic, descendants. However, although descent links from father to son and between brothers are the model of segmentary group structure, they may not reflect actual genealogical ties. Because boys follow their fathers to the men's house and inherit land within clan territory, their ties to the settlement area, and to one another, are life-long. The translation of these practical arrangements into a descent theory is no great step: The father-son-brother ideology of male, group relationship is, for the most part, common and comprises the basis of descent theory of highlands society. When orphans or sons of divorced women are adopted by another man, or when a brother-in-law becomes a host and sponsor, the father-sonlike and brotherlike relationships that result easily fit the model. However, the literal-minded analysis of Western observers, who desire blood-test demonstration of parenthood, rather than the highlanders' ready welcome of kinsmen into the family, suggests that the anthropological terminology is imprecise.

Since the family is not a Western-style, isolated unit protecting individual rights and property, and especially as the men's house is an expandable group of intense interaction and mutual aid, guests can readily be incorporated into a highland family or group; such male guests become as sons or brothers to those members of the group who are actually related by birth. A newcomer is first tied to a male sponsor, from whom he or she gets all rights to membership. Wives must always be incorporated from outside groups and, eventually, a wife's relatives from outside the group may also be incorporated into the community. Sisters marry and move outside the group; their offspring belong to their husbands' group. Divorce or separation of wife and young children is rarely accepted by a husband and his group. However, in special circumstances a family migrates to join the wife's relatives or other kinsmen. This may be a temporary or permanent move.

A patrilineal ideology identifies the local group of men. In Chimbu, *boromai suara*, "one blood," is used to describe the men's group; the Hageners apply the term one blood cognatically as well as agnatically. Highlanders speak of one father, one line, one family, one name, or one men's house, all of which carry an idea of agnation, unilineality, and continuity. Anthropologists have often called this a lineage group, recognizing that a strict, genealogical adherence to patrilineal descent is not usually found in the highlands; patrilineal lineage is an ideal or folk model, not a genealogical reality. The larger groups, also based on belief in a male founder and his descendants, are subclans, clans, and sometimes phratries or tribes.

Boys are allied through boyhood ties and mutual property interests; they are united in defending their security and pursuing group prestige. Leadership and programs for building reputation and strength for mutual advantage begin in the local group. There may also be a need for order, involving the allocation of rights and privileges, among members of the local group. The group is not independent and cannot survive without a larger area of security than its own neighborhood. In land alone, individual holdings are interdigitated with those of other segments of the territory. For large-scale relations and exchanges the men's house groups of a clan, village, or tribe may combine as a unit opposed to others. Certain activities are more appropriate to certain sizes and scales of groups than others, for example, menstruation ceremonies are small gatherings of the neighbors and close kinsmen, whereas marriage involves the clans of the bride and groom, and many other relatives. The opposition of groups at all levels, the support and solidarity of men, and the attraction of followers to leaders make a constantly adapting, flexible, group structure.

SEPARATION AND BONDING BETWEEN MALES AND FEMALES

Because husband and wife are brought together by their elders from unrelated families, their loyalties may be in opposition. A man's loyalties are firmly set in his home place, while his wife's are established elsewhere. A wife must acquire a new set of loyalties as a result of the marriage transaction. Only the men form a ritual community, based on common interests and male initiation into a cult of some sort. Male separation begins with the boy's incorporation into a men's house. A group of boys together undergo introduction into a cult. There are no comparable women's cults, and no elaboration of sexual fears by women. Everywhere, sexual opposition and separation are reinforced by beliefs (Brown and Buchbinder 1976). Sexual differences may be ideologically exaggerated to include a mutual ambivalence, sometimes antagonism, mistrust, or fear of the opposite sex. Female sexuality, menstruation, childbirth, the body substances of blood, vaginal secretions, and semen are considered both potent and dangerous. Men must prepare for marriage and sexual relations carefully, as it requires that men bring strangers into their homes. During courtship men visit nearby settlements, and occasionally girls visit the men's community. A certain restraint, derived from the boys' unease among strangers and with sexuality, and from beliefs that women and strangers are dangerous and debilitating to young men, pervades these courtship gatherings. Men wish to be vigorous, glowing with oil, smooth-skinned, and shiny. Men believe that women may make them shrivel and dry, that they sap their juice. This general form of belief is embellished in the male cults and initiation ritual to take many particular forms.

A group of youths, from their late teens to twenties, of the same village, clan, or subclan, are a close group. Interclan courtship parties may be attended by such a group, who practice the songs and follow leading singers. Smaller sets of age-mate friends are constant companions who may share a house, loaf, visit distant relatives, and meet with a few girls. They sometimes join in work parties or fighting excursions organized by the older men of their local group. Few young men take an active part in exchanges, but some own chickens or pigs, usually fed by their mother, or grow sugarcane and bananas in their family garden plots to distribute at ceremonies. Marriage is the beginning of an independent household in production and transactions. A man then must plan his garden and pig production with his wife's cooperation to establish his position as an independent householder with exchange partners among his kinsmen and affines, especially his wife's close relatives. The wife's productive activity is stimulated by her expectations of giving food and pigs to her relatives (M. Strathern 1972).

INITIATION AND MALE CULTS

Associated with the alliance of men in ritual and political activities is, in different ways, a cult or cults and the initiation of boys into the men's group. In the highlands, many of the classic features of *rites de passage* are present – planning by mature men, information and meanings concealed from the uninitiated and all women, rituals held in seclusion, paraphernalia prepared in secret, surprise carrying off of novices to be initiated, infliction of pain and tests of endurance, taboos and deprivation of food and water, instruction in proper manly behavior and in significance of symbols, and public presentation of initiates after seclusion. Initiation is one of the first rituals to be discarded in conversion to Christianity and cultural change.

In some areas the initiation group is small, composed of coevals, whereas in others initiation is performed at intervals of ten or more years and does not similarly serve to form a group of age mates. Age-mate groups then emerge in courtship and social activities. The Chimbu *yaglkuna* are age mates in a subclan – about four to eight men with about a three-year age span. They attend courting parties as a group and with age-mate groups of the whole clan and sometimes with a larger group. The sizes and age range of such groups varies; accidents may deplete an age group, and short-term sex ratio variations may make groups of unequal sizes. The group is a life-long association, broken only by death or group dispersal. An-thropologists in recent years have become aware of the force of change on men's age-groups, which now may not be so bound to men's house, sexual separation, warfare, and secret ritual. Young men nowadays often attend mission and government schools, leave the area for further training, and work for periods outside the vil-lage, and have no experience of ritual seclusion and warfare. In the past, however, initiation was a most important event in the lives of young men in the highlands.

The following description of an initiation is derived from Read's account (1952; 1965) of the eastern highlands' initiation of the Gahuku-Gama group of tribes, where Read lived during 1950–51. On this occasion boys from several tribes were taken into the cult together. The sacred *nama* bamboo flutes announced the proceed-ings. Each subclan had its own pair of flutes and tune, which could only be played by the initiated men. Boys and women may have been told that these were bird cries and that the birds carried off boys for initiation. Then one day men of many groups, in paint and feathers, came together with their boys to be initiated. At a secluded spot near the river, adult men displayed their genitals in a show of male strength, then forced abrasive leaves up their nostrils to pro-duce bleeding, in simulation of menstruation and for purification. Long canes were forced down the throat and into the stomach. Boys were made to bleed and vomit, and the discharged material was carried away in the river. The boys were thus introduced into male ritual, and then the whole body of men took them away from the river. Afterwards, the women attacked the men's group with sticks and stones enacting sexual opposition and the loss of their sons.

The boys were secluded for some weeks, instructed, and informed of taboos; then they emerged to the public, as men, to dance and feast in the village. The pairs of flutes that were used to play each tune were said to be age mates, and were believed to be sexually attractive to women. Young boys and all females may not see the flutes: They are concealed by leaves in the men's house and often covered when played outside. The first view that boys have of the flutes is at one early phase of initiation, between the ages of five to seven; they return to their mothers afterwards. Boys ten to fifteen years old experience the painful blood-letting and vomiting induced to remove what is believed to be the contaminating influence of women. After being told about the making of the flutes, the boys continue to practice vomiting and blood-letting and have only minimal contact with women. As novices they fetch water and firewood and cook for the men. Boys fifteen to nineteen years old pass through the rites again, and have a period of seclusion from working, abstain from drinking water, are instructed in their adult rights and duties, and learn to play the flutes. At this time the elders may arrange the boys' marriages, and they remove bachelors' headdresses and emerge with new decorations for the *idza nama* festival.

This sequence of rites and period of isolation separates the boys from the mother's house and domestic life. During the initiation period, the boys do not eat food cooked by women and, in company with age mates, learn the traditions and history of the group. The greatest solidarity and closest ties are between age mates in the village men's house who pass through the rites together. But the collective tribal or subtribal rituals at the river, where blood-letting and vomiting are first performed and the sexual dichotomy dramatically portrayed, emphasize the cohesion and strength of the large group of men. Through the rituals and seclusion the youths achieve physical and sexual maturity. Male dominance, an important value in the society, is asserted through warfare, ritual, flute symbolism, and other institutions that justify the lower status of women. It culminates in the *idza nama* festival, where pigs are killed, men dance, and guests receive pork. The tribe presents its new initiates as proof of its masculine power to visitors from all surrounding tribes.

These striking and dramatic demonstrations point up the male values of solidarity and strength. The initiation procedures and seclusion do not allow young men to participate in domestic activities; their role is as warrior and they perform rituals and practice for manhood. The Gahuku-Gama seem to practice an extreme form of sexual separation. Some reports of initiation elsewhere suggest that the severity and length of seclusion have been relaxed in recent times; initiation was not practiced at all among many western highlands peoples.

In central Chimbu, initiation is a minor phase in the preparation for pig feasts, and includes boys of a wide age-range. Those in their teens are subjected to seclusion and discomfort, including putting nettle leaves in the mouth to induce blood-letting, being kept in hot rooms without water, and shown the flutes and how to play them. The time of initiation and seclusion is adapted to plans for the pig feast. A minor rite is held by the Kuma in which the novices are made to experience some discomfort and are lectured by their elders.

Young men are introduced into cults of several sorts in the western and southern highlands. In some cults all participants are men, but these do not always include all the men of a group. One such cult is the Sandalu or Sanggai among the western Kyaka (Bulmer 1965) and some other Enga groups; these cults are led by a mature bachelor. A house is built in the forest, where young men are secluded to learn the sacred chants and symbolism of sacred plants, purify themselves, eat food prepared by men, and remove the ill effects of association with women. After a few days, a final ceremonial dance, cult songs, and ritual end the seclusion. Married men do not participate in these rites. The bachelor cults, each with its own form and ritual objects, have some features in common with initiation rites. The seclusion of bachelors which takes place several times for boys between the age of fifteen and the time of their marriage, usually in the early twenties, is a ritual intended to remove the effects of what males fear is the pollution of women. It cleans, strengthens, purifies, and newly adorns the bachelors of a clan who emerge in public ceremony. Groups of young men and of girls from other clans attend the emergence, the men of other clans to show their strength and importance in opposition to the bachelor cult group, and the girls to lure and taunt the bachelors. The older host clansmen act as police to prevent fighting. In the final steps, the shining skins and new dress of the bachelors are displayed to be admired by visitors (Meggitt 1964). Among the Huli, not all youths join the bachelor cult. Those who do are secluded from contact with women for about two years, in which rituals are conducted to make their skin firm and their hair grow.

These rites underline the highlanders' concern with strength and health in men. The medical studies which show the slow growth and late maturation of some highlanders, and the lack of a clear-cut sign of puberty in males, make this concern understandable. In many societies a short man is considered ugly and may fail to attract girls. Some highland fringe peoples seem to show greater anxiety about the achievement of manhood than do these central highlanders. Where children are betrothed, the girl may reach puberty before her intended spouse is full-grown. Young men fear early marriage will prevent their full growth. Initiation and bachelor cults are absent in Mt. Hagen, where instead men have spirit cults which protect them from what they believe is female, menstrual pollution and insure male, generative prowess. The ritual practices of the Wahgi and Hagen area are not devoted to making boys into men, but rather to demonstrating the dominance of men over women. This deemphasis on male growth seems consistent with the findings in studies of growth and adult physique, for these people are the tallest and best-nourished highlanders. There is less anxiety over growth of boys in this region than in other parts of the highlands, so that severe and universal male initiation is not practiced. If both girls and boys can grow up without intensive ritual protection, the girls may also be strong. Is this why the male cult aims at dominance?

Big man is a euphemism, but highland leaders must be powerful, and many highland leaders have been larger than average men. Physical strength is admired, and necessary to success in fighting; exceptional physical energy is required for organizing and controlling people (Berndt and Lawrence 1971). The belief that men should be strong and dominate, and that close association with women is dangerous to men, is held by all highlanders. The taboos and rituals to achieve male strength take many forms, expressing a range of beliefs from anxiety about weakness and vulnerability to assertion of masculine generative power.

The greatest change that has occurred in the highlands has been the pacification brought about by the suppression of intergroup warfare. There is no longer a pervasive fear of enemy attack. We may imagine that the life and attitudes of young men in former times were quite different from those observed by anthropologists of recent years. Renewed tribal fights of the 1970s have revived some of these fears and avoidance of enemy groups. Initiation and training of youths had an important aim – the protection of the group against hostile neighboring groups, and the development of in-group solidarity. Initiation developed a cohesive group of age mates.

COURTSHIP

Adolescence in the highlands is generally a period of little responsibility and of pleasure, visiting, courting, and friendship with age mates. Girls are relaxed and friendly with the girls, boys, and young men of their settlement and clan. These young men are forbidden to marry within the clan, and act as chaperones or protectors of girls in their courting parties with the youths of other groups. While the adolescents are at home, and throughout their lives whenever they visit, a close kinship relation exists between them: It is not the rivalry of brother and sister for parental attention, or the nervous anxiety of a suitor and coquette, but a congenial, reliable, familiar tie between age mates of a settlement and clan group. For each, the kinship circle is enlarged by maternal relatives – the sons and daughters of the mother's kin – and by the children of clanswomen who have married into other groups. The kinsmen who normally reside in other communities are frequent guests and hosts, as adolescents in small groups attend courting parties and visit widely. The ties of age-mate friendship may be weakened when girls marry into distant groups, but they are revived in festivals and visits to the home clan and in exchanges. Where marriage arrangements follow certain kinship-links, a special relationship may develop between betrothed or marriageable kin (Glasse and Meggitt 1969).

Before marriage, young men have few interests in gardening, pig raising, payments, or exchange; they devote themselves to group festivities, displays, and fighting to enhance group prestige. The parades and dances as well as the courting parties give them opportunities to show off their physical appearance and ornaments, thus representing their groups and winning the admiration of women. There is an important symbolism and association of values among the Chimbu and some other highland peoples: The feathers and plumes of birds of paradise, especially – and to some extent other birds – oil, iridescent shells, paints, and other items used for adornment and cosmetics, represent health, beauty, masculinity, and wealth. Birds are fleet, brilliant, untamed; young men want to resemble them. Physical courage, fighting skill, speed, glowing skin, strength, and size are admirable: They win favors from girls and respect from their own group. Associated competitive activities are still vital as ceremonies: Exchanges are attempts to outshine and outdo other groups. These events are especially important to young people, although for older men the festivities are occasions of prestige rivalry in exchange and repayment and of group recognition (Brown 1972).

Local and clan exogamy are usual practices in the New Guinea highlands; intergroup visits are occasions for acquaintance of marriageable youths. At formal ceremonies, the marriageable youth are often on display, made attractive by cleaning, cosmetic application of oils and paints, new clothing, adornment with fresh leaves, flowers, and colorful ornaments of feathers, shell, fur, and other goods of value. To take the Chimbu as an example: On an appointed night, unmarried teenaged girls await the visitors; they dress in some finery, and sit with their backs along the walls of a large house. The young men, invited as a group from a nearby clan within or outside the tribe, have rehearsed some songs and approach the house, singing in falsetto voice, the form used in serenades. They enter and sit in a circle with their backs to the center, facing the girls. The young men decorate their faces and heads with paint, leaves, and feathers; their falsetto singing and waving of heads seems to imitate birds. A small group of the best singers, often including some young married men, stays near the door and leads the serenade, beginning each new phrase which is then repeated all along the room by the men. After a few minutes, when a song is finished, the men in the room move one place along to face the next girl. At first they all seem uneasy, and remain at some distance from one another. In the dark, with only an occasional flicker of light from the fires, and heavily covered in grease, paint, and feathers, the individuals are hardly recognizable. As the singing and changing of partners proceed, some couples lean close together, the girl's legs placed across those of the boy; they touch faces and roll cheeks and forehead from side to side. This is known as "turnim head" or "carry-leg" in Pidgin English. Some of the older couples may creep to the secluded rear of the house, or leave the house, for greater intimacy. The younger boys and girls seem too shy to choose a partner, and those who have joined the party but have special friends in another group may avoid close attachments in these rather public gatherings.

More private courting occurs at the invitation of one or several girls. The favored boy may be asked to bring his close friends, age mates from his subclan. The evening is spent in singing and conversation between pairs. More intimate sexual contact may develop in these smaller courting parties. However, preferences are usually in couples, not between sets of age mates. In these courtship parties some young people find a desirable mate and ask their elders to arrange a marriage.

There are many songs, and new ones are composed frequently. The form of courting songs differs somewhat from those sung at ceremonies or while working. The phrase *wa ya*, somewhat modified to *wai, waye*, is frequently repeated at the end of stanzas and between songs until one of the leaders strikes up a new verse. The songs commemorate places, people, birds, trees, and so forth. The verses may be translated as, for example, "the girl is like a *druage* flower," "a bird cries that the girl has gone away," "if you take the road, I can follow you," "the rain comes to Dani," or "there is cloud in the morning at Yungawo."

In Chimbu, small courtship parties are frequent, with the larger parties organized by older people, often in the dry season. A single girl, or a group of age mates may pay a visit to the kinsmen of one of the age mates, and courting parties are held especially to entertain the guests. Some young people are shy or feel unattractive, but in Chimbu courtship can be bold. A girl may be so attracted to a young man that she goes to his home settlement, staying with a woman, often his subclan brother's wife, for some days, as a sort of trial marriage. If she gets along well with the adults of the group as well as the young man, her parents may agree to arrange a marriage. However, the more frequent outcome is that after a few days the girl is anointed with oil and pig grease, decorated with ornaments, and goes home to continue courting until a marriage is arranged for her. The large festivals, for which men spend many hours applying cosmetics and arranging ornaments in a headdress, are important occasions to meet young people and be invited to serenade girls. A surprise visit of girls, accompanied by some men of their clan, to a men's house of another clan was a former practice. The surprised host-clan responded with nonstop singing and courting by married and unmarried men; men and women provided food, including meat, to the guests. After some days of courting and feasting, the visitors went home, and perhaps some marriages were then arranged between the groups.

The variety of Chimbu practices does not exist in all highland societies. Sexual intercourse is rarely permitted in most highland societies. Bena Bena parties include the youths of two clans in one house; the girls of each clan have one side of the house. Each girl calls for a man she favors to lie beside her, and they sometimes make love. The girls change partners from time to time throughout the night. Kuma girls visit men's houses for courting ceremonies. In these situations – in Chimbu, Bena Bena, Hagen, Mendi, and Kuma – the girls have the advantage; they choose, seek, visit, and invite boys. The boys make themselves attractive with cosmetics and finery, practice singing, and achieve prestige if girls seek them out. They always avoid courting members of their clan and other prohibited marriage partners.

A girl may marry the man she chooses, but this rarely occurs. Often the young man the girl chooses does not wish to marry yet, or does not care enough for the girl. Men, who in their initiation have been cautioned about the uncleanliness of women, and susceptibility of young men to the debilitating effect of continued sexual relations, often are reluctant to marry. Nowadays many go to work away from the settlement, so that they achieve both some financial independence and a delay in marital responsibility. But the main block to a marriage of choice is the elders' wish to place the girl with a different group, and the unwillingness of the boy's kin to provide a payment to the girl's group at the time. If the girl is rejected, she is taken home by her kinsmen if she does not go herself. The girl's determination is rarely strong enough to overcome these barriers, for marriage must be a public ceremony and exchange.

The strain of an arranged marriage sometimes becomes intolerable for the young woman. I was told of a number of cases of suicide in which the woman's desires were disregarded by her family, and she was forced to marry or to remain with a man whom she did not like or who mistreated her by excessive beating. Hanging from a tree was the usual means of suicide. The incidence of suicide seems to be decreasing, however, probably as a result of Catholic mission influence and a greater acceptance of a woman's wishes. In Chimbu there does seem to be a greater frequency of marriage by choice and a growing trend is toward allowing young people to choose their mates. This is influenced by mission teaching, and by the contribution often made by a young man – who has earned money of his own while away at work – to his own marriage payment. Migrant labor both delays marriage and gives the young man more choice and independence from his elders. Nevertheless, in 1976 a high school girl in the eastern highlands told me that she would have to marry a man her elders select. It may be that education will not bring independence for these young women, at least for some time.

The courtship practices we have discussed are characteristic of highland societies where young men are not so inhibited by fear of contamination that they do not enjoy courtship and sexual contact. The Chimbu and Wahgi peoples, and some, at least, of the eastern highlanders are included. During the Enga bachelor initiation, young men visit and sing to their betrothed, and girls dance up to and snatch at the men they select, but relations are never intimate. Fear of sexuality and pollution dominates the courtship practices of the Enga men. Early betrothal, with protection and separation of the betrothed until they reach the approved age for sexual relations, is found among some highland peoples – for example, Gahuku-Gama, Fore, and Daribi. Eastern highlanders who have initiation seclusion and purification may prohibit young men from having sexual relations. Promiscuity is nowhere approved in the highlands, and the rare illegitimate child is a disgrace for the mother and her family. Kapauku youths, who have no initiation or cults, are independent bachelors who seek out girls. The girls are closely watched by their elders, and are generally thought to be selective, yet sexually willing and sometimes aggressive. Feasts bring opportunities for meeting and social contacts, but elopement often leads to intergroup conflict and is thus disapproved.

These courtship practices reveal the local variations possible on the ambivalent theme of male strength, solidarity, and dominance, and female sexuality, pollution, and danger. The extremes of male anxiety and subordination of women must be adapted for the interdependence of people and the unity of the group. However unwilling a bride or groom may feel, they know that mature and independent adulthood in the highlands is only achieved by establishing a married household and family.

MARRIAGE

As everyone knows, courtship and personal attraction are not synonymous with marriage. In the New Guinea highlands, they are hardly connected at all. Courting parties, visiting, and elopement rarely culminate in settled married life. When they do, public recognition of the marriage, exchange of goods and approval by the relatives, and tacitly by their clans, is necessary. A disapproved liaison is forcibly broken up by the older male relatives, and no payments are made. Selection of mates is controlled by the parents, guardians, kinsmen, and the senior and leading men of the groups, who may be influenced by the young people's wishes only if intergroup negotiations are also favorable. Marriage between members of the same settlement, locality, subclan, or any kin group is not permitted. However, when clans have become large and segments are distinct, marriage between members of the clan segments is sometimes possible; in Chimbu it is a step toward clan fission. Occasionally young people reside with kinsmen and marry a member of the kinsman's clan, but the link must not be close.

Each study of a highlands people reports a different, particularistic, set of exogamic rules, which shows the combination of descent group and kin exclusion. Most often, the clan, large or small, is defined as a group of common patrilineal descent, more or less localized, in which marriage is prohibited. The clan settles together on its territory; its men are initiated and fight as a unit. They do not negotiate marriages with one another, compete with one another, or quarrel over women. Where population is sparse and dispersed, some idea of common heritage among separate local groups may not prevent marriage between them, because the negotiating groups are not one unit. The relatives of the bride and groom, outside their clan, also take an interest in the marriage. Although they are excluded from the group that might provide a spouse, they may act as intermediaries, guardians, or sponsors and often provide some of the goods given in marriage of their kinsman; they are not possible spouses themselves. The typical central highlands' pattern of widespread marriage ties is not typical of all New Guinea.

Among many interior New Guinea people there are distinct patterns of marriage exchange. One form, practiced by the Maring,

Manga, and Daribi, is sister exchange: In the narrow sense this is an arrangement between two family groups, each with a marriageable son and daughter. The daughters each marry the son of the other group; as a result each man is married to his sister-in-law. The exchange is equal. Thus both marriages are guarantees of good treatment, for, if one couple separates, the other is affected and may also break up. The groups see this as a balanced relationship between families, and the children perpetuate the interfamilial ties. One can see how small, dispersed groups on the margins of the highlands can view sister-exchange marriage as contributing to good relations with the other small groups in their vicinity. And the principle of exchanging daughters to be brides is widely accepted among people who have no formal law-enforcement to secure their rights. Intermarriage has always been a way of cementing political relations. Several other forms are outgrowths of this principle. One is a sort of delayed sister-exchange or patrilateral cross-cousin marriage in which, after a marriage in which the bride comes to a man, the man is obliged to have his daughter marry a man from his wife's group. That is, the exchange is carried from generation to generation, a girl marrying into her mother's group as a return for her mother. Since the woman's clan has lost a woman through marriage, it is considered right that the woman's clan should gain a wife from her offspring. This, like sister exchange, can occur between families, but in the highlands it is more common between subclans, or between larger groups. The reciprocal idea is extended to larger groups, and carried over time. The Siane and Kuma have such forms of reciprocity.

The concept of continuing relations between groups can take another form – for example, when a subclan or family sends its daughters, generation after generation, to certain groups, and gains its wives from certain other groups. In this arrangement the relations between each pair of marriage groups is always the same. They either give daughters or receive wives from another group in the area. It can be envisioned as marriage of a man to his mother's-brother's daughter, or matrilateral cross-cousin marriage. The Fore and some other eastern highlands people prefer such marriages, although they are not the exclusive practice. These forms, and others that favor marriage to groups with which there are or have been marriage ties, all aim to perpetuate friendly intergroup relations and ensure that wives are available from friendly groups. Where life is precarious and intergroup ties often hostile, loss of manpower and low reproductive capacity due to a shortage of wives is a serious threat to group survival. The advantage is with the group that has many wives. Polygyny carries the advantage further.

Women, who give birth to new members of the group, must be brought into the group; they must bear healthy children and raise them well, so they will be valuable members of the husband's group. The abiding concern for group autonomy and continuity is expressed in the marriage patterns. Because a woman marries and lives away from her natal group, she may find a dispute developing between her own relatives in her childhood settlement group and her husband and adult attachment; thus, her loyalties become divided, perhaps irreconcilably. Her husband and his associates may not trust her when intergroup hostility is serious. Thus women are sometimes suspected of carrying information or possible sorcery substances from their husband's group to their brothers. In some communities it is thought that a woman can deliberately injure or weaken her husband and his age mates by contaminating their food with her menstrual blood. A mother's substance or blood is transmitted to her children, and the close ties of mother and child may also tie them to her family. This threatens her husband's group with the loss of manpower. Marriage, then, because it is exogamous between autonomous groups, and produces children who are primarily members of their father's group and yet held by kinship to their mother's group, is a matter for intergroup arrangement, negotiation, and often guarantees.

But the couple whose marriage has been negotiated by their seniors may sometimes balk at the partnership and refuse to participate, or a girl may run away after the wedding. It may be possible to arrange and hold a marriage without the groom, if he is away working; but he may refuse to accept the bride later. Indeed, with all the apparent concern of the elders for good intergroup relations, marriages are unstable. Child betrothal and marriage are an attempt to establish a relationship before the young people can be attracted by individuals of their own choice. The child bride goes to live with her mother-in-law or sister-in-law. In Bena Bena the girl is usually treated much as a daughter in the household of her future husband, while the two have little contact, are never alone together, and the boy undergoes initiation and seclusion in the men's house. Marriage may be arranged for all of a group of age mates, and they may begin to cohabit with their wives when all have been released from seclusion, or are fully mature at twenty years old or older.

EXOGAMY

Rather than encouraging the perpetuation of ties between small groups, as results from sister exchange or cross-cousin marriages between families and small groups, most of the central highlanders have some concept of larger scale reciprocity between clans or tribes, and often will not permit marriage between families or subclans which are related by a former marriage. For example, the Enga do not allow a man to marry a woman of the lineage of his mother, mother's mother, mother's-brother's wife, mother's-sister's husband, father's mother, father's-sister's husband, or to the daughter or daughter's daughter of a clanswoman. Huli may not marry any close cognates, and the Hageners may not marry into any subclan with which there has been a marriage, or any mother's close kin. The Chimbu may not marry into the subclan of the mother, and Mendi exclude any clan with which there has been many previous marriages. The effect of all these prohibitions, in their different ways, is to make each marriage the beginning of new ties between families and subclan groups. While there may be a number of marriages between people of two clans, the actual pairing is between different subclans, so that each subclan and family has its marriage ties to several different units in several other clans. This provides a wider basis of exchange and cooperation, and distributes the ties. Over the generations, good relations between neighboring clans and tribes lead to further intermarriage, the stitching together of neighboring groups by a multiplicity of marriages.

There are limits to the dispersal of marriage ties, however. Because each clan or tribe has a territorial base, any marriage negotiation involves some link over a distance. Highlanders do not venture far from home without intervening friendly hosts. They have few intermediaries who could arrange marriages to very distant groups. Intergroup relations are tense, and marriage to a distant group is only desirable if it initiates friendly exchange, access to trade, and mutual attendance at festivals. The woman who marries afar has few or no kinsmen in her neighborhood, is rarely visited or able to visit her home, and feels lonely and isolated. The marriage can hardly accomplish the interlinking of distant groups, unless it is followed by more marriages between the groups – perhaps other subclans of the clans, visits of cousins, and exchanges.

There may thus develop special links between clans and tribes, intensified by marriages over the generations and exchanges between cousins and kinsmen. For example, certain clans, and subclans within them, in different Gururumba tribes are bound by numerous marriages into alliances of kinsmen and affines (Newman 1965). This may serve to reduce intertribal friction, or at least to restrict it to those clans that are not so interlinked. The hostilities can be only between certain clans and do not involve whole tribes. Also, men of the closely intermarried subclans may attempt to mediate between the hostile elements in their own and kinsmen's tribes. At the time of their discovery in 1930, the eastern highlands' village groups were in a nearly perpetual state of hostility with other communities; alleviation or attempt at peacekeeping was facilitated through intervillage bonds of common clanship, interclan alliance into tribes, and interclan marriage and kinship links. A man would not wish to kill or injure a relative or affine, and thus only a reduced and restrained fighting force could be mobilized between villages much interlinked by marriage. On the whole, the ties of kinsmen – for example, cross-cousins or the offspring of a brother and sister – are more likely to be a deterrent to fighting than affinal relations of brothers-in-law. Competition and hostility between men in different groups is not eliminated by the marriage of a man to the sister of one of an enemy group, but the sons of these brothers-in-law, growing up as kinsmen, visiting and eating together in one another's settlement, are closer and would not wish to harm one another. These kinship relations and visits are often the beginning of immigration, adoption, and incorporation into another man's group, subclan, and clan.

The exogamous group is small among many of the smaller and less densely populated highland groups; the Fore, Maring, and small eastern highlands tribes often marry into settlements nearby or within the territorial group. In the larger central highlands groups, however, between Siane and Enga, the locality is only part of the exogamous unit. There are no cross-cousins or affines in clans of several hundred people which may sometimes number over 1,000; the whole clan – sometimes great clan, or subtribe, or clan cluster – is exogamous. The exogamous group is expected to be peaceable and unified; no marital disputes or difficult marriage negotiations take place between men of a clan. The goods exchanged at marriage should go to unrelated people, not be given and received by the same groups. A comparative analysis of territories, population, and the exogamous, local clan-group showed an average range of one to 3.3 square miles as the area of an exogamous local clan (see Table 8). Thus affines and kinsmen may be no farther than a few miles away.

There is, then, a marriage range within which negotiations are pursued – not so close as within the clan or exogamous unit, and not so far that there are no ties between negotiators. The Mae Enga prefer dispersal of marriage ties: 37 percent of marriages are within the phratry (a group of allied, localized clans), 61 percent to neighboring and allied phratries. In central Chimbu, 44 percent of the marriages are within the tribe, 46 percent in neighboring tribes, and the remaining 10 percent to more distant groups. Most Gururumba marriages are outside the tribe. Usarufa have a small zone of intense interaction, in which both fighting and marriage are concentrated: 41 percent of marriages are within the intensity zone comprising four districts. The Melpa assess cases: An exogamous clan with a few hundred members may favor marriage within the tribe if they are on bad terms with neighboring tribes, but smaller tribes may favor marriage and alliance with other tribes. The obvious effect of intratribal marriage is to concentrate affinal and kinship ties; the effect of extratribal marriage is to disperse them. Although one does not contract more marriages with the same small subclan after a marriage, marriage with other parts of the clan are favored; the idea of reciprocity is extended to the wider group. Such practices bring close relations between individuals and small groups; many people have kinsmen in the several subgroups of a neighboring clan and tribe. As we have discussed, the close feelings of kin, reinforced by intergroup reciprocity in exchanging sisters to be wives, act as some restraint on intergroup conflicts and fighting.

The relations between people connected by marriage ties are complicated. They always contain the seeds of conflict, because husbands and wives may quarrel, and children are affected by marital disputes. Then brothers-in-law may clash over the marital quarrel, treatment of a wife and sister, or rights and duties of affinal relations. Since each marriage is between groups which may have other sources of disagreement, the married pair and their close kinsmen may be in conflict over these other questions and this affects the relationship. A long-standing or serious dispute between neighboring groups involves many marriages and kinship ties, and thus, many people are affected by fights between their kinsmen and clansmen. When such conflicts break into open warfare, many of the men who would join the fray are somewhat restrained because they do not wish to face affines and kinsmen on the battlefield. Thus the separatist tendency of local groups and clans is partly dispelled by the cross-cutting ties derived from marriage and the kinship of each person to his mother's clansmen. In many areas, special ties between clans which become allies may develop; the reciprocal exchange of sisters as wives binds together the sons of these sisters. But by concentrating marriages betwen certain clans, there are fewer between the others, and a dispute between clans which are not extensively connected by marriage ties may more readily become a fight. While two clans are fighting, they do not exchange sisters as wives, but this may be a temporary interruption, or truce may be reinforced by marital exchanges. There are, then, three categories of exogamous relationships: (1) family, including people of both sexes, men and children of one clan but wives and mothers necessarily from another; (2) clan or exogamous group, often localized, and territorial; and (3) for each person, a second group or category of prohibited marriage partners, close kinsmen of family members. All of these are usually closely allied and interdependent, and disputes between them never reach hostility.

RELATIONS BETWEEN GROUPS

The preferences and tendencies to marry among more distantly related groups, exchanges between clans and tribes, reciprocity, and the concentration or dispersion of marriage ties concern relations to all other groups. Some highland people see the social world outside their realm of exogamy as wholly enemy territory: Each marriage is viewed as marriage to an enemy group. But other highland peoples distinguish between traditional enemy groups, with whom marriage negotiations are not often made, and the large category of outside clans and tribes with whom some marriages have been made and further are possible. With these clans there are ties of kinship – a sister or father's sister married to a clansman and her sons, the mother's brother and his sons, and other relatives who are frequent visitors and whose celebrations are attended. The region of neighboring clans and tribes, within a visiting distance of perhaps a few hours' walk, is the usual region of intermarriage and kinship.

Beyond this, few people have many kinsmen or are likely to arrange a marriage. The links required for negotiation become more tenuous with distance, and there are fewer kinsmen at both ends who will support and encourage a match. Distant people are not trusted, and the opportunities for visits and exchanges are fewer. Today, work in towns and travel by road has dispelled these restrictions. There is an advantage in having affines and kinsmen in distant places which might offer trade and other opportunities. However, previously, unusual determination was needed to arrange such a marriage, for most girls did not want to go far from home. Town life is a new attraction. When I was first in the Chimbu area, the fact that I had come so far from home to live at Mintima gave me the nickname "Mintima Mam." The same name was given to a young woman recently married from a distant tribe who had said, "Yes, I want to live at Mintima." In this special case we call one another *dina* or namesake; we share a nickname.

Ordinarily a child is named for a person of the same sex who is a close friend and helper of the parents. Girls are given the name of a woman who helped the mother during pregnancy or childbirth; boys are named after a man who helped the parents, usually someone in the local group. Many boys are named after a leading man in their father's group who may have helped in the marriage. A big man will have many *dina* or namesakes in the subclan; a practice which I at first found confusing, and later, when they were identified, informative about interpersonal ties. Kinsmen, such as mother's brother, mother's sister, father's brother or sister are often the namesakes, and when the name is unique in the locality it is usually an expression of the close ties of siblings outside the clan group.

While moieties have been noted by anthropologists in several parts of New Guinea, it is the Dani of Irian Jaya who base their political, ceremonial, and marriage relations on a division of society into two exogamous moieties. The political confederacy is made up of two subconfederacies. Each clan has a local territory, but may have sections in other areas; each clan is classified as being in one moiety only. A typical confederacy is composed of two main clans, one of each moiety, and several subsidiary clans, which are also classified in one moiety or the other. The confederacy can be largely endogamous, as most marriages are between the two exogamous moieties within a confederacy. This does not mean that one marries into the same subclan as one's mother, but there is a preference for intraconfederacy and mother's-clan marriage, so that these constitute a large proportion of marriages (O'Brien 1969). Outside the confederacy there are more marriages to allied confederacies than to enemies. There seems to be a surplus of women, perhaps due to loss of men in warfare. Many men have two or more wives. Often affines of the same confederacy live together to cooperate and exchange regularly.

The term endogamy has sometimes been applied to a Dani confederacy, as to groups of neighboring tribes in other highland societies, but this suggests an exclusive practice and division of the area into endogamous districts. The actual form of marriage patterns is often better portrayed by considering each clan as the center of a zone of intermarriage: The nearest neighbors are often the most frequent marriage partners. The pattern of choice is also affected by short- or long-term enmities between groups, and the cumulative effect of past marriages that prohibit certain choices – for example, marriage into subclans of kinsmen. The political and ceremonial structure of larger groups also influences marriage choices, and this will be discussed later.

Polygyny, the marriage of a man to two or more wives, is practiced by New Guinea highlanders, but is now declining under mission influence. A polygynist can have his wives employed to his advantage, in providing garden produce and feeding pigs. He also gains in affinal ties to other clans, and must be involved in exchange relations with these groups. This is important to prestige and in transactions. The marriage of eighteen- to twenty-year-old girls to men of twenty-five or older, high mortality of men in warfare and disease, and some permanent bachelorhood were all conducive to the practice of polygyny; some early observers found that one-third to one-half of the married men were polygynists. Big men had a group of dependents including wives and unmarried men.

Every highland marriage is confirmed by a public announcement, ceremony, and exchange of food and goods between the elders, guardians, and leaders of the groups of bride and groom. Marriage arrangements often require protracted negotiation accompanied by demands for larger and better payments of valuables and pigs by the prospective bride's kin and agnates, and are frequently broken off by disagreement over amounts. Sometimes the unwillingness of the bride or groom prevents the marriage. But even before contact with the Australian government, when locally available goods such as stone axes, dogs' teeth, fur pieces, feathers, pigs, and perhaps cassowaries were the main portion, only occasionally including small shells and other objects of distant trade, the groom was never expected to assemble the payment himself. Nowadays, money is an increasingly important element. Young men who have earned money at work may make an important contribution to the payments and have more say in the selection of the bride. However, they cannot bring a bride into the group without the help of older relatives. Their age mates can give little. Ordinarily, the main contributors are close agnates of the groom; older men of his men's house group, and some friends in his subclan provide more than half the goods, and clansmen, his close nonagnatic kinsmen – who are not members of his clan, of course – and scattered friends contribute. The bride's supporters are a comparable group, but usually a little smaller and make less contribution. They attend to receive a share of the groom's payment.

A CHIMBU WEDDING

A description of wedding ceremonies, as I observed them in Chimbu, will show the intergroup character of the proceedings, but it should be noted that some groups prefer child betrothal, sister exchanges without payment, different delayed payments, or different goods. Chimbu payments are large and elaborate, including shells and many bird of paradise plumes and feathers placed on a large wooden display board, which are not usual in the highlands.

Other highlanders give pigs, some shells, and a few other objects such as stones, salt, oil, axes, and net bags.

Pigs and food are produced by all peoples; the giving and sharing of cooked pork is a most important symbol to announce new and renewed relations between groups. Many highlanders believe that food may carry sorcery or poison substances, so that an exchange of food affirms trust between donor and recipient. A marriage between previously unfriendly groups brings them together in the sharing of food and pork – the symbols of trust, kinship, and value. This point is often emphasized in speeches during the marriage ceremony, when the intention of all to regularly exchange visits and food is said to follow from the marriage of this pair. The timing of payments varies from place to place, with the age and maturity of the couple and the time of cohabitation.

In Chimbu, when a young man is in his twenties, and his subclan seniors feel the time for his marriage has come, they begin to assemble goods for a payment. If the young man has a regular courting relationship with a suitable girl, her family may be willing to discuss marriage. But if he has no such girlfriend and does not find a suitable girl, his father and other members of the men's house begin to pool valuables, promise pigs, and inquire among their friends and kin about eligible girls in the eighteen- to twenty-two-year age range. An immature girl may be married if she, her female relatives, and her father's men's house-group agree to the match. This is more likely if the family already has kinsmen in the groom's group, which would ensure that the girl will be protected from harsh treatment. The couple need not be acquainted, and I have seen weddings in which they both held back and only saw one another at the end of the ceremony. Sometimes marriage is arranged for a young man away at work.

The groom's kinsmen visit the houses of eligible girls of their acquaintance, sometimes going to a distant tribe with a kinsman or clansman who has connections to the girl's group. On an appointed day, the men of the girl's group come to the boy's settlement to view the goods offered. The girl is not usually present. The boy's sponsors – senior men of his subclan and senior kinsmen – press their relatives and debtors for contributions. Then a display is set up; banana stalks form the base into which bird of paradise plumes and feathers on bamboo sticks are erected. In the 1960s large, whole goldlip mother-of-pearl shells and sometimes a few bailor, green snail, or other decorative shells were laid out. Before 1950, marriage goods included dog's teeth necklaces, headbands and strings of cowrie and nassa shells, which are no longer used. Finely-polished stone "Hagen" axes, which we noted were made at a few places and traded throughout the highlands, were an important item. During the 1950s steel axes and knives, early trade items from government and mission gifts and trade stores, took the place of stone axes in exchange and work. Then both were so widely available as to be disdained in marriage payments by the 1960s. Feathers and plumes of a few types were favored although others were no longer used. Finally, money supplanted nearly all other goods; the goods were mainly a festive addition to the monetary transaction. In 1976 the payment consisted mainly of money, usually several hundred kina or up to $1,000. Long, black plumes of *Astrapia stephaniae* and certain parrot feathers were sometimes added, and an exchange of cooked pork and food followed. If the money and goods offered are satisfactory, or nearly so, and the bride's group can also agree on the number of pigs to be killed, cooked, and presented by both sides to one another, the conditions are very favorable for the marriage to take place. Further visits and more detailed discussions about the time, other goods included, live pigs to be donated as the beginning of the married couple's livestock holding, and the agreement of other relatives, as well as the couple themselves, then go forward. There may be problems, delays, or a cancellation during these negotiations. But when agreed, while the groom's relatives prepare the goods for transmission and cook the pigs, the bride's relatives bring together the agreed-on return payment, some goods to present and exchange with the groom's relatives, and cook pigs. On the appointed afternoon some of the groom's group bring cooked pork to the bride's home – most commonly to the men's house of her father or guardian. The space beside the men's house is a gathering and small feast-area, where cooked pork is exchanged and shared and the guests eat pork and vegetables. Later in the evening, the bride is taken to the rear of a house, and vegetable oil and pig grease are applied to her whole body to cleanse her and make her skin glow beautifully. The older women talk about married life and sing as this is done. Men, mostly of her father's men's house-group, lecture her about the responsibilities of a wife: Hard work, gardening, pig raising, cooking, and sharing food are the main themes. She is told to remain faithful to her husband and his group, not to go visit her parents too often, or to be lazy and gad about at markets and in towns. These preparations and discussions may last most of the night, as a farewell to the bride.

The next day, the groom's group gather to arrange and carry the payment to the bride's home. Preparations include attaching feathers and shells to circular boards which are carried on sticks, and often applying cosmetic paints, charcoal, and oil to the men and women who carry the gifts. Some goods, such as axes and feathers and the display boards, are carried to show them off. Pork and some goods are placed in women's net bags. The group proceeds along the footpaths to the bride's house. As they approach, they call and hoot so that people quickly gather to receive them.

The bride is oiled, painted, and then decorated with a magnificent headdress of feathers and bird of paradise plumes, goldlip shell necklaces, beads, fur pieces, and armbands. This is her moment of greatest display of health and wealth, and she will bring the goods she wears as ornaments to her husband. Pork and some other goods are also laid out for the exchange. The bride has one or two girls as attendants; they are usually younger girls and wear few ornaments. Some men of the groom's group who have some ties of kinship and friendship with the bride's group are also decorated with some feathers. The girls may accompany the bride and visit her for a while, and the men act as hosts and protectors for her; their attachments to both groups serve to mediate any problems. The newly arrived groom's group is greeted, and puts down the goods. Some exchanges of feathers or shells between individuals may take place, and the goods offered by the bride's group are displayed. Although the transaction has been called bride purchase, in fact the couple's cooperation is essential, and the later phases promise good will on all sides.

The leading men of both groups make speeches, which mention previous marriages between the subclans and clans of bride and groom; the past relations of the groups are described as closely linked, friendly, or distant. They proclaim that the new marriage will renew or initiate friendly exchanges, visits, and trade. The groom is usually in the background and must be summoned for the bride bestowal. Pork is brought forward; then the decorated bride is given an axe and carried to the center where the groom and bride together eat from one piece of pork – a symbolic union of sharing the good things of Chimbu. Shortly thereafter, the groom's group packs up the pork and goods, and the bride and attendants go with them to the groom's home. On one or two occasions I witnessed a symbolic protest by the women of the bride's group. They attacked the departing group with sticks and clusters of stinging leaves. This is usually in fun but occasionally announces an objection to the removal of a girl from her parents' home. Afterwards, each group divides the goods, mostly to men who arranged and contributed to the exchange.

The bride and any girls who may accompany her stay quietly with women of the groom's group – most often the wife of one of the men of his house. After a few days, another exchange takes place, this time at the groom's home. The bride is presented with household goods, as in a bridal shower. The women of her husband's group are the main donors, but some other relatives, men and women, may also give things. Previously, bark-cloth strips and net bags were the main goods; more recently cloth towels, blankets, blouses, lengths of cloth, enamelware basins, dishes, mugs, cutlery, cooking pots, and other store goods have been included. These are presented to the bride and she is told who gave each item. It is the first step in her household establishment and at the same time places her in a mutual network of gifts of food and domestic goods.

Large stacks of vegetable food, especially bananas, sugarcane, yam, taro, nuts, fruits, and other festive foods, rather than the everyday sweet potatoes and greens, are set up by each group and given to the other. The stacks are divided between the members of the groom's group, who eat food from the bride's relatives' gardens, and members of the bride's group, who eat food grown by the groom's relatives. Food grown by men and women is included. Speeches on this occasion are minimal. Affirmations of future exchanges are made. The bride's group leaves after having seen that she is well-treated in her new home.

The bride lives quietly with the older women for some time, gradually beginning to help in gardens and tending sections of new

After a marriage in Chimbu, a celebration is held at the bride's new home. She is seated and still wears some of her shell and bead necklaces. Her relatives, and the people of her husband's settlement, present her with blankets, cloths, enamel basins, and other personal and household goods.

gardens allocated to her. She has little privacy with her new husband, but he is expected to be preparing garden land and later to build her a house. She should cook for him and also others of the men's house-group. A shy couple, who have not been friends before marriage, may be slow to begin cooperation and cohabitation. But more recently, some couples were intimate before marriage and a husband may quickly build their own house.

A bride may run away from her husband in the first months of marriage. If so, the men who arranged the marriage, and her female relatives, will press her to return. Brides who run away several times, or who refuse to work, are called lazy and obstinate by all their elders. They may succeed in breaking off the marriage. If it is clear that she will not stay and work with the groom, the men of her group must try to return some of the marriage goods, and may hope to do this by finding another husband for her who will make a suitable payment. Girls who run away from two or more marriages get a reputation for stubbornness and laziness; eventually they may have to marry a man with a similar reputation who has not been successful in holding a bride. A young man in divorcing blames his wife and tries to avoid being known as a bad husband, because his elders will not so willingly contribute to his second or third marriage-payment if little has been returned in the past. Female divorcees are usually married within a few months to another man, and young widows also are married soon. Before 1933, young men were sometimes killed in fighting, resulting is some disproportion in the ratio of adult men to women. A few men who have been too unattractive, disagreeable, or incompetent remain single or divorced, but Chimbu have no class of permanent bachelors. In the past, men had two or more wives if they could afford it. A big man is known to be wealthy and attracts women whose relatives welcome the connection. Wives are a social and economic asset, providing garden produce and pig care to support a man's ambitions and exchange relations. Many women take pride in the families and food they raise, making it possible for the family to present food and pigs for group prestations.

The Chimbu believe that repeated sexual intercourse is needed for conception. A pregnant bride or unmarried girl is thought to be promiscuous; it is believed that the baby has been fathered by "all the men," and her husband may deny responsibility. Since physical maturity is rather late, brides are not so likely to conceive quickly, and by the time they have settled into comfortable relations and regular cohabitation with a husband, the baby usually will be accepted. Some forced abortion and infanticide are practiced, though usually such actions are kept quiet and may never be admitted. A 1963 study of reproduction, counting only children that survived for one year or longer, showed that married women aged sixteen to thirty had an average of 0.9 children, whereas women thirty-one years old and over had an average of 2.3 children. The relaxation of restrictions on intercourse after childbirth, and improved hygiene and health have increased family size. The average birth interval of 3.8 years, which we found in 1963, has certainly been reduced, but no current data on family size and birth intervals are available.

After a birth, the long taboo on sexual relations between husband and wife may ensure that the child will not quickly be displaced by a younger sibling. It is this practice that appears to be disappearing, and this restraint is not without infractions. The few accusations and admissions of adultery I knew of were mostly said to be initiated by men, and sometimes the guilty man paid damages to the husband. A man who attracts women, or who is able to pay for a second or third wife, or takes a widow and fosters her children, may have more opportunities for sexual intercourse and father more children. By the time of most anthropological studies in the highlands, mission endeavors to encourage monogamy had been pretty effective. Some early observers and census reports show a prevalence of polygynists, and many bachelors unable to obtain a wife. A polygynist can provide much food and pigs, whereas bachelors must attach themselves to a family or big man and may not have independent status. Now monogamy and larger families have become usual, resulting in an increase in population in Chimbu. Other highland areas which are more restrictive in sexual relations may not show the same trend. A general preponderance of males has been usual throughout the Pacific islands, for reasons not fully understood. Because population growth is measured in relation to the proportion of women of childbearing age, the growth rate is affected (McArthur 1976).

A married woman has many occasions for visiting her relatives, and if the distance is not too great, she may have a garden on her parents' land. She may frequently help her parents and relatives in small ways, and usually attends feasts and celebrations at her father's men's house. When she bears a child, her husband is expected to cook a pig and make a gift to her parents. A mother takes her baby and small children with her in visiting her parents and siblings; later they can visit separately. These close relations are the basis of kinship outside the father's clan, and continue with small gifts, loans, garden land, invitations to feasts, and exchanges of large amounts of goods and food throughout life. When a grandparent dies, the relations continue with aunts, uncles, cousins, and nieces and nephews. These close ties serve as a sanctuary and second home whenever the need arises. In widowhood, a woman may bring her children to her own settlement, and her brother or another relative may become their guardian. A man in need of land, or in a desire to help his father-in-law or brother-in-law, may move his family to his wife's home. The move may become permanent, with the family granted land in the woman's territory. By participating, contributing, and sharing in marriage exchange, kin have a special interest in marriage and offspring.

These details concern the central Chimbu of Mintima as I observed them; however, my reading of other accounts of highlanders suggests similar forms and attitudes.

KIN RELATIONS

The interest of kinsmen in the life of a woman of the settlement group continues throughout her life, and is carried on to her children. She actively encourages continued visits, help, and exchanges of food, goods, and pigs among her family and kinsmen. A woman raises and feeds the pigs and grows the vegetables for her husband and children. She may give or receive vegetables, and urges her husband and sons to allocate gifts to her kinsmen. When her husband's group receives goods, pigs, and food from people of her home settlement, she shares in this. On visits, a woman and her family receive food, shelter, and gifts from her kinsmen.

An important and sometimes dramatic expression of kin relations occurs at the death of the woman and her children. An adult man's death is also observed by his maternal kinsmen, but if a woman is old and long married she may have lost ties to her mother's kinsmen. The observance in Chimbu depends somewhat on the closeness of relations during recent years.

At the time of death, people in the settlement gather to mourn and send word to the kinsmen in other settlements. The next day, sometimes hundreds of people, including groups from other clans who are kinsmen of the deceased, come to express their sorrow. They bring some bananas, sugarcane, and other foods for refreshment of the mourners, and also bags of sweet potatoes to give the people of the settlement group whose mourning prevents them from working in the garden. Valuables, especially shells, axes, and money, are given by exchange partners to members of the mourning group. The group of men at the men's house of the deceased allocate the valuables, set out small piles of sugarcane and bananas for the guests, and then begin speeches. The close kin of the deceased are honored in speeches and given many valuables as a recognition of the regard

At the center of a settlement the cooked pork is laid out. It will be distributed among guests invited to this funeral. On the left is a corrugated iron store, on the right a shaded shelter. Dwelling houses are in the modern "mission" style.

and obligations of the settlement group to these relatives of the dead person. The occasions in which the dead person received hospitality, help, and friendship from these kinsmen are recalled. In this way the life-long associations and exchange of food and goods between relatives are publicly acknowledged. The audience, receiving refreshment, is told of the obligations of kinsmen. On a later occasion pigs may be cooked and distributed. Killing and sharing pork is always a memorable way in which to honor the transaction.

In the lives of highlanders, kinsmen are associated with food and help. The local settlement is the first place of attachment for children, and they are there first recognized as persons, and as family and group members. Boys and girls are also known to visitors to their home settlement – their mothers' kinsmen, the married sisters, and sisters' children of the men of the settlement. Kinship terms and categories are applied to these relatives, and the children come to regard the home settlements of some of these people as a second home. I have used Chimbu examples to show the quality of these ties and cannot be certain that they hold throughout the highlands.

Although several different types of kinship terminology and classification are found in the highlands, a few are especially frequent. The terms for parents, siblings, grandparents, children, and grandchildren are applied to everyone in the settlement group and clan by members. Often, the terms distinguish elder or younger members of the kinship category. The children of father's brothers and mother's sisters (parallel cousins) are classified with brothers and sisters. An important distinction is between these parallel relatives and the cross-category of father's sister and her children and mother's brother and his children. These are in different groups, derived from marriage and affinity, with whom some competition and exchange may be expected. Thus the whole clan or subclan of cross-cousins is an exchange group. Relations of affinity and kinship are similar, from the group viewpoint, because the exchange patterns which are initiated at marriage are continued into the lives of the offspring, or longer, between cross-cousins and their children.

The Chimbu have some practices which are of special interest. The proper kinship terms are used with older relatives – father, mother, grandparents, mother's brother, father's sister, cross-cousin, wife's father. Among contemporaries and with juniors, personal names, affinal terms, sibling or cousin terms or other friendly and joking terms are used. In friendship, one may call a man or woman "father of my namesake" (*dina nim*) or "mother of my namesake" (*dina mam*) to suggest that they name a child after him, a friendly act rather like godparenthood.

Among the Kamano, Jate, Usurufa, and Fore someone from the cross-cousin category is considered an ideal marriage partner (Berndt 1962) – another way of combining affinal and kin categories. The relationship between male cross-cousins is of comradeship and is perpetuated by further marriages of kin.

Among Siane, the eldest man of his generation in a lineage is called "eldest brother"; he holds a distinctive position of authority, acts as guardian of lineage property, and makes decisions involving the whole lineage for ceremonies, participation, and marriage payments. Senior and junior relatives are recognized throughout; for example, the senior or mother's brother is acknowledged as having some claim over the junior, whereas cross-cousins of the same age are equals.

These variations, where circumstances, relative age, and personal relations are expressed in the choice of terms used to address friends and relatives, make one feel that the highlanders do not follow a formal kinship system; rather, they devise special terms to convey their feelings and intentions in a particular situation. The formal kinship systems in the highlands are mostly what anthropologists refer to as the Dravidian-Iroquois type, but with some differences.

Dani, who have local intermarrying moieties as we have seen, have also an Omaha-type system of terminology in which generations are not distinguished in the mother's lineage. Whereas the confederacy includes several clans, in each area there are members of both moieties. The local clan is not territorially distinct. It is the intermarriage and exchange between moieties that dominates social relations between groups and individuals. The several Dani groups are probably all of a kind, as contrasted to the highlanders in Papua New Guinea. The latter see the social world as their own settlement, clan, and larger territorial group, surrounded by other clans in which there are kinsmen and families that are intermarried with their own.

5

Cohesion and competition

The structure of larger groups in the highlands is to some extent related to settlement form and population distribution. However, highlanders' concepts and practices concerning rights, descent, origins, continuity, and alliance are also involved. In this chapter we will discuss the level of the largest social, ritual, and political groups in the highlands – clans, tribes, phratries, confederacies, and alliances. Their structure and common activities will be shown to be forces for cohesion, whereas the mobility of individuals and families, the rivalry of big men, and the conflict of groups act to produce fission and recombination.

GROUP STRUCTURE

We might follow de Lepervanche (1973) in defining a highlands structural type:

In most Highland societies each parish consists ideally of an exogamous patri-clan whose members claim exclusive rights to parish territory . . . In general, each Highland parish, particularly through the efforts of its big-men, tries to maintain its strength and reputation, retain its autonomy, and simultaneously ensure its own security by keeping some channels of exchange open and by entering into alliances with neighbours. (pp. 31, 32)

These features distinguish highlands from lowlands political groups, and also demonstrate the interaction between local autonomy and relations with neighboring groups. But as Langness (1973) says, the use of conventional anthropological terms, such as clan, village, tribe, or phratry, which suggest that each type of group has always specific functions and sovereignty, does not convey the real situation. Rather, the network of individual ties and obligations, and the variety of activities instigated by leaders, mobilize different sets of individuals for each event. Therefore, in discussing group structure

I will consider (1) the ideal and actuality of group structure, and (2) leader-follower formations.

The earlier observers of highland life were concerned with the stability and continuity of corporate groups, following what was the usual emphasis in the study of groups in social anthropology. A segmentary structure is, indeed, in the ideology and tradition of most, if not all, highland societies. To take an example from the eastern highlands, Read defines a subclan in Gahuku-Gama as a village or village section, and a clan as one (sometimes more) village with a population of about 100. These groups are localized, territorial, exogamous, have a belief in common descent, and form a unit in ceremony and warfare. Two or more clans make a subtribe, which may also be exogamous, localized, and conduct initiations and pig feasts as a group. But again, the largest group, a tribe of hundreds of people, also is by tradition of one origin, patrilineal, territorial, and sometimes a fighting unit. The tribe, however, is not exogamous and is not unified in ceremonies; furthermore, some fights may arise between segments of the tribe. This Gahuku-Gama tribe is smaller in population than the phratry of the Enga. The terms phratry, parish, and tribe in the highlands have been used to designate a set of clans that are politically allied, or a localized, territorial unit, considered of common origin, which may hold some ceremonies as a group.

Central or Mae Enga (Meggitt 1965) whose homesteads are dispersed, have a similar pattern of segments: The lineage, subclan, and clan are localized, territorial patrilineal-exogamous groups, which hold ceremonies and fight as groups. The clans range in population from 100 to 1,000 people, with an average population of 350 people. The rights of members to land, inheritance, and membership recognition is by birth as sons of clan members. The Enga phratry is said to have been founded by a single ancestor, who was the father of the clan founders. The whole phratry, one territory with several thousand inhabitants, is a segmented lineage-structure, all derived from the clan-founding sons of the phratry founder. The subclans and their subdivisions are also seen as lineage segments, down to the small lineages of living men and their sons.

These are two common types of structure in the highlands of

Papua New Guinea as first described, and to which subsequent studies have shown some variations. However, later studies have repeatedly demonstrated that highland political groups are open to kinsmen born elsewhere, not restricted to agnatic descendants, and emphasized the very important role of big men in redefining action groups. We have, then, a theoretical or ideological, segmentary descent-group structure, which places activities in a structural context. But close inquiry into residence, land use, participation, and involvement shows that birth is the main but not the only way for a man to become a member of a group. This is not to say that highland social structure is bilaterial or cognatic. Only the Huli of the Southern Highlands province have been described as cognatic (Glasse 1968), because land and residence rights are available to all descendants of the founder, through daughters and sons. Often, Huli men have gardens and houses on several group territories, with multiple membership.

In studies of the highlands, many assemblages of people in their capacity as territorial, local, ceremonial, exchange, and war units are named. In any activity the name that is known to have a position in the segmentary system of tribe or phratry, clan, and subclan indicates the group size or the scale of activity in terms of the level of interrelations of groups. For example, Read stayed in Susuroka, a small village inhabited by two subclans. One men's house served all; in larger villages each men's house is used mainly by men of different subgroups.

The large Enga clan of several hundred people is a discrete social and political unit, with a ceremonial ground used for important group occasions. Ceremonial grounds in Hagen, however, are settlement sites of important big men and their following, not exclusively associated with a clan or segment.

The idea of segmentation – a common origin or founder of tribes or phratries, with the passage of many generations and successive divisions into segments – is a ready and appealing image for continuing social groups. Father-son succession may dominate in the formation of a group and is usually followed by the division of next-generation families into those of the brothers. If the group expands, it does so by births of men, their marriages, and the adoption and incorporation of junior kin as sons of leading men. A big man, with several wives and dependents, can himself found a group with five to ten next-generation segments. If the central highlands' population has rapidly expanded in the past several hundred years, this is likely to have been the process – pioneering, occupation of territory, expansion of land holdings, men's houses established, women bearing sons, and the breaking of the group into segments. The ideology is patrilineal and segmentary, with successive generations becoming the founders of sections. A clan can thus contain a complex, nesting set of subdivisions, but the occasions for coordinated action, the distribution of territory and need for defense, and the numbers required for assembling on ritual occasions or for intergroup exchange determine the choice and recruitment on each occasion. Local and familial matters involve a small segment. Chimbu marriage and death exchanges concern primarily a men's house-group, which may be supported by other men's houses of the subclan. Chimbu clans are among the largest in the highlands; they collaborate for large exchanges of food and interclan or intertribal warfare.

THE QUESTION OF DESCENT

Our description of property, land, settlement, marriage, and kinship all point to the transmission of group membership and inheritance from father to son. Wives bear children who are recognized as offspring and heirs to their fathers. Children are automatically members of their father's settlement, clan, and tribe. The male head of the mother's household, her husband – or, in rare cases, her father, elder brother, or lover, if she is separated or not married – takes on the functions of fatherhood. Subsequent moves of mother and child may lead to their being adopted and incorporated into other groups.

The normal, expected social classification of offspring is agnatic (patrilineal). This is the principle and ideology of the system. Groups are conceived as continuing in a line of male ancestors. In most situations of stable marriage, patrilocality, continuity from father to son in land holding, and local and group attachment, the succession of generations of fathers and sons forms a patrilineage. However, a continuously expanding lineage is actually rare in the highlands. War, death, migration, divorce, adoption, recruitment by big men, joining of kinsmen or affines – all the practices we have observed – break the continuity of descent. It is rather rare for a lineage to survive in a locality and clan without loss or accretions. More often, some lineage members are detached or die without sons, and nonagnates (kinsmen and affines) are brought in. These and their sons may come to be regarded as true members, having inheritable land rights and adopting the group ritual. Their sons are initiated and incorporated fully into the group.

If we could trace the descent of highlanders from their ancestors, say, 1,000 years ago, we might find the distinct language and cultural group founders of some of the present phratries or large clans, living in the region of their present-day descendants. And we might find some continuous lines of patrilineal descent to the men in the clans today. However, we would also find many instances of movement and membership change, with a lineage begun by a migrant extending into the present. Those which occurred in the distant past, hundreds of years ago, have long been absorbed as full members in the host group. Even those of 100 years ago have been absorbed; no one knows the details of genealogy, the occasion of migration is forgotten. Most anthropologists studying highlands groups have found few people who could recount long genealogies, and two to three generations are the most that can be recalled with precision. However, highlanders often think of their clans and subclans in lineage terms: They believe that sons have always succeeded fathers, and remain in their natal clan settlements. An individual move and adoption is seen as a particular situation, but not a significant exception to the rule. Furthermore, adoption, fostering, incorporation, and participation in the group are sufficient to assume patriliny. True biological fatherhood may be uncertain, but fatherly, brotherly, and filial behavior can always be recognized. Highlanders often care more about the behavior expected of close kinsmen than the assumption of blood relationship.

Among highlanders, the Mae Enga seem the most concerned genealogists: They told Meggitt of a multigenerational, agnatic lineage-system connecting the sun and sky beings to the phratry founder, clan founders, subclan founders, patrilineage founders, and living people. Such a mythic framework appears to the Mae Enga as fixed relations between agnatic groups. Nevertheless, the Mae are aware of changes in specific groups that do not fit this ideal schema.

As reported by anthropologists, most other highlands people do not see their groups in such formal terms. They think of groups as originating and perpetuating through agnatic descent, but in any context certain relations are stressed and others disregarded. The anthropologist may try to put it together, but discrepancies are unavoidable. For example, the Naregu, whose local and clan ties were described previously, told me that the tribe founder had three sons – Penta, Numambo, and Komba – who founded three clans. The founder of the fourth clan, Gamgani, was a brother of the Naregu founder, some of whose descendants migrated far to the west. Now the Gamgani are very small; the time since origin is no indicator of size. The Chimbu have been known to rearrange their structural genealogy in other situations, as when Gamgani became a minor appendage of Numambugu. These observations suggested to me that, in Chimbu, at least, contemporary group and political action is important, and genealogical belief is adapted to present reality. Without written lineage records and without a trustworthy oral history, genealogy cannot be absolutely authenticated; to the Chimbu, the only matter of real importance is present reality, cooperation, or separation.

Glasse and Lindenbaum (1971) say that the Fore think of their parishes as "one blood," descending from a common ancestor. They speak of descent as a means of conceptualizing residence. But the concept of descent-line is not developed into a genealogy; rather, it is recognized that the parish is a conglomerate group. Common residence is symbolized by an ideology of descent.

GROUP SIZE AND FUNCTION

Given the natural fluctuation of group size, the rate of natural increase, and the fortunes or misfortunes of intergroup conflict, we would not expect groups of equal population with equal land areas throughout the highlands. But we might expect that, in any area, villages, clan territories, and tribal populations would be within a range: that there would not be great variation in the mean size of a village, clan or tribe. Knowing that groups split or segment when numbers become too large for the usual activities, and ally or fuse when they become very small, we expect the hierarchy of segments to fall into a pattern, say five subclans to a clan, or two to four clans in a tribe. We also ask how the population is related to the size of a group's territory.

Each group has a particular history of its formation, of the way in which it has come to its present size and function: Some groups have continued to grow and segment internally without being forced apart by fighting, migration, or other disruptive forces; others have separated, become depleted, formed new alliances, or otherwise changed so that their tradition describes such dispersal and new formation into contemporary tribes or alliances. As part of the relations between groups, a sort of opposition of nearly equal units develops. Thus the exchange and rivalry of equal-sized units develop and become stabilized. Any great loss of manpower adversely affects the group's ability to hold its own in competition; if it does not increase by bringing in new families, it may be subsumed under a dominant group or wholly dispersed, and its territory taken over by more powerful neighbors. The irregularity of group growth, population loss, and misfortune results in unequal group sizes, and these are only partly adjusted by segmentation, migration, and fusion processes. Thus when anthropologists attempt to record oral traditions and tabulate clan and tribe size and territorial extent, some of the figures they accumulate vary over a very great range. Such has been noted by Bulmer in his studies of the Kyaka. In certain contexts, such as exogamy, a clan of 100 members and a clan of 25 members may have the same status. But they are not equal in territory, sovereignty, or relations with other groups.

A small group of men, such as we discussed in the men's house group and activities, is important in local cooperation and mutual aid in a great many highland societies. Together with their wives and children they are the basis of larger groups. But in each region there seem to be characteristic patterns of intergroup opposition, so that parallel groups compete in exchanges, as dance units, and defend territory. Yet the groups are by no means of equal size. The range of clan and tribe size indicates that some are ten or more times as big as others. The larger groups have many more people who can produce food, pigs, display valuables, and fight and their territory is that much larger. In every ethnographic account of the highlands a similar, very great size-and-population range is noted for groups evidently at the same status. Such groups, which share the same status but vary according to size, necessarily maintain an uneasy equality, the small threatened by destruction, the large by fission. A closer look shows that clans that vary in terms of size are not in fact equal units in competition. To understand the political and ceremonial groupings and activities, we must also examine the organization and mobilization of groups. For the group taking action may be known by the clan name, though it is in fact an augmented or diminished clan group. Participation is in fact voluntary, although urged by leaders to make a showing against competing groups. In rivalry the groups emerge as near equals or one dominates as the other must submit. Collective action is in the name of a clan, but the participants are not all or only clansmen.

The clan is not always an independent group: In fact, more often several clans, perhaps of unequal sizes, make up the larger political unit. When common ancestry and patrilineal descent are stressed, and it is believed that the original clan has so grown as to divide into several clans, the larger group might be called a great clan or a phratry. Sometimes the larger group is exogamous, but more often the constituent clans intermarry within the phratry. One or more of the several clans may have migrated, so that a phratry need not always be territorially unified. When dispersed, marriage between clans is usually permitted, and sometimes favored as common origin and friendship is then strengthened by affinal and kin ties.

A group of clans holding a territory in common, often with discontinuous land blocks, can be allied as a clan cluster or tribe. Here there is no dogma of common ancestry or segmentation from an originating clan, but local tradition accounts for alliance, friendly interchange and intermarriage, joint defense of territory, and ceremonial coordination. Tribes, even more than clans or phratries, may need to stand as equals, independently guarding their land and people. The structure can adapt to incorporating fragments of dispersed groups, and marriage between unrelated members increases intratribal affinal ties. The confederacy of Dani is a special subtype of this tribal form, with two main clan groups, of different moiety, in close exchange relationship and sharing territory. Alliances among the Dani of the Balim include numerous confederacies, with a total population of 2,000 to 8,000 (Peters 1975:54).

Vayda (1971) gives the example of the Kauwatyi clan cluster, the largest in Maring. It maintains its solidarity in fights with neighbors, with strategic alliances, and recompense to allies. A small group might not be able to maintain its independence and alliance against competitive enemy groups.

DENSITY, GROUP SIZE, AND TERRITORY

In our study of the relationship between population density and some cultural and social characteristics, Aaron Podolefsky and I tabulated data on some seventeen groups of highlanders and, when possible, placed them in rank order and in categories of high, middle, and low, and in high-low. This was then analyzed according to the Spearman rank order correlation (rho), gamma (γ), and Yule's Q (see Chapter 2, Tables 6 and 7, and Map 2). We used two general group categories, the local, exogamous clan and the largest political unit. Table 8 presents data on the population and areas. We would expect that the highland fringe and other sparsely settled peoples would have smaller clans and political units than the more densely settled highlanders. The relationship was statistically tested in these three measures.

In the correlation of population density and the population of the local clan group we found:

$$r_s \;\; = \;\; .564$$
$$r_s^2 \;\; = \;\; .32$$
$$.025 \; > \; p \; > \; .01 \quad \text{one tail}$$
$$\gamma \;\; = \;\; .574$$
$$Q \;\; = \;\; .538$$

For population density and largest political unit we found:

$$r_s \;\; = \;\; .723$$
$$r_s^2 \;\; = \;\; .522$$
$$p \; < \; .005 \quad \text{one tail}$$
$$\gamma \;\; = \;\; .863$$
$$Q \;\; = \;\; .818$$

These figures show that: Population density is directly associated with exogamous, local clan-population size; and population density is directly associated with the population of the largest political unit.

The relationships between population density and group size are positive, and this is especially true for the largest political units.

Table 8. *Areas of clans and political units*

Societies by density rank	Mean population of local clan	Mean areas of local clan (miles²)	Mean population of largest political group	Mean areas of largest political unit (miles²)
Dugum Dani	N.A.	N.A.	4,200	10.14
Chimbu	650	2.89	2,400	10.67
Mae Enga	350	2.19	2,290	14.31
Gururumba	375	3.32	2,300	20.35
Huli	N.A.	N.A.	500	4.42
Kapauku	200	1.92	600	5.77
Mt. Hagen	280	2.86	820	8.37
Gahuku Gama	100	1.10	750	8.24
Raiapu Enga	270	3.0	1,072	11.91
Bena Bena	188	2.11	750	8.43
Gadsup	N.A.	N.A.	293	3.71
Siane	200	2.70	840	11.35
Kakoli	318	4.68	318	4.68
Kuma	383	7.82	475	9.69
Maring	40	1.05	200	5.26
Kyaka Enga	200	6.25	780	25.00
South Fore	39	1.26	180	5.81
Correlation with density	$r_s = .564$ $r_s^2 = .32$ $.025 > p > .01$	$r_s = -.002$ $p > .10$	$r_s = .723$ $r_s^2 = .522$ $p < .005$	$r_s = .186$ $p > .10$
Mean of means		3.08		9.88
Range of all cases		1–7.8		3.7–25
Range of less extreme cases		1–3.3		3.7–11.9
Percent of cases used		79		82

Some further inquiries in terms of the relation between group population size and territorial extent are suggested by these findings. When we find a range of societies at different population densities, will this be associated with constant group territories, so that a clan and tribe will everywhere control approximately the same amount of land while population varies, or will there be clans and tribes of about the same number of people but with larger territories where population is sparse and smaller territories where population is dense? We have shown that population size varies with density. Now we may ask: What is the range in the size of group territories? In attempting to answer this question, we used the field research statements concerning the population of local clans and largest political units, wherever the information was available, and divided this by the population density to obtain a figure for the group territory. This is no more than an approximation, and could be compared with a field researcher's statement of the extent of a group territory in only a few cases. In these cases in which the field researcher presented data on the extent of territory and density, the same pattern of relationship held for the most part, so we felt that our approximation could be used for the whole series. Our calculation (see Table 8) shows that the general pattern is that group territories are about the same in high- and low-density highland societies. The low and insignificant negative and positive correlation with density fails to confirm the hypothesis that there are clans and tribes with about the same number of people but with larger territories where population is sparse and smaller territories where population is dense. We found that in about 80 percent of the societies, the mean territory of a local clan is between one and 3.3 square miles, the mean of means being about three square miles. The mean territory of the largest political units averaged about 9.9 square miles with a range of 3.7 to twenty-five square miles. We then eliminated extreme cases and reexamined the data. Clan territories varied from one to 3.3 square miles. About 80 percent of the largest political units were between 3.7 and twelve square miles. Some extreme cases, where larger territories appear, may include an exceptional amount of nonarable or unoccupied land, as perhaps in Kyaka, or refer to an aggregation of clans or subtribes that rarely combine into an effective political unit, such as the Mae Enga phratry.

The noncentralized societies of the highlands, where the maximum political unit may number between 100 and 5,000 people, depend on interpersonal contact among clans, communities, and leaders for the coordination of social, political, and ritual activity. Neither population density nor settlement type seems to affect the size of the territory; rather, average territories fall mostly between three and twelve square miles, and fellow members of a political unit may be kinsmen or clansmen, and collaborate in political, military, and ritual action. When density is low, the clan and political unit have a smaller population, so that social ties are generally within the same area or same territorial range for all highlanders.

The size of a clan's territory can be seen in relation to courtship, affinal, and kinship relations. If the local exogamous group is rarely greater than three or four square miles, courtship, visiting, land borrowing, and close interaction with kinsmen and affines may readily occur outside this area. As we have seen, most marriage and kinship is among neighboring clans.

In terms of the territory of the largest political groups, mostly under twelve square miles, communication, planning and coordination of group festivities, and warfare are within an accessible area. Often most men's houses, hamlets, and villages are concentrated in the central core of the territory, where plans and rituals are carried out.

The relations among settlement form, density, and social groupings were also examined. We have noted that most of the eastern highlands peoples live in villages, some with populations of 1,000 or more people, although men's houses and hamlets, house clusters, or scattered homesteads are found in other highlands areas. No relationship between density and settlement type was found. It may be worth noting that scattered homesteads combine well with large-scale pig raising because pig houses must border the forage areas. When villages are large, there may be inconvenient distances to scattered pig houses, a disadvantage (Hide, personal communication, 1975). Chuave, Sina Sina, and some Asaro Valley peoples are the most affected by this problem. Scattered homesteads may be also advantageous for defense, control of diseases, and lessening of disputes and sorcery accusations.

The exogamous, local clan-group, found in many but not all highland societies, is often a cooperative group with common territorial interests and joint action for defense, organizing ceremonies, and conducting its affairs. Members have kinsmen and affines in many of the surrounding clan groups. They will have close ties, visits, and interchange of goods and services with these relatives. If the clan territory were circular, the majority would have a radius of less than one mile.

The tribe, confederacy, or other group of clans that forms the largest political unit is the maximum group for coordination of interests and cooperation in political, military, ritual, or festival activities. Within this unit, many ties of kinship and marriage between the clans reinforce the bonds of friendship and common interests. For the majority of these groups, assuming a circular territory, the radius would be less than two miles.

The preceding estimates, based as they are on approximate and generalized density and territory measures, cannot be assumed to hold in every case. However, we can see how social life is locally concentrated, and that no expansion of political centralization has developed to control large territories. The variations in political unit are primarily variations in population associated with density rather than area. These highland social and political units may be contrasted with those of the fringe peoples. Fringe groups are small in population, with large group territories. They are sometimes separated from other groups by one or more days' walking distance, and intergroup contacts are infrequent.

BIG MEN

In Melanesia the leader is the big man – the one who has triumphed over his rivals and achieved his position of influence, prestige, and wealth. His followers are not ascribed through membership in a genealogical segment, but members of his clan segment and locality form the group's core with those whose allegiance is achieved by the leader's strength. This indefiniteness of relationship provides the opportunity for increasing the size, prestige, and power of a group by attracting individuals connected to the big man as exchange partners, affines, debtors, kin, adoptees, friends – any sort of personal associate. Any follower may join another group; the leader performs no essential service or ritual duty for persons related to him in any way. At any time there may be a number of active rivals for prestige in a community: These may break apart, or reinforce one another; some segment leaders regularly support one of their number as community leader. The competition of rivals may affect any enterprise; a leader cannot rely on his usual followers to support him in an unpopular undertaking. The big man keeps his position while he is wealthy and influential; his prestige depends on the size and wealth of his following. Big men make large contributions to displays and feasts, and have many exchange partners. But the wealth is dissipated in distribution at feasts; it cannot be accumulated and transferred to a successor. A big man's realm of influence may grow, but his following does not become a politically united community to be led by a successor; any charisma, mana, and so forth he may be thought to possess – and this is not a necessary part of leadership – cannot be passed on.

We should observe that each small group has a recognized leader or leaders: Each settlement, subclan, hamlet, village, or clan has one or more men who initiate new activities, prod their fellows to complete or expand production for feasts and ceremonies, and represent the group in its dealings with others. In this, some men are more successful and commanding than others. They attract followers to their settlements and schemes. They gather a group of followers and dependents who carry out their suggestions, provide food and goods for feasts and payments, and attempt to enhance the group's reputation for size, wealth, and strength. Fighting and oratory are the big men's most important skills, but a big man's personality and reputation is compounded of personal qualities – physical size, strength, courage, a commanding appearance and style to intimidate enemies and attract women and followers, and knowledge and judgment in personal and intergroup relations.

The accounts of exceptional leaders – the big men of a phratry, tribe, or group of clans – show that their leadership qualities are not always the same. Leaders or despots everywhere have an individual style which must be adapted to local circumstances and needs, but which includes bold imaginative programs for group achievement. Success requires a following and some demonstration of success, domination, esteem, and awe-inspiring qualities. One example is Matoto, who was a leader of Tairora in the Eastern Highlands province (Watson 1971) and was especially known as a large, aggressive, and courageous man who killed many enemies by stealth and ambush, incorporated whole groups of refugees into his community, attracted many women to be his wives, traveled vast distances into unknown territory without fear, and flagrantly fornicated with women. Although his own following was perhaps 2,000 people, his dominance and esteem extended to other groups, who sent emissaries and consulted with him, not venturing to offend him and risk retaliation. Matoto's extensive network of political ties gave him a wide influence. But he was also the target of sorcery and attempted vengeance. An invitation to receive a gift once became an ambush to destroy him. Matoto is characterized as a "bad man," widely feared and dangerous. I knew some men in Chimbu who were known as fighters and killers. Often they would lie in wait for travelers and kill them. These men were feared rather than admired. They did not often become respected leaders, organizers of exchanges, and orators.

Another big man might be known more for his economic manipulation and acquisition. Chimbu big men are often energetic traders and travelers, combining strength, vigor, skill, and a wide network of exchange partners in areas where valuables can be obtained. Their success in the exchange system, speaking as leader, organizing, and dominating ceremonies gives their following pride and satisfaction in intergroup relations. Melpa and Enga leaders of *moka* and *te* exchanges gain prestige in this way.

The Mae Enga big man (Meggitt 1971) who in the first place is acknowledged leader of a patrilineage segment, holds authority as representative of his group. His ambition and participation in payments and exchange may give him prominence in the affairs of his subclan and clan. To be successful in clan leadership, that is, effective in speaking, planning, arbitrating, negotiating, and exchanging, he must also have support for kinsmen, affines, and exchange partners in other clans. He may extend his influence beyond the clan and his followers. He may stand preeminent in war and in transactions of pigs and pearlshells as long as his group is united and undeterred in warfare. But overexpansion makes the group liable to internal conflict, with new, ambitious big men competing for power.

Fore, Maring (Lowman-Vayda 1971), and some other groups have been said to have recognized two or more types of big men. One is the warrior leader, with characteristics of strength, vigor, and aggression; some of these could count up a long list of victims. A second type excels in persuasion of his followers for production and exchange. He is often a great orator, negotiating between groups and amassing food and goods for ceremonies. The role of spirit director, curer, magician, or diviner, that is, a practitioner in the arts of medicine and magic, requires knowledge which is learned from a qualified specialist, and perhaps also personal contact with spirits. Cults are numerous: A successful practitioner is often admired and sometimes feared for his influence and ability. When combined with the other personal qualities of a big man, the spiritual specialist may be a powerful leader. But the magical abilities alone do not make a big man.

Success in leadership may take one or more of these forms, but some Chimbu men who were feared individual killers had no ability to attract a following or expand group prestige. Matoto in Tairora combined these qualities. Overall leadership includes warfare directed by a big man who can lead fights, organize groups, and follow up a successful battle with oratory, ceremonial exchange, and display of wealth, and attract followers from other groups to expand his own. Such a multifaceted big man is rare; he develops a large supporting group, expands his territory, and achieves prestige over a region. In the highlands, such exceptional men of great renown never established a long-term domination of any large group. No kingdom, establishment, permanent control, or continuity of leadership has ever occurred there. Highland leadership has always been the big man's personal following, from his clan, tribe, kin, and affines, which did not survive him. It is difficult to imagine any long-lived political unification emerging from such a pattern. Where such unification has developed it has been based on stratification and enforcement by officials.

OPPOSITION AND SOLIDARITY

In a noncentralized social and political system, groups and intragroup and intergroup relations are defined in terms of action and opposition. Segmentary opposition develops whenever two individuals interact in dispute or competition. Each party can usually count on support for his rights among his closest agnatic kinsmen and followers. If the disputing persons are in the same settlement or subclan, each may be backed by his brothers, but others will often mediate, urge agreement, and stop the conflict from spreading. It is in the interests of all to limit and resolve such intragroup quarrels.

One who is persistently troublesome will not be supported even by his close kin against others of the settlement. A man's kinsmen and affines in other settlements may not publicly come to his defense, but they may provide a temporary sanctuary for him, and he can visit until the matter is resolved or forgotten. An insoluble conflict may be the occasion of a family migration or schism in the group.

Interpersonal conflict develops within the clan or larger local group from accusation of theft, property damage, adultery, or similar attack, and from a fight or demand for damages from the accused. If the offense is real and known to others, the guilty person may make amends, or withdraw for a time. If both parties claim to be right, there may be no resolution. In Chimbu there have been some fights between subclans in conflicting land claims and theft of pigs; such disputes may lead to a redefinition of boundaries and strengthening of fences. Most highlanders attempt to restrain quarreling clansmen, and fights with major weapons – bow and arrows, spears, or clubs – were rare and considered wrong between clansmen.

The bold and aggressive behavior of a big man might include taking over goods, pigs, produce, and wives of others without fear of reprisal. Followers in the settlement and clan support his demands; they lack the force or courage to oppose his wishes. He rules, it might be said, by his own strength and the absence of organized or firm opposition. He is beyond retaliation. His achievements, killing of members of other clans, and intimidation of opponents may allow him to dominate others in his own group. They may accept this domination because it gives the whole group power in intergroup relations.

In the New Guinea highlands, it would seem that intragroup cohesion is uneasily maintained without political or legal authority, and that the big man is not traditionally a force for intragroup solidarity. Men are bound to one another by mutual reciprocity, debts and obligations, and the need for protection by powerful and feared individuals and alliances. A small clan, depleted by quarrels or misfortunes, cannot long retain its position in relation to larger groups. An aggressive leader might draw supporters from outside his own group, build up his following, and reestablish the group's prestige in intergroup competition. Otherwise, the remnants of a group may form a new alliance or become an adjunct to an established group.

In the names of places and groups, the tradition of former independence or migration may be retained. We often find group names that are paired, commemorating the alliance of distinct groups, perhaps of separate origin. This naming device points out an opposition and an alliance, in different contexts. Sometimes, as in Chimbu clan-section names, there is a distinct level of grouping. For example, the large clan Numambugu is composed of seven subclans, varying in size from 60 to 203 people (1962 figures). Some of these are grouped into local clusters, sharing men's houses and land, so that they are known, and often appear, as a unit rather than separately. Thus two of the largest subclans, Baugu and Aundugu, are known as Bau-Aundugu (population 370), and may appear at feasts or exchanges as one unit, whereas the other group of five subclans, collectively known at times as Minegu (population 477) acts as a unit in opposition. I recall one occasion when logs were needed to repair a bridge, and a group of Minegu men went into the Numambugu forest slope, cut down a big tree, and hauled it down to the road through Numambugu gardens. The situation became complicated as several men in Bau-Aundugu raised objections, some because the tree had been cut from an area of forest and fallow land that they claimed as theirs, and others because of damage to fences and gardens in bringing the log down. Collectively they accused the Minegu of disregarding the rights of the Bau-Aundugu, taking their property, and damaging their crops. Minegu replied that the Numambugu as a whole were responsible for providing materials and work on bridge repair, that they were carrying out clan responsibility. They said they doubted that Bau-Aundugu had exclusive rights to the trees, and insisted that the garden damage was slight. As in so many such instances where some individuals feel injured, there is no real solution but a mounting list of grievances which contribute to the intergroup tension. In this way, with accumulating grievances, a serious dispute can set off a fight between all who have felt resentment. A fight in 1963, in which many men were jailed, required food exchanges for resolution. One phase of the resolution had been completed, but in 1976 the next phase was being organized. The exchange is not only reciprocated, but escalates with mounting debts to create competition. If settlement is not negotiated, or the people are not satisfied with payments, opposition predominates over unity. The sections will only cooperate to give or receive in helping one another in payments to larger groups. And in Chimbu when a clan section population reaches about 400 or more, it increasingly acts independently without its partner section. This often results in two clan sections becoming effective clans in action and exchange with other groups. Finally, clan sections may agree to remove the exogamic rule and arrange a marriage between the sections. When this occurs, the clan sections are considered separate clans. In the traditional history of the Naregu tribe, Pentagu and Numambugu were sections of one clan three or four generations ago. They began to form separate territories as the Kombaku clan was given land at the boundary and came to hold a strip of territory between Pentagu and Numambugu. The split was finalized by marriage between a Pentagu man and Numambugu girl. Subsequently, the paired sections of each have developed almost to the point of another split. This is the process of growth and segmentation. If one group is driven off in a fight and migrates to a new area, or the opposition intensifies to long-term enmity, a fission can occur between sections.

Of course, quarrels and accusations of theft, trespass, and adultery arise most often between people who live together. Among the most common quarrels are marital disputes in which a partner is accused of neglect, disregard, or cruelty. This often involves members of two clans, if the wife runs away to her parents or to a friend elsewhere, or is accused of neglecting her husband, his pigs, and gardens in order to be with her family. When a divorce is contemplated, there may be expectations of return of the marital payment. Since these goods were distributed by the bride's family to her clansmen and relatives, and subsequently became part of other payments, few of the goods can be returned, and none of the recipients wants a divorce that would require such repayment. It is in the interests of all to prevent separation, but everyone also wants to avoid serious injury, beating, or suicide of the unhappy wife – which may provoke a greater conflict between the clans of wife and husband. The disputes that polarize two social segments can only be resolved by negotiation between the sides or, when possible, by an outside or superordinate authority. This was not found in the traditional system, but has developed in the magistrate functions of government officers and local courts. More recently, cooperative negotiation of elected councilors, committeemen, and village court magistrates have attempted to settle such conflicts.

Alliance of two clans or subtribes is the most developed form of New Guinea highland collaboration. It is found in special form among the Dani. The Dani language and culture group is very large and covers a huge area. Several anthropological studies in different subregions present different aspects of the group's structure. Although the local settlement pattern of a compound with a men's house and several women's houses is found throughout, the largest alliances include populations of thousands only in the densely populated Grand Valley of the Balim. Less populated areas surround these on all sides; peoples west, north, and east have also been studied. Patrilineal and exogamous descent-groups are recognized all over. Frequently, they are composed of several local subgroups who have the same name. But the territorial organization is basically a confederacy of these local groups from the two moieties. The two largest local groups usually dominate, with a confederacy name as a pair of these names, for example Wilihiman-Walalua. Other smaller local groups are included. The moiety system of exogamy and local intermarriage between the two main groups makes a close-knit confederacy of these groups. A single village or local area may have men of both moieties; it must always have wives of different moiety than husband.

Local concerns and the interrelations of kinship and marriage bind together the people of a confederacy. The population of the confederacies in the Konda Dani area is 200 or less (O'Brien 1974), whereas 400-500 people live in the community territory of others (Ploeg, on Wanggulam parish, 1969; Koch, on Jalé Pasikni village, 1974). But in the Grand Valley of the Balim, Heider describes Dani confederacies of 1,000 to 3,000 that are territorial, protect their land, and recognize leaders who organize large-scale warfare and pig feasts. A very great leader may form an alliance of his own and other confederacies; one included 5,000 people who were led by Gutelu into war with other alliances and organized the initiation of boys into the moiety. Activities involving such a large group are rare because such powerful leaders are not equally able to coordinate the people of so many confederacies. Supraconfederacy alliances are often short-lived; if any campaign fails, the supporters fall away, and a successful fight cannot bring the defeated into long-lasting alliance with a conqueror. The necessary controls are not available; no government-military system exists.

A somewhat similar confederacy organization is described for the Kapauku, but without moieties and alliances its organization resembles the tribal form of the central and eastern highland area (Pospisil 1958).

We can conclude our observations on group structure by comparing these highlands societies with the corporate unilineal segmentary descent-group type. There are several characteristics.

Corporation. This involves the collective rights and responsibilities of birth members to property, titles, positions, and so forth. It is found among both birth and adopted members in most highland societies. Such groups elsewhere are often sanctioned by authorities, genealogy, and ritual, which are not highly developed in most highland societies.

Unilineal descent as a mode of recruitment. Highlands group membership is not limited to agnatic descendants; rather, other types of incorporation and adoption are widespread, and immigrants do not always suffer disabilities. Patrilineality is ideology rather than a genealogical charter.

The segmentary pattern of hierarchy and opposition. This is generally present in the highlands as the schema of interrelations of groups and subgroups. An image of common descent and father-son continuity is characteristic. In practice, growth and decline of segments, incorporation of migrants, alliance, and the adaptation of group territories and boundaries all influence the organization. Both land and descent concepts enter into grouping. And these are changeable with group activities, leaders developing new groupings, and expansion into new land. The corporate functions may break down in the process.

Duality, as opposition, contrast, and combination, is a pervasive theme in human societies. In the highlands it provides a framework for opposition, alliance, and exchange. This appears in the segmentary structures of the highlands and in the moieties of Dani and others, symbolized further in the opposition of the sexes, domestic and wild, allied clans, age mates, and pairs of birds, plants, and other objects.

Ritual, marriage, exchanges, and alliances all express the duality, opposition, and pairing ideas in the relations between groups. By payment or rearrangement of status, there is a balance or shift of the intergroup relationship. If one of the pair does not reciprocate, the status relationship changes, and the balanced opposition fails. Thus when one group declines and cannot make a transaction, it must make an alliance at the appropriate level and may lose its status. If it grows beyond its opposed unit, it must engage in transactions at another level.

CONFLICT AND COHESION

We have already seen that interpersonal disagreements occur as often in New Guinea as anywhere – perhaps more often. The propensity to dispute and fight have often been named as special characteristics of New Guinea highlanders, and some reasons for this have been advanced. But perhaps there is no single reason for these disputes, and that, instead, the force for cohesion affects some situations rather than all.

Individual disputes involving misbehavior, accusations, insults, theft, and property damage are common within the family, settlement group, and between kinsmen and neighbors. When they develop into shouting, fighting, and injury, the attention of others is drawn, and one or both parties demands settlement, usually with compensation. In addition to the conflicts between people due to their own actions, the depredations of pigs, their care, abuse, and constraint or loss by theft or secret killing involve the relations of people and groups.

The relations between people in families are often based on a mass of expectations and dissatisfactions; harsh words and accusations of neglect, laziness, preference, and failure are common and this is often accentuated with striking or fighting. A person insulted or injured may complain to a sympathetic kinsman, gain support, run away, or otherwise extend the dispute in seriousness or to other persons. Marital and family quarrels thus spread to kinsmen and may provoke a dispute between affines, separation, or division between kinsmen. If the dispute involves marriage partners, a woman is usually urged to return to her husband and domestic duties, and might be refused support by her kinsmen. Without comfort from her family or husband, a woman might commit suicide by hanging, and this is quite often reported. Death in these circumstances may require mortuary payments and exchanges between the kin, who are humiliated by the publicity of the death and their treatment of her. Suicide in bereavement, over the death of a close relative, in illness, in shame, and in fear is also reported in many parts of Melanesia. It is a way of making public one's distress, and perhaps repaying a wrong. But the many situations that provoke suicide cannot be subsumed in a single category in New Guinea any more easily than elsewhere.

Pigs are the most common form of payment, compensation, and truce exchange, so they are highly valued as property, security, and sources of prestige and status. The usual recommendation for a dispute settlement is a payment or exchange of pigs. A man's worth is linked to his pig herd, its growth, security, and welfare more than to any other property. Because pigs are dangerous, unreliable, and threatened property, success in raising pigs is a measure of agricultural efficiency, and any threat to pigs endangers self-esteem. Many quarrels between relatives involve care of pigs and their management.

When marriage disputes or pig thefts involve members of different clans or tribes, many people may join in a fight. The incident itself may hardly seem sufficient to provoke a fight, but the group involvement is high. The incident arouses suppressed hostilities and rallies whole clans and tribes to attack. On these occasions there is no evaluation of rights or wrongs; the other side is the enemy, attacker, or thief, and the mass action is in revenge for many past injuries, insults, unavenged killings, losses, or sorcery, and the aim is to subdue, evict, and remove the enemy from the border land.

Pig theft – which can sometimes be accomplished without the theft being detected – is a typical incident of intergroup aggression. A pig theft provides an occasion of celebration and feast by the thieves, and can sometimes be justified as retaliation for a debt or damages when the pig was permitted by its owner to get out of control and break into gardens. The pig's owners may know the pig's habits, and attempt to find a missing pig. The pig is called by name, sought in its usual haunts, and may be traced to a broken fence or place of abduction. If the search fails, the pig has usually already been killed, cooked, and shared by the thieves, and the incident becomes known to relatives and neighbors of the thief who have shared the meat. Often the secret is revealed to friends or kinsmen of the owner, and the owner will be supported in an attack and demand for compensation. The indignant owner and his party may leap on the thief or anyone who may have shared the loot, to attack them, damage property, and steal pigs in retaliation. The next stage may be further retaliation by both sides, as each can demonstrate injury without satisfactory recompense. But if the thief offers compensation, or the attack party is satisfied with its revenge, there may be no further fighting. An important element in the resolution is the past relation of the two parties. If a long series of incidents and grievances has not been compensated, and anger grows, the fight may escalate to a war including more distant kin, clansmen, tribesmen, and supporters. Men may be killed, houses and crops burned, groups evacuated, and a deep division developed between two groups. But this is uncommon, for many potential supporters have kinship ties to both parties and try to avoid such escalation.

The role of a forceful, persuasive partisan can be crucial in escalating a personal dispute into a large fight. The group may respond to a call to retaliate and chase the offenders off their land, making them flee to the grassland, the forest, or live in caves. Raid is answered with counter raid until the two parties are tired and stop, or someone is killed. Then the shock of loss may provoke settlement and payment of compensation. Alternatively, a renewed resolve to destroy the enemy may bring on more extensive fighting. Every day is uncertain; there may be an attack or provocation. The outcome is seldom definite or the settlement permanent. There is no real armistice or treaty to end such wars. All belligerents are never satisfied. A truce involves the payment of compensation and reward to supporters, and an exchange of pigs and goods between the major opponents. It is often years before such payments can be accumulated, and new grievances may develop. Any satisfying truce exchange is likely to be short-lived. However, alliances between groups wax and wane during and between periods of tension and hostility. A constant flux, realignment, and new sources of conflict characterize intergroup relations.

A highly provocative element in the strained relations between groups is the action of aggressive fighting men, such as those we discussed earlier, who ambush and kill strangers. Neighbors of nearby settlements withdraw in resentment and fear. The aim of the fighting men is self-aggrandizement and the enhancement of their group's reputation for superiority and vanquishment. Solitary travelers and isolated farms and homesteads are the targets of the attacks. In areas in which fighting men are known to exist, men never travel beyond the settlement without weapons, such as bows and arrows, which might be used for shooting birds as well as for self-defense, and axes, which are used both as weapons and as tools.

A local and territorial aspect of intergroup hostility is involved in individual attacks, in pig theft, in personal quarrels, and in most other conflicts. The parties to a dispute and fight must meet, and the meeting place is public or private territory to which both have access. The land itself may be the source of the dispute, for example, when a plot of fallow land is cleared by a man and another claims it is his land. Fences, crops, buildings, and trees on land can be damaged or taken, or ownership and rights may be disputed. There may or may not be a real shortage of land or property, but theft or conflicting ownership claims are matters of dispute between individuals and groups. Often the conflict is not over land scarcity, but over access, convenience, or a particular resource such as wild pandanus trees in the forest. When a group is defeated and forced to flee, seeking refuge with allies and kinsmen, its land is looted and laid waste. The conquerors may not wish to occupy the enemy sites, but want the border extended to an unoccupied no-man's-land. Then they need not fear attacks or reprisals. In the studies of conflict and aftermath of war, Chimbu and Enga, both densely populated areas, do fight over, conquer, and occupy enemy land. Among the Dani and many other peoples competition for land is not given as the precipitating cause of war, but a redistribution of people and relocation of boundary is a frequent outcome. The conquered land may be unoccupied for years before it is reclaimed by former owners or taken up by new settlers. In the short and long term, there is reallocation following a large, group victory. Some battles are so destructive that many men of a local group are killed or disabled, women and children die, and the remainder flee. When fighting is not so destructive, people are not routed, and property is not destroyed; people may or may not temporarily abandon outlying fields and houses, but do not relinquish their land claims. Yet the land may be liable to enemy encroachment and attacks over open land. However, the danger of encroaching on another group's land is heightened by the fear that magic may have been used to protect the territorial margins.

When a group is closely settled for protection, it concentrates gardens and houses in the center of its territory. But pigs must forage outside the garden land, where they are vulnerable to theft by enemies; more pig thefts perpetuate the antagonism between groups.

WAR

The Dani believe that warfare is essential to their welfare, and demanded by their ancestors (Peters 1975). Dugum Dani warfare is photographed and described most vividly in Robert Gardner's film, "Dead Birds," and the book, *Gardens of War* (1968). Opposing alliances in the Grand Valley of the Balim are separated by a frontier overlooked by watchtowers, from which each group can foresee the onslaught of an enemy raid. Attacks and counterattacks are a feature of everyday life. Group security is unattainable, yet health and welfare depend on success against enemies. Ghosts demand revenge; if their death is not avenged, they harass their neglectful kinsmen. A war leader may decide that a battle is demanded, and his band of warriors challenge the enemy. Then the call goes out, and men of the various communities prepare themselves with feathers and paint and assemble at the battleground. Ritual preparation may be elaborate. War leaders conduct divinations to determine the course of the battle. The fighting begins by agreement of both sides, on a battleground. Members of both sides meet with arrows and spears in a skirmish, and new parties of warriors come into the arena from time to time. Fighting is intermittent, with some warriors retiring and others taking their place. At close quarters the fighting groups must be very agile to dodge arrows and spears. The enemy may be trapped in an ambush, in an area where tall grass permits concealment. The barbed arrow points break off when embedded in the flesh, and must be removed, and the wound bandaged. After a day of fighting, both sides withdraw, perhaps challenging the other to a continuation on another day; a guard force remains near the frontier during the night. Raiding parties of ten to twenty young men may steal to the frontier and penetrate enemy territory and attempt to kill by attack or ambush. If they succeed, they have attained vengeance, but the victim's kinsmen will later attempt retaliation. In this exchange, hostilities are endless. Because an alliance has enemies on every side, many frontiers need to be watched, and raids are possible on all fronts.

Throughout the highlands, most deaths in war occur as a result of injuries in ambushes and raids. Enga fight in small raids and in large phratry encounters in which two large groups meet at a prearranged site. In preparing for battle, shouts and insults are exchanged at a boundary between the opposed groups. Chimbu fight in several separate groups. Barbed and decorated spears and axes are used by a few men in hand to hand fighting at a prearranged battleground. Shields made of wood, and held by a strap, are large enough to hide behind for protection, but heavy and cumbersome in fighting. To back up the spearmen, men with bow and arrow, at a greater distance, aim at the enemy spearmen and others on the opposing side. They try to make a man drop his shield. The weapons are not accurate at a distance. Skirmishes are brief, and only rarely do the two sides meet for a protracted series of engagements. For these, an open battleground is selected and agreed upon by both sides. Such a war could go on, intermittently, for months.

In the eastern highlands, most fighting occurred in surprise attacks, ambush, and retaliatory murder. Stockades, escape tunnels, and other defensive fortifications were used in villages. The usual venue of fighting, however, was outside the village, an attack against one or a few people on paths or in gardens.

Unusual surprise tactics are attempted by fighting leaders to trap the enemy or prevent retreat. In exceptional success, the fleeing enemy is pursued by conquerors who loot, burn, and destroy houses and gardens, and force the vanquished group to seek refuge with kinsmen. A long period of attempts to revenge and regain territory might follow. In the village, a men's house might be surrounded, the door made fast, the house set fire, and escape prevented while it burns. This can only be countered if an escape tunnel is already dug. In a raid, enemy forces may burn fences, trees, houses, crops, and fallow, creating a wasteland that cannot be occupied for years. The loot taken by the enemy forces may include food crops and pigs.

When the opposing forces are exhausted or one side is overcome, the exchange of raids, injuries, and deaths can be stopped by agreement to a truce, peaceful exchange, and payments. A thanks or indemnity is paid to allies, for example, men of another clan who have joined in the fight. If allies suffer injury or death, the payment must be adequate. I encountered cases in Chimbu in which, after an ally was injured, his clansmen supported the opposing side to inflict injury on those who allowed their clansmen to be hurt.

Among the Jalé Dani, pigs are exchanged to terminate fighting. The initiators of the war share a pig, and each side compensates allies for their injuries and losses. Warfare within a confederacy takes place on open battlegrounds, but is limited in time. Victims in such fights may not be eaten, as they are known to the enemy. A war between confederacies or districts is carried out in a series of raids and counterraids; enemy dead, strangers to their killers, are eaten and their relatives must avenge this. Thus interconfederacy wars can rarely be terminated: A vengeance raid may be undertaken at any time (Koch 1974).

Compensation for enemy casualties comes when both sides wish to stop attacks and establish peaceful relations, including friendly exchanges and marriage. The *moka* cycle may be initiated, as will be discussed later. Compensation for casualties in warfare between groups establishes conditions for visiting, marriage arrangements, ceremonies, trade, and exchange, but these cannot be regarded as permanent. A continued peaceful exchange, without incidents, arguments, demands, and, finally, raids or attacks, hardly exists between New Guinea highland clans. No superordinate authority can prevent the escalation of personal differences to intergroup conflict. Some truces are less threatened than others, when people on both sides do not encroach or steal, and married couples do not quarrel and involve their relatives. Such restraint may come when a wide interclan no-man's-land separates the settlements, or one group is preparing for a festival that will honor their friendship with the other, or both are diverted by conflicts with other groups. When serious hostilities develop between two clans or tribes, the nonbelligerents are drawn in as allies of their kinsmen in the opposing groups. This may easily lead to casualties, the involvement of more people, and demands for compensation. When kinsmen and affines are on opposite sides of a battleground, they stop fighting, retire, move to a different front, or somehow avoid injuring close relations. On another occasion, these same relatives might support the clan who is, at present, the opponent. There is a rallying of allies who reside near the scene of hostilities – to support a clansman or affine, or to grasp an opportunity to redress a grievance.

RETALIATION AND COMPENSATION

Most of our information about indemnity and compensation is derived from recent cases, in which the presence of a colonial authority, determined to stop tribal warfare, influences actions. Sometimes a police force is called in to arrest the initiators and participants. At other times the dispute is taken to administrative authorities. In the past few years, the elected tribal councilors and committeemen have become informal adjudicators who discuss disputes and sometimes award damages to an injured party. Land disputes often persist after a court judgment is given. Such disputes have been responsible for recent fights in Chimbu, where occasions of intertribal conflict have, if anything, become more frequent in recent years. Death in road accidents is treated as killing which requires large compensation payments. These demands have often led to fights.

In most of Papua New Guinea the establishment of patrol posts was followed by appointments of locally responsible headmen, later replaced with elected local government councilors, whose duties included reporting fights and bringing disputants to headquarters for trial. Fighting was repressed, and miscreants jailed or fined. Still, grievances remained; the jailing of thief or attacker gave little solace to the injured.

There is some difference in principle. The law believes that injury or killing can be accidental and excused. However, most New Guineans disagree; they believe misfortune is always due to sorcery, witchcraft, or other human or spiritual causes and can be counteracted or avenged. Recently, there have been many new outbursts of vengeance fighting, killing, and demands for compensation. They sometimes culminate in payment as the following article in the *Papua New Guinea Newsletter* (2 July 1975) illustrates:

After more than 50 years of fighting and bitter feelings, members of the Niniga and Kumai clans have settled their differences as a mark of respect for Papua New Guinea's Independence year. At a meeting in Minj recently, attended by 4000 warriors, the Ninigas made a settlement of 200 pigs, four cassowaries and K2000 in cash, and the long standing feud was over. Most of those present could not remember what the years of fighting were all about and only a few old men remembered the day when a Kumai man was killed in a food garden by a party of Niniga warriors. It was thought to be a Niniga garden, but no one could really remember after so long. Certainly no one remembers the man's name. Assistant District Commissioner at Minj, Don Simmons, who attended the ceremony, said the compensation payment was the second by the Ninigas. The first, made many years ago, consisted of 500 pigs and traditional riches but was considered inadequate. Fighting had continued until this meeting and compensation payment had been arranged. Mr. Simmons said the two clans would now live in harmony and understanding.

Huli expect the initiator of a war to indemnify an allied victim's family and bilateral kinsmen with at least thirty pigs, which are supplied from his own herd and that of others in his locality and among his kinsmen. Huli who kill a man in a minor war may compensate his kingroup. This is to deter retaliation, and prevent major war. However, between long-established enemies, retaliation in attack and further fighting are used.

We might attempt to classify types of hostilities and appropriate reactions or outcomes, but each case has distinct features in the initiating offense, relations between opponents, assemblage of supporters, casualties, damages, retaliation, mediation, or truce. Intergroup, interclan, intertribe, interregional, and interconfederacy relations are generally tense and hostile, punctuated with acts of aggression and exchanges which may include compensation. Alliances are short-lived, threatened by internal conflicts and division by support of opposing sides.

Tsembaga Maring hold a major festival, the *kaiko*, as a truce-confirming pig feast (Rappaport 1968). At the end of a serious fight between major local groups, or clan clusters, when each group desires truce and is confident that its opponents will not attack again, truce rituals are held separately by each party with its allies. Pigs and wild animals are eaten, and a red-leaf variety (*rumbim*) of cordyline is planted. Some years later, when sufficient pigs have been acquired, this *rumbim* cordyline is uprooted to signal the beginning of the *kaiko* festival. Territory abandoned during the war is reclaimed by planting stakes at the boundary. Feast preparations include planting of food gardens for the feast, fattening pigs, tabooing minor feasts and ceremonies, and preparing the ceremonial ground and houses where the hosts and guests will stay. The ritual lasts for a year with special events: marsupials and pandanus oil prepared in special ovens, sacrifices to the spirits, songs to commemorate the war, wearing paint, shells, and feathers, dancing, entertaining the invited guests who also dance while elaborately painted and adorned in leaves and feathers, courting of local girls by guests, and trading between hosts and guests. The killing and sharing of pigs is the culminating event of the ritual cycle. It serves many social functions, but primarily it is a display and demonstration of the wealth and cohesion of the hosts, to announce their recovery after warfare, pay indemnity to their allies, and to demonstrate that they have subdued their enemies. A new war may begin after the *kaiko*.

Traditional forms of private vengeance include sorcery, which may be used by those who cannot succeed in physical confrontation. It is widely believed that specific sorcery techniques, known to some people and perhaps taught or inherited, using personal materials of the intended victim, or projecting injurious materials into a victim, can cause illness or death. Since they depend on secrecy, stealth, and magic, they are not accessible to investigation and testing. Witchcraft, which is believed to be an intrinsic malevolent power of the witch, may inflict harm without the intervention of material carriers or spells. Witches may attack within the local group, but sorcerers in the highlands are nearly always thought to be in enemy groups.

Outsiders who hope to use sorcery must have some means of acquiring materials associated with the intended victim, which are then bespelled or destroyed, to hurt or kill the enemy. Counter-magic, divination, and treatment may cancel or reverse the ill effects. Thus sorcery is risky, and only determined people are thought to attempt it. The magical propelling of disease-carrying substances, another form of long-distance sorcery, may also be reversed by skilled counter-magic and injure the sorcerer. It is possible that poisonous substances are sometimes used, but there is no conclusive scientific evidence of this as yet.

In the highlands, the use of sorcery by disgruntled and resentful people to retaliate for a theft, insult, or injury is believed to be an explanation for illness or death. The offended person resorts to sorcery when direct violence is not possible, such as when the offended person is a woman, elderly, or distant from his provoker. Vengeance is either specific to the one who has caused the offense, or general to his or her local group. When sorcery is given as a reason for illness or death, and blamed on a particular sorcerer, the victim's relatives attempt vengeance by violence or sorcery. Thus sorcery accusations precipitate attack against the sorcerer or his community, and may begin a war.

The belief that sorcery is practiced by persons in other communities contributes to intercommunity tension and hostility. The individual sorcerer need not be named, only his settlement; any member of the settlement is exposed to attack to achieve vengeance. The sorcerer uses sly means to attack his antagonists; he may be avenged by counter-magic or open violence. The accusation and death of the sorcerer can be interpreted as a false charge by his settlement, in which case the accused sorcerer's death must be avenged by his kinsmen. Again, the intergroup conflict is perpetuated by accusation and retaliation.

However, although sorcery beliefs can perpetuate and increase the tension between groups, they can also serve to strengthen intragroup cohesion, pointing to an external enemy and reinforcing the interdependence and joint responsibility of members of each group. Outsiders are blamed; insiders avenge. At the same time, the group of the accused sorcerer shares his blame; the whole group may be attacked for the injury the sorcerer is believed to have caused the other group.

A quite different effect is felt in those cases of witchcraft, such as *kumo* in Chimbu, in which the witch is accused of killing a relative or member of his settlement group. When a loss is suffered, it is believed due to a witch of the victim's group. This is very unsettling, endangers others, and demands the killing or removal of the *kumo* witch. In the past, *kumo* witches, who are thought to have a spirit animal within their bodies that forces them to destroy people, often admitted their guilt and were executed. Only by exile or execution could in-group solidarity and mutual trust be restored. The treatment of witches here is similar to that in American and European communities in the seventeenth century.

The same sort of belief is found among the Kuma of the Wahgi

Valley, where the witchcraft is called *kum*. Reay interprets killing or banishment of a witch as a way of rebuilding community solidarity.

Whether or not the persons identified as witches are actually traitors, as alleged, the ideology of witchcraft enables the group to shed those individuals it would be better without. Persons who are unsociable and unsocialized, who fail to conform with custom and etiquette, who are grossly gluttonous or addicted to adultery, who have an inordinately gloomy disposition and may even have contemplated breaking the strong taboo on sampling human flesh: these are the people who are put down as witches. Witch belief provides the idiom for the group to strengthen custom by getting rid of them. (Reay 1976:6)

The public performance of a "man named sky" among the Konda Dani announces the avengeance of a killing to the ghosts and reestablishes good relations with ghost spirits. Such a man may also be a witch who kills enemies in other groups, but not in his own (O'Brien 1974).

Beliefs in the inheritance of special abilities, such as sorcery or witchcraft or the involvement of ghost and ancestor spirits in human affairs, remove some of the responsibility of people from social events. If a man is believed to be under the control of spirits, his actions of placating a ghost, or following the instructions of a spirit, are involuntary. One who is victimized by a sorcerer, or attempting to avenge sorcery, is not guilty of aggression. He is saving or protecting himself and his kinsmen against forces that would destroy them. He thus removes the evil-doer, avenges wrongs, and secures his group. Most of this public intervention is by men on behalf of groups, for political ends. The internal accusations and disruptions of *kumo* witchcraft and some other forms of witchcraft in which local, resident women are accused, point to a group's mistrust of those who are not birth members, and the divided interests and loyalties of married women. Identifying and removing the disruptive element may open the way for new communal cooperation.

In a similar way attacks on and thefts from strangers and members of other clans are approved: They are good for the perpetrator's clan and enrich it in relation to the other. When a large, attacking force was amassed against a small, local group, which sometimes occurred in Chimbu, the larger group overwhelmed, plundered, and destroyed, and then often appropriated the land of the conquered who fled or were killed. This is outright expansion and acquisition of land and property to the victor's advantage.

FESTIVALS

Highlands ecological adaptation, cultural values, and social activities culminate in ceremonial practices. Wealth is demonstrated in the provision and display of agricultural produce, pigs, and valuables such as bird feathers and shells. The strength of the group is shown in the agile dancers and the weapons they carry. The greatest values in highland society are expressed in the great festivals and exchanges, in which the achievement of big men, clans, and tribes, especially food and pork in quantity, shiny valuables, decorated and greased bodies, and skills of the dancers are displayed. The audience is made up of affines and kinsmen, and these represent communities, clans, and tribes who are rivals and enemies. In many places a great feast is the culmination of years of work, accumulation, and preparation, and a large tribe must be coordinated for the maximum display. Certainly the Chimbu regard the pig feast *bugla gende* as their greatest achievement, the basis of their reputation among other tribes. In order to make the feast great, leaders will forbid or defer fights and payments of pigs or goods while actively preparing for the feast. Trade in valuables, and access to resources, is essential to the displays and choice of display goods. Prior to the introduction of money and manufactured goods, trade within the highlands and via the highland fringe was the source of goods from the lowland and forest, including feathers and shells, and some cosmetics. These fringe areas did not have the agricultural resources or population to mount large festivities, but they provided a trade network that supplied the central highlanders with some of their festive goods.

Birds, especially the many species of birds of paradise, with their colorful, long, often iridescent plumes, are greatly admired. In some ways the plumage symbolizes a masculine ideal of glowing health, light, and quick movement. The theme is further developed in the *nama* flutes, or *koa* in Chimbu, where the sacred bamboo flute and its music, known only to initiated men, are said to be birds. The Siane associate birds with the sun, another important, almost universal, symbol of health and success. Birds are associated with death in warfare by the Dani.

Human welfare and fertility of plants and animals are believed to be the result of a combination of circumstances – the absence or remission of bad influences such as demons, ghosts, and sorcerers, and the beneficial effects of personal effort, proper ritual, purification, ancestors, sun, and other favorable spirits. When a group is numerous and productive, it displays its food, pigs, and wealth in festivals to awe and intimidate rivals. Delayed exchanges give each group a period of success following a feast, and then the other groups hold their feast to repay and enjoy high prestige. Debts and credits alternate.

The highland fringe peoples do not have the potential for large groups and settled communities. Their soil is quickly depleted in heavy rainfall and run-off, requiring new locations, and they utilize widely scattered resources, trading some lowland products into the highlands. They have few domestic pigs and lack the quantity of sweet potato or other agricultural produce to maintain large herds. Although it has been suggested by some field workers that the fringe peoples' diet is better balanced and more nutritious than that of the highlanders whose meals are mostly sweet potatoes, this must be qualified by saying that the fringe peoples' diet is characterized by variety rather than quantity. In the highland margins the population remains low, with a low rate of reproduction and higher infant and young adult mortality rate than that of most highland groups. These differences are revealed in the beliefs and rituals of the fringe peoples, who seem obsessed with the problems of growth and maturation. Group and individual survival is hazardous; religious beliefs are primarily concerned with fertility.

In central highlands ritual, fertility is a theme, but not a matter of such anxiety as in the fringe. It would appear that central highland people, crops, and livestock are naturally fertile. Many practices, beliefs, and rituals limit reproduction in humans and in pigs; the emphasis in highland men's initiation and bachelor cults is purification, the separation of the sexes, and limitations on fertility and sexuality. Some ritual and belief, most notable perhaps those of the Enga, stress the excesses of female reproductivity; others seek dominance for men and submission by women. Sexual avoidance and taboos are common, with the ambivalent interpretations of danger to men and children as a result of pollution by fecund and menstruating women. But the highlanders do not on the whole fear crop failure, or hunger; gardening magic is sometimes performed, but food displays and gifts seem to be easily accumulated. Population in the central highland area shows an impressive trend in increase, with only a few groups recounting a history of severe illness, deaths, and dispersal, although malaria and respiratory diseases affect young people. The highlands' environment is apparently healthier than that of the lowlands, and the land more productive where sweet potatoes are the main crop.

Highlanders' prestige is gained in the show of plenty – heaps of food, masses of plumage, and lines of pigs. The big man of Hagen wears a neck pendant of bamboo sticks, which provides a record of exchange activities. Large platforms, central plazas, display boards for marriage payments, strings of shells, and hanging pig jaws on a branch are ways of publicising the group's transactions. A highlands man who is considered a failure, or lazy or incompetent, is called a "rubbish man": He usually has small gardens, no food surplus for gifts and entertainment, no big pigs, and no valuables, and his skin is dry and shriveled. If he has a wife, he cannot make presents to his affines; often he becomes a bachelor dependent of a prominent man's household. The successful man has many dependents who work so he can present food, pigs, and valuables to affines and rivals. His name and his local group are known by their gifts. Whenever a birth, marriage, puberty, or initiation of one of the dependents of a successful man occurs, the gifts are many and the fame of the man and his group spreads. The range of productivity in the highlands is between adequacy, available to just about all normal people, and largess, which requires planning, energetic application, and the cooperation of local groups. Each household, with proper planning, has at least one productive garden with sweet potatoes and some festive foods at all times. Seasonal shortages might result from warfare, illness, or poor allocation of time in various activities.

Small gatherings in the men's house and settlement, when visits or plans bring people together, are occasions for communal food preparation and sharing with guests. Every family's farms can provide some extra sweet potatoes, and something of luxury – the uncommon vegetables, fruits, nuts, or tobacco, which make the meal a feast. Pigs are reserved for special prestations, but bananas, sugarcane, pandanus nuts, and nowadays imported rice, tinned meat and fish, bread, and beer may be included. When a group of local people spend some hours or a day helping to clear land or build a house, they are given a meal by the host. Occasional special harvests of wild or cultivated foods, beans, or nuts may be celebrated with a party for the neighborhood and invited friends. When one person receives a portion of pork at a distant feast, he brings it home, where it may be recooked with vegetables and shared in his locality. These small redistributions make the special foods go further, and are part of the give and take of every highlands community. This is possible because of the quantities available, the close proximity of friends and relatives, and the frequency of visits and occasions for sharing. In contrast, the isolated hamlet may be a close, internal sharing-group which has few opportunities to give to or receive from other local groups. A serious epidemic or crop loss may destroy such a group, whereas highlanders would find relatives elsewhere to assist with food supplies and shelter.

HARVESTS AND FOOD EXCHANGE

Different areas and groups throughout the highlands vary in the frequency and scale of their festivities. Ceremonies contain ritual and prestige elements, but many also have a specific concern with initiation, marriage, death compensation of allies, or the establishment of truce. A single village or local clan may conduct a small festival every few years, but a large clan or tribe that aims at a huge display may coordinate efforts over ten years or longer. Intermittent smaller celebrations may serve as markers of the group's potential, and promise of a festival to come. Kapauku feasts are held by rich men as occasions for trade as well as celebration.

The Chimbu *mogena biri* (vegetable heap) is primarily a distribution of vegetable food, often occasioned by a large harvest of pandanus nuts or oil fruits. Because pandanus nuts grow only at high altitudes (6,500 ft. or 2,000 m or higher), whereas the oil pandanus is present below 6,500 feet, (2,000 m), a group with good supplies of

A Chimbu man and young woman are elaborately dressed in bird of paradise and parrot feathers, woven head bands, kina shells, woven arm bands, and marsupial fur pieces. The woman wears a string skirt and holds an arrow, and the man wears a decorated apron and carries a spear. They are attending a Chimbu *mogena biri* feast.

one variety is likely to have little of the other. A clan or tribe whose supplies complement those of the donor group are appropriate recipients. When a *mogena biri* is planned, special fruits and vegetables are also grown, marsupials hunted, and other foods accumulated, so that the heap, perhaps 50 to 200 feet in diameter and six feet high in the center, is made up of bananas, sugarcane, yams, taro, corn, and other vegetables, and is ornamented with very many decorative foods – the red oil pandanus or the wheels of nuts wrapped in cord and trimmed with leaves and moss, red *gembogl* fruits, bandicoots, kuskus, other marsupials, bunches of colorful fruit, and any exotic foods such as coconuts, beef, eel, or horse that the donors can obtain. The *mogena biri* is a pile made up of thousands of separate parcels, each gift from one person to another. These are assembled in sections by subgroups. Most are made by men, who prepare and build up the heap. Men of the invited clan or tribe arrive as a dancing troupe. The dancers rush forward in a threatening posture, armed with spears and bows and arrows, vividly expressing the rivalry between the groups. They circle the vegetable heap as an attacking force. Then the items in the heap are distributed: Each parcel or item is a unit, and the recipient's name is called out. Even with the simultaneous shouting of different sections, it takes many hours to distribute a large *mogena biri*. The relations of marriage and kinship between individuals are the basis of these gifts; a man gives to his sister's son, his wife's sister's husband, his daughter's husband, and his mother's brother's daughter's husband. Although women are present, see, and share in the gifts, they rarely receive directly unless they are widows, or represent absent husbands. Each gift is a unit in the exchange relationship of donor and recipient. On the next occasion, the present recipient must return an appropriate gift to the donor. Women shout and dance when a gift is carried in by a husband.

A vegetable distribution between tribes is much larger than one between clans, or smaller groups, which may be more of a harvest and compensation gift to a group to maintain or reestablish good relations after a conflict. On such occasions pigs may be included, and the former antagonists show their peaceful intentions by sharing food. The occasion is also conducted as an indemnification to allies. But similar, special group presentations are made as an element in the *bugla gende* pig ceremony in Chimbu.

Chimbu *mogena biri* have reached very complex and large dimensions, with purchased foods dominating local produce, and an extensive set of preparatory gifts preceding the main event. I witnessed such a series in April and May 1976 when each of several nearby and neighboring tribes made separate gifts, with dance and large distribution, consisting of thousands of bundles or parcels of foods, to the Siambuga-Wauga tribe. All of these were received by kinsmen, affines, and friends on more than five separate occasions on different days in a three-week period. Each time, some food was consumed and distributed to neighbors, kinsmen, and friends. The culminating gift, from the Siambuga-Wauga to the Nogar subtribe of Gena, was bigger than any of the contributing gifts. It was said to be a repayment for pandanus nuts, which the Gena, who live in the high-altitude zones, presented to Siambuga-Wauga some years ago. Oil pandanus and peanuts, both lower altitude crops, were the most important elements in the gift. The total heap was about fifty meters in diameter, including cartons of beer, fish cans, meat cans, cooked pork and other meats purchased for the occasion, along with bananas, sugarcane, taro, yams, and corn. Decorative features were split bamboo bound around tins of fish, and bamboo poles and boards to which flowers and paper money in two *kina* notes (about $5.00) were attached, and long sticks holding beer cartons, peanuts, and red pandanus fruits. Live cows and pigs are also given at such feasts. The crowd of spectators, donors, and recipients must have numbered many thousands, and with many men calling the recipients, the distribution lasted five or six hours.

Such an event is planned for many months, sometimes years, with special planting of peanuts or other foods, gathering of pandanus in season, and the coordinated assembling, decorating, and presentation of great numbers of individual gifts. In preparing for such a big festival and series of gifts, the main donor tribe or subtribe must prepare land and plant considerable amounts of the special foods to be given. When tree fruits, pandanus nuts, or oil fruits are given nearly all of the produce of a season is set aside for the gift. Many other tribes grow or set aside special foods for their gifts to the main donors, and planning is thus coordinated among thousands of people. When cattle, purchased goods, and other foods are included, the necessary work and money from sales of coffee and other activities must be directed to the effort. Thus the leaders of tribes debate the merit of a food exchange plan, and the willing cooperation of each family is essential to its success. The adornment and massing of dancers, speech-making, and preparation of donors and recipients for carrying and dispersal occupies much time and interest. In this series all of the surrounding tribes and members of many others, a total population of perhaps 20,000, had some part in several phases of the series and both gave and received as a result.

Any individual has wife's relatives, sisters' husbands, and matrilateral and other kinsmen in several tribes. He gives, helps, and receives something at several phases of such a complex series, and enjoys the spectacle of heaps of food and crowds of people. Hosts, visitors, and spectators mill around greeting friends and relatives, exchanging news, sharing food, and watching the main events. The high points of the completion of the heap, the chase of the male dancers, speeches, and the excited admiring shouts of recipient women provide a spectacle of wealth and plenty for all to enjoy. Each individual transaction, of the many thousands that are made, recognizes debt and relationship between two persons of different groups and is an essential part of the continuity of intergroup and interpersonal relations.

Some marginal peoples, for example the Gadsup (Du Toit 1975) and perhaps other eastern highlanders, are not described as holding large intergroup food displays or pig ceremonies. Pigs are raised and distributed on ceremonial occasions, such as initiation and marriage, but on a much smaller scale than in the central highlands – Sina Sina, Chimbu, Hagen, Enga, Dani, and Kapauku. Eastern highlanders may have fewer or smaller pigs which are distributed in different ways at smaller and more frequent ceremonies.

PIG FESTIVALS

Eastern highlanders, for example the Kamano (Berndt 1962) who conduct pig festivals, may do so on a cycle of three or more years corresponding to a boy's initiation ceremony where the bamboo flutes are demonstrated. The themes of fertility, growing of crops and pigs, honoring of creative spirits and ancestors, and male dominance are expressed. The symbolic association of men, flutes, penes, and arrows with fertility and masculinity makes the initiated boys into men. Pig festivals for the clan or larger group are the combined effort of several villages which act as hosts to kinsmen of other districts. A temporary peace is required, but intergroup competition and preparation of youths for war are involved in the ceremonies. Siane feasts also accompany initiation.

The *nama* cult is especially developed in Goroka and among the east-central group, with resemblances to the *gerua* and *koa* of the Chimbu area. Bamboo flutes are the key symbolic element; initiation ceremonies include demonstrating flutes to the boys and culminate in a large pig festival, the *idza nama*. This can only be held when sufficient pigs are raised. Each patrilineal group in the subtribe has a pair of flutes, which are played in its distinctive tune. A youth, during initiation, must learn to play his own patrilineage flute tune. Ordinarily the flutes are concealed from women and the uninitiated, and kept wrapped in leaves in the men's house. The large pig festivals are held after initiation but also serve to indemnify allies in neighboring subtribes and acknowledge the status of the leading men and host group's ability to raise large pigs. Flute playing announces the forthcoming festival, and an allied tribe or subtribe is invited. Each invited guest is given one or more whole or half sticks which serve as a promise of a pig or half pig from a donor to a recipient. The hosts cook pork and sweet potatoes on the appointed day. Guests enter in a procession, hosts ceremonially greet them with weapons upraised, and then individual guests are called to receive pork. Speeches recount the alliances, battles, and deaths, and a main presentation of food is accepted to be carried home. Festive preparations, making decorations, and playing flutes continue. An exchange of valuables, bark cloth, and cowries is made at a later ceremony, in the villages of the guests, who then are responsible for providing pork. A thousand or more people, including observers from other groups, may come together at the conclusion of the festival, when the heavily decorated guests and hosts dance and distribute the largest pigs. The subtribe will be renowned for lavish hospitality throughout the valley, and the recipients will work energetically to provide a return feast.

This procedure has many resemblances to feasts in other highlands societies. Chimbu *mogena biri* similarly assembles a large feast for another tribe or subtribe with an accumulation of individual gifts. The Chimbu *bugla gende* or pig ceremony is not given in honor of one tribe, however, but for kinsmen, affines, and friends in every tribe. Crowds of many thousands come to the culminating dances of a Chimbu pig ceremony, representing all nearby tribes and many distant ones, even including people from different language groups who have some acquaintance in the host group or accompany a friend.

A Dani alliance group of several thousand people holds a pig feast every four to six years, in which marriage, initiation, and memorial ceremonies are all involved; in order to provide the maximum amount of pork and celebrate all events, transactions that require pig gifts are deferred for the feast (Heider 1972). Marriages are arranged at some time in advance, and on an appointed day the brides are dressed in new skirts, and then several days later are escorted to their husbands' homes. A series of pig, stone, and cowrie shell gifts and exchanges begins, to be made at intervals, when children are born, sons initiated, daughters married, or children die. The local groups of husband and wife are usually in the same confederacy and alliance: This phase is largely an exchange between families within the alliance group.

A major ceremony commemorating the recent dead and placating the ghosts is held at the settlement of the alliance leader. This brings the whole alliance population together, with guests, some 5,000 to 8,000 people, for pig cooking, driving away ghosts, and distribution of pork fat to named individual persons – the leaders of enemy groups, the war dead, other dead, and relatives. The legs, ribs, and other pork joints are distributed. This phase of the ceremony is especially directed to war compensation and proclaiming the military superiority of the alliance leader; gifts to persons in other alliance groups are made.

A form of boys' initiation establishes moiety membership status for all boys in Waija moiety, in a procedure which lasts over two weeks. To make them grow up to be warriors, the boys of this moiety are purified, dressed in a new penis gourd, taken to the sacred place, introduced to battle, trained to throw spears, hunt, and participate in special meals. Heider concludes, "The Grand Dani Pig Feast is thus a compound ceremony with a complex interweaving of rituals which dramatize individual passage from one status to another and which promote social solidarity and integration of the group through dramatization of social structure" (1972: 196). Peters (1975) says the feast is held every three years, and boys of a wide age-range may be initiated. Peters draws special attention to the use of pig grease as a symbol of prosperity, health, and strength, to satisfy the ancestors and renew these values for the community.

Very large feasts, such as are held by Sina Sina, Chimbu, and Dani, require the ceremonial coordination of pig and food raising for guests and participants, assembling of other valuables, site preparation and house construction, gathering of stones and firewood for cooking, and practice and decoration of singers and dancers for a whole tribe or alliance. These are the largest gatherings highlanders ever have. Whereas the Dani feasts mostly celebrate events within the alliance, with moiety divisions prominent in initiation and marriage, the Chimbu pig ceremony is held by each tribe; several thousand people present whole and halfsides of pork to their kinsmen, affines, and friends, especially those in other tribes.

Chimbu planning and ceremony follow a long sequence, from the time that the flutes *(koa)* are first played in the men's houses to be shown to the boys and announce the intention to hold a feast, to the final disbursement several years later. During this time, the tribesmen stop breeding pigs so as to concentrate on fattening sows and geldings. The tribe may select some new sites, or clear and begin building at traditional ceremonial grounds where land is relatively flat and shade trees have grown. Each tribe has four to eight sites. New sites are chosen, or old sites redeveloped, as a demonstration of territorial ownership rights. The traditional ceremonial center is marked with a large, open, dance and cooking area. A series of pie-slice segments are allocated to subclans, who build a men's house *(gerua ingu* or ancestor house) near the center, and subsidiary and long guest houses on the flanks. There is accommodation for hundreds, sometimes thousands of guests. While men and women concentrate on food raising for themselves, pigs, and guests, and place some pigs with relatives in other tribes for fattening, young men and girls practice dancing and songs. Plumes and feathers for headdresses, new woven belts, armbands, wigs, painted *gerua* spirit boards, decorated long dance aprons, and other ornaments are made ready. Each dancer wears an elaborate headdress of feathers and other ornaments representing wealth. In the final weeks of dancing, visiting troupes from outside come to dance in all the grounds, and the host tribe dancers visit other grounds in their tribe and in other tribes who are also preparing for the feast. These visits present the youth of tribes to one another. The nights are spent in courtship parties, often leading to intertribal marriages.

The ceremonial ground becomes the center of social life for people whose usual dwellings are scattered throughout their territory. Additional gardens, often distant, are planted, and pigs kept away until the last days of the ceremony. Children are given ancestral emblems – the *gerua* boards and wigs to wear at the ceremony. Boys' initiation is conducted in and near the dance ground, and marriage payments finalized at the dance ground. Death payments are made to kinsmen. Indemnity payments to allies are made when the first, smaller pig feast is given. Usually, each man kills one or more pigs for his special payments or contributions to the group. These individual and group payments of pork are considered "spirit meat" *(gigl kambu)*. In the dances, weapons are flourished, tribal successes are praised in song, and girls admire the youth of other clans. Some important themes are fertility in people, pigs, and crops, wealth as measured by quantities of shells, plumes, and pigs, male military strength, the welfare of people, and the honoring of the ancestors with painted *gerua* boards, wigs, and by killing pigs in the cemetery. Pig jaws, blood, and fat are placed on the *bolum* shrine. A culminating pig killing, the largest quantity, follows these individual payments and ritual activities. Here, I believe, the display of the Chimbu has its greatest moment. All morning, large pigs are killed by clouting with a heavy stick. They are laid out from the *bolum* as spokes to each men's house, for all visitors to see the numbers and compare the sizes. Each household kills several pigs. Then the owners, with helpers, remove the pigs to singe and butcher. Women wash the entrails and stuff them as sausages to cook in a drum. The whole and half sides are cooked in huge pits of hot stones and steaming leaves for a few hours. The following day, individually, the recipient affines and kinsmen carry away their whole or halfsides, to be shared in their home settlements. The aftermath, for the donor, is the urgent need to replenish depleted supplies, build, plant new gardens, and trade finery for pigs to initiate a new cycle.

When pork is cooked in the ceremonial ground, stones are heated and the food steamed. Hanging to smoke are puddings of blood, fat, and herbs, wrapped in banana leaves. Such puddings are a Chimbu delicacy.

About half of the Chimbu attempt to hold their feasts at one period, within several months of one another, and the other half, several years later. Thus, the need for more intensive food growing, for pigs and guests, alternates and evens out the demand for sweet potato production. A family usually sends some pigs to be fattened by relatives in other areas. Chimbu pig ceremonies are attended by people from all tribes, and the pork is widely distributed by being carried back to the guests' homes. Because the guests always inform others of where they received the pork, a gift of pork always enhances the reputation of the host tribe. For married women, their natal tribe's pig feast is an occasion of homecoming and renewal of kinship ties; their husbands and sons receive pork.

The tribe's prestige benefits by the efforts of all its individual members. Yet the members must call on their extratribal relatives for help in feasts. The vegetable distributions usually require obtaining some supplies, especially of rare foods, from relatives outside the tribe. And for the pig ceremony, valuable items for the headdress and help in the agistment of pigs are given by relatives outside. These relatives might also be involved in helping to subdue an enemy, or giving asylum to defeated kinsmen. Thus the relatives in other tribes, who receive the pork and distribute it to spread the reputation of the donor, are an external link for the feast giving tribe; they help both in providing and distributing the food. A man with two or more wives can raise more food and pigs, and also has more groups of affines outside the tribe. A polygynous big man is engaged in more transactions with more groups, and may kill ten or more large pigs at a feast. He will also receive proportionately more at other feasts.

Still another variant on festivities occurs in Kapauku, where a big man sponsors a feast (Pospisil 1963). A feast site is chosen, and a dance house is built. Then groups of men and women come to dance and sing, the songs telling of events of the dance group. Men compose courtship songs for the girls they desire, and couples may retire together. The ceremony culminates in the killing of several hundred pigs, distribution of meat to exchange partners, and trade in meat, salt, manufactures and raw materials for cord, bow strings, carrying bags, bamboo containers, feathers, and ornaments for shell money. The sponsor's pigs are augmented by those of his associates and supporters, and all local people and visitors participate in the trading. In this combined festival and exchange celebration, shell money is used in transactions. Trade and barter in feathers and plumes, especially for those who have killed their pigs and therefore wish to acquire piglets, follows a Chimbu pig feast but is not a central feature.

The spirit cults of the western Papua New Guinea highlands area also connect the ancestors and fertility with initiation of males. Initiation into some of these cults is voluntary, and not all youths participate. Occasionally a ceremony developed by one group is widely believed to be efficacious, enlisting the help of important spirits for group and individual benefits. Such cult practices may be learned by initiating guests, who then carry the practice to other areas. In this way, cults and their spirits are carried into new areas. Often a new cult replaces the traditional practice, although for a time both may be celebrated.

MOKA AND TE OF THE WESTERN HIGHLANDS

A transition in festival practices appears to have been in process in the Western Highlands: The *moka* ceremonial of the Mt. Hagen area (Strathern 1971) has extended into Kakoli, Enga (Meggitt 1973, 1974), and Mendi areas as the *te* cycle. This has been expanded recently, as the great increase in goldlip pearlshells and other new valuables since 1935 has stimulated exchange in goods and pigs, and the development of roads and communication has interlinked previously independent exchange regions and language groups. These western highland exchange-systems differ from the eastern highlands, Chimbu, and Dani in a number of ways. Organizers and initiators are individual men, not clans or tribes, and the many individual transactions of pigs and goods take place at the big man's ceremonial ground, which is a large clearing decorated with flowering plants. Beginning at one end with a series of initiating or soliciting gifts, men thus inform their debtors, associates, affines, kinsmen, and friends that they expect pigs in an exchange. Traveling, for example, from west to east, the solicitory gifts pass from man to man. Then each counts up his obligations, and allocates the pigs he holds and the pigs he can expect to those who have initiated the cycle. Over a period, live pigs are passed from man to man along the chain in reverse from east to west. At each ceremonial ground there is a dance and display to visitors, and hundreds (or perhaps thousands) of pigs given. Some pigs move several times along the chain, while others are held by recipients. The final step is the cooking of pork and giving of meat, in reverse, from west to east, as a thanks. Only part of the pig gift is returned as pork. Thus the recipients usually finish with some live pigs for future breeding. The quantities increase each time. Several years later the process is reversed – soliciting gifts from east to west, main gift of live pigs transferred west to east, and cooked pork east to west. Although many men participate in a small way, with their own gifts and support of a big man, the central figures are big men who funnel goods and pigs into their ceremonial ground, for dance and display, and then distribute them to others.

These festivals are not identical. The Hagen people have exchanges of goldlip mother-of-pearl shells (*kina*) which they shape, frame in clay, and decorate with red clay. Shells have become plentiful with European trade, and large numbers are used, also serving as currency. A war payment may start the *moka*, and payment is made in shells, live and cooked pork, and other special goods. As the exchange cycle alternates between two partners, they give and return gifts of increasing size, to top one another. There is prestige in giving extra pigs, shells, packages of salt, axes, cassowaries, oil, or other valuable and rare goods to a recipient who may have limited access to these resources. The goods given were rare in the local economy; now they may be purchased for money in trade stores. Values and equivalents have changed (Strathern 1971).

The Enga *te* has entered from the east and takes a slightly different form. Ideally on a four-year cycle, the solicitory gifts of small pigs, salt, axes, shells, and plumes are made over a period of two to three years to exchange partners all along the network. Then the participants throughout the network call in their debts and assemble their livestock. The main gifts of pigs are made in a series of public ceremonies at each local center. A man visits the man from whom he expects a gift, along with many others, to receive his pigs, and perhaps pearl shells or cassowary. Next, on his clan home territory, he gives some of these pigs, plus some of his own stock, in a ceremony. I saw the line-up of stakes for this phase in 1976. Each man of a group had a column of stakes, one for each pig, to mark his gifts. Some men had twenty, others up to fifty, at one place near Wapenamunda. When the sequence has reached the end of the chain, the return gifts are called for. Then, beginning from the end that last received, pigs are killed and cooked, and meat is distributed to those who gave pigs, approximately in the proportion of one halfside for a live pig. The meat is distributed all along the line, sometimes the same pieces of decaying meat passing through several hands. In principle, about four years later, the cycle should reverse, but recently the cycle has repeated in the same direction at times. Success in the *te* and prestige in Enga is measured by the transactions a man is engaged in: the number of partners, quantity of pigs, cassowaries and shells he gives and receives, and the range of his contacts. Kinsmen and affines are usually involved, although a big man seeks out distant big men as partners, often neglecting his obligations to lesser men nearer to home in his ambition for a widespread reputation.

Enga and Hageners manipulate the exchange activities for wealth and prestige (Strathern 1969). The ambitions of men are expressed in the intensity of their participation in the exchanges – the lending and borrowing of pigs and goods, obtaining helping gifts from clansmen and distributing the gifts they receive to clansmen and exchange partners, pooling pigs for an impressive display, and allocating them for maximum reputation. Many thousands of men are involved in the larger, Enga chain of transactions, to produce a standard of exchange and prestige system that connects groups formerly unknown to one another. The immediate partners are in nearby clans – kinsmen, affines, and friends. The total system transcends these local acquaintances to link people with quite different resources, population pressure, and supplies. The rare pork meat is distributed over an area of hundreds of square miles. This spread and interregional integration has expanded since European contact and the introduction of imported goods and money. A transaction chain of this magnitude probably could not develop in precontact times, before pacification. It requires truce, the control of raids and warfare, and agreement between leaders and organizers throughout. The Chimbu pig festival is held by each tribe as a unit, with loose intertribal coordination in an alternating grouping of tribes. If one tribe or subtribe fails to hold a feast, the others are not prevented from theirs. But a group suffers loss of prestige if their feast is greatly delayed.

In comparing the ceremonials of highlanders, we can see some common features and themes, and also some differences which point up regional ecological and social contrasts. Pigs are the most important object of exchange, the main universal local product, whereas many other objects have an outside or limited source. But even pigs are not equally available in the highlands. The Maring, many eastern highlanders, marginal peoples, and a few central highlanders include wild pigs in their economy by breeding boars, bringing in and rearing young pigs, and sometimes capturing or hunting wild pigs for feasts. Other wild animals may be provided at certain stages of festivals as a requirement for initiates, and cassowaries are sometimes important. Not all peoples breed or raise sufficient domestic pigs; they obtain young pigs in trade, and have domestic pigs raised by friends or relatives in other groups. Highland pigs depend on sweet potatoes; when pigs are raised in the central highlands, the sweet potato gardens must be fenced to keep out pigs, and pigs being fattened for festivals consume as large quantities of sweet potatoes as do adult humans. For the Enga *te*, pigs must be numerous, but need not be large. Furthermore, all are not killed; the transfer of live pigs, rather than the feast of cooked meat, is the main event. Chimbu preserve the jaws of pigs they kill, and point with pride at the evidence of their size and number. After a festival, hardly any grown pigs remain, and herds must be raised anew. Hageners count their festival participation with a neck pendant of bamboo stick markers which indicate numbers of objects transacted, not the size of pigs.

Festivals are occasions both for the display of rare, often imported goods such as shells and plumes, and for the gift and trade of these things for pigs, stone, salt, oil, or other valuables. A few of the goods highlanders desire are available in the forest, or can be manufactured in some areas, but many enter from a distance through trade partnerships. The central Enga comprise a dense enclave surrounded by land with less potential for settlement. The *te* brings in some of the rare resources of the fringe Enga, and this facilitates exchange (Meggitt 1973).

Festivals combine the productivity, achievement, exchange partnerships, and prestige of individuals into a group effort. They are vital community festivals. The initiation of youths is common in highlands ceremonies, and the timing of successive initiations requires a festival periodically. Major ritual themes are fertility, community welfare, the beneficence of the ancestors, growth and increase of crops, pigs and people, and prosperity and strength of the group. Presentation of youth as dancers decorated in valuables, participating in courtship parties, and arranging marriage is both a display of group success and a forging of future ties to other clans.

The big men of the group – the clan leaders, owners of ceremonial grounds, and organizers of *te* and *moka* – are on display and under scrutiny on festival occasions. Their ability to bring crowds of exchange partners, their followers, wives' kinsmen, and spectators to their displays and distributions is the basis of individual prestige and group renown. Size, wealth, and strength are measures of power. Many of the rituals include carrying weapons and dancing in an attitude of war, underlining the association of wealth and power.

The festivals often include ally indemnity and enemy compensation, with speeches praising allies and promising future good relations. But inadequate reparation, slights, and disparagement must be met with opposition. A gift may imply the proof of the donor's superiority, and the recipient's inability to meet the challenge. The rivalry between big men and between groups focuses on wealth and strength.

Ritual elements of pig and other festivals and cults, such as the Hagen *amb kor*, *wop kor* (Strathern 1970a, 1970b), Kuma *bolim* (Reay 1959), Chimbu and Kuma *geru*, and eastern highland *nama* express many of the important themes of group welfare, fertility, and strength. The ancestors, sun, and other spirits or gods that can help men achieve plenty are called on. Some particular themes – for example the glowing beauty of shells and birds, shining with oils, fertility stones, and wealth in pigs – are associated.

Display is important in the highlands festivals as a public demonstration of fertility, strength, and wealth, proof that the gods are on the side of the celebrants. For some, birds symbolize a wild beauty, their plumage captured for the adornment of man, and to attract women.

The contrast and combination of wild and domestic, forest and garden, and the products, animals, and people of the several highland areas is another important highland theme. In this system of symbolism, fringe peoples and places away from settlements form a natural wild domain in contrast to the densely occupied, domesticated, pig-raising central highlands peoples. In ceremonies and feasts the products of one domain may be provided to inhabitants of the other. Wild fruits, nuts, and game may be contrasted with cultivated sweet potatoes, other vegetables, and pigs. In the growth of large, settled communities there is a loss of wild products and an increase in domesticated and cultivated ones. The New Guinea highlands are a vivid example of this development. The contrast and unity of nature and culture is a major theme in the ritual and folklore of the highlands and, as such, the rituals of the highland peoples reflect one of man's universal themes.

Conclusion

In concluding this study of the highland peoples of New Guinea I briefly recapitulate the main points and show how ecology, culture, and society make an interdependent whole. The book began by considering environmental, technological, and physical characteristics as resources and proceeded to discuss the uses to which they have been put.

The New Guinea highlands as a cultural region is in some respects distinct from other New Guinea types, but it must be characterized within the general Melanesian type. We can then view the highlands as a concentrated, settled, specialized cultural development from the general interior New Guinea type. In order to point up cultural differences and important special developments of the central highland peoples, we have compared these to cultural characteristics of some interior New Guinea peoples who live in the highland fringe. Between these and the central highlanders are many peoples of highland cultural type but less concentrated and of a smaller scale; these have sometimes been called marginal to distinguish them from the central highland societies. People of the highlands received agriculture, food crops, tools, trade goods, and cults through trade contacts for thousands of years. Innovations and trade goods passed from coast through interior mountain and highland fringe peoples, with modifications and additions at every stage before reaching the highlands. Much of the highlanders' distinctive character appears to be of indigenous invention. The influence of Malayo-Polynesian culture which is important in coastal New Guinea and Oceania seems very indirect.

A combination of natural conditions and human, cultural, and social forces produced the highlands way of life. Environment and resources, population movements and growth, agriculture, technology, trade, the introduction of new goods and ideas, production, allocation of property, group structure, social activities, cooperation, alliances, competition, and patterns of dominance combine to make the distinctive highlands society and culture. The New Guinea highlands had developed into an acephalous, tribal society – which was actively engaged in agriculture, pig raising, exchange, warfare, and feasts – before it was discovered by explorers in the 1930s.

In the highlands, the transition from mixed subsistence – hunting, gathering, and general gardening – to more intense and more settled, denser populations may have begun over 5,000 years ago. Agricultural specialization in the highlands is mainly local and linked to local conditions and needs for protection, drainage, and so forth. When sweet potatoes – which can be grown in cooler regions – were introduced, this stimulated higher altitude settlements free of malaria, and generally permitted population expansion and more permanent settlement. As a result, agricultural specialization was intensified. In Kapauku, the Balim Valley Dani, Enga, and Chimbu centers, development has approached maximum density in terms of the present technology of these regions. In the eastern highlands, southern highlands, upper Sepik-Star Mountain, and marginal areas for the most part only low- to medium-density has been reached: Agriculture has proceeded from shifting to long-fallow, sometimes becoming short-fallow in a few places (*e.g.* Bena, Gahuku-Gama, Huli, Melpa, Kakoli) where some more intensive techniques have been used. The particular need for creating drier conditions in flat and swampy land was met by constructing drainage ditches and raised beds in the Wahgi. The difficulty of gardening on steep slopes was handled by placing stones and fences to hold the soil in Chimbu. Composting for protection against cold was utilized in Enga; permanent beds were created by ditching and building up beds in the Balim. All of these techniques were used to increase fertility and, for the same purpose, casuarinas were planted in fallow in several areas.

The settlements of the Chimbu may be dense because the Chimbu have not been threatened by the occasional frost and drought that affect other parts of the highlands. The Enga have reached the limits of settlement where drought and frost periodically force settlers to leave high-altitude garden areas. Epidemic illnesses, earthquakes, volcanic eruptions, and other uncontrollable phenomena have had important effects on population and have stimulated technological change.

An important finding, established statistically, is the close association of population density and agricultural intensity, with individualization of land tenure closely linked to agricultural intensity. However, as yet there is no demonstrable causal or historical process behind this phenomenon. Population density is not a simple measure if considerations of land use, arable land, or forest and other resources are included: Gross density is only comparable as a very crude measure of the way people occupy their land and tells us nothing of the living conditions. Agricultural intensity is a complex phenomenon, which can include frequency of cultivation, labor intensity, technology, and adaptation to specific environment and crop requirements. Even within a region such as the highlands these vary: There is no general form or sequence of intensification for the highlands as a whole. Thus the relationship between population density and agricultural intensity is no simple causal sequence, but an interaction and demonstration of human adaptation and inventiveness.

The larger scale, denser, more intensive gardeners in the New Guinea highlands are mostly concentrated in the central area of Papua New Guinea, from Chuave to Wabag. Through this region there are many local differences in group size, population density, and land occupation, but on the whole the tribes and clans are bigger, agricultural productivity higher, and festivals (*bugla gende*, *moka*, *te*) on a larger scale.

On all sides of this central concentration, both among long-established peoples in the east, south, and west, and in what may be marginal or overflow areas where sweet potato agriculture may be more recent or less intensive (*e.g.* in the lower altitude Jimi Valley), tribal size and population density are both lower. Another concentration is in the central Dani of Irian Jaya, which is surrounded by medium-density settlements of smaller groups. The Wissel Lakes Kapauku to the west are a third area of concentration.

The correlation is perhaps not unexpected, yet the factors involved must be very complex. One set of factors is environmental, which may be extended to include social and cultural isolation; the pattern of health, fertility, and mortality of the people may form a partly independent set of factors, too. These areas have much in common: The dense populations are supported by intensive and semipermanent agriculture, individualized land rights, and organized, community defense of territory. Outside these central areas, density is lower, tribal groups smaller, agriculture more shifting, and intergroup contacts less fixed.

Continuous settlement, tenure rights, and improvement of the land with trees, long-term garden plots, house sites, ceremonial grounds, burial places, and other more permanent property and territory uses and symbols of occupancy have developed in the highlands. Even among the sparsely populated peoples, there are traditions and attachments to favored sites and their resources, natural or man-made. These include plants, trees, groves, rocks, caves, and shrines. Houses are rebuilt on traditional sites with materials available from the territory. These locations are defended against invasion; if forced to flee, a group often attempts to reestablish itself on traditional sites, near the ancestors.

The Chimbu are concentrated in large clans and tribes. Their intragroup and intergroup relations are of a larger scale than other highland peoples. This is correlated with their greater population density. Chimbu tribal alliances and the feast-war pattern are led by big men, not by institutionalized leaders. The Chimbu of 1930 recognized the strain of land competition and the rivalry of big men and their tribal followings. Dani also have large group alliances organized by big men. The dense populations of both the Enga and Dani are permanently settled, with large central groups and less-concentrated hinterland areas. These are not so developed in Hagen, Kapauku, or the eastern or southern highlands. Between the central highlands and the fringe, we find such peoples as the Maring, Fore, and Gadsup to have smaller and less-concentrated population groups.

Patrilineal clans, or lineages, are a common form of social group in inland New Guinea. They are often conceived of as having a single ancestral origin, frequently attached to a locality and land area. As generations succeed one another, the men who remain in their father's locale form a continuing, cohesive group. They share in ritual and initiation, cooperate to defend their territory, help and protect one another, care for widows and orphans, and form a local core-group that other relatives may join. But there is still some flexibility and mobility, so that some men leave to reside with other relatives, temporarily or permanently. Sometimes wars or misfortunes disperse the group and new branches are established in other territories, but the common ancestral bond is still acknowledged.

Such a process, in slow or rapid population expansion or redistribution, is very widely found in New Guinea; it may be basic to nearly all societies. Natural disasters, epidemics, and wars may drastically affect some peoples. These fluctuations in size and distribution are further affected by beliefs about the nature of illness, sorcery, witchcraft, or spiritual influence, which may stimulate cohesion, conflict, dispersal, or realignment.

The theme of group continuity is symbolized by ideas of lines or ropes of men, sharing ancestry, blood, and group experiences. The knowledge is imparted by the elders in story and through ritual. Male initiation into the clan group and a patrilineal ideology, including male dominance, is characteristic of the highlands. It is reinforced with sexual separation, men's houses, ritual seclusion, painful initiation rituals, secret symbols such as flutes, and knowledge of spirits, ancestors, and ritual action.

Male solidarity supports the dominance of men over women, especially as women leave their home groups at marriage. The women of a settlement have come from many different groups and have no rituals that would consolidate them. Sexual antagonism or hostility of men toward women does not unify women. The mistrust of strangers and expectation of enemy sorcery is a divisive force that affects women especially. In contrast, the dominant male idea, expressed in leadership by big men, coordinates group action for power and prestige. Big men enlarge the group with their followers and enhance the group's reputation through successful competition in fighting and ceremonial exchange.

The unity of groups is reinforced by the pervasive ideas of opposition and reciprocity. All intragroup relations include both elements: Warfare and exchange ceremonies are the major group activities, necessarily involving opposition and reciprocity. Cooperation in production for displays and ceremonial distribution of goods and food has reached a high development in the highlands, and especially in the great festivals of the Chimbu, Dani, Enga, Hagen, and Kapauku.

Individuality and reciprocity are expressed in these exchanges, but the emphasis is not always the same. Enga *te*, Hagen *moka*, and

Kapauku ceremonies stress the individual achievement of the men who organize and present goods and pigs. In contrast, Chimbu and Dani pig feasts glorify the largest groups, tribes, or alliances. They combine individual transactions into a huge ceremony attended by crowds of spectators and recipients from all other groups.

Flexibility in group composition is necessary in this environment of uneven population growth, limited and variable resources, and the absence of centralized authority to enforce the allocation of resources. This is achieved mainly by individual mobility, with flexible groups in the big man leader-follower pattern. An energetic and successful leader attracts followers and establishes a local group and enlarges his group's territory and membership. For the period of his dominance he controls land and assembles people for ritual, feasts, displays, wars, and other competitive or large-scale activities. This group may expand and force others to join or flee, thus extending the local core on a favored site and building up the size and strength of the group until it dominates a larger area than its neighbors. Alliances may form and the scale of organization increase. Then, after considerable expansion, intragroup conflict, factionalism, and fission may develop and break up the alliance. This is usually followed by dispersal and the formation of new alliances.

I see the values of strength and wealth as of greatest importance in the highlands. These are the basis of cohesion and competition of individuals and groups, and they are expressed in countless forms and on countless occasions. These values, and the forms of expression, distinguish highlanders from other peoples. Compared with highland fringe and coastal peoples, the festivals and fights of the central highlands people are more competitive and on a larger scale. The most populous, largest groups of highland peoples compete in strength and wealth at a high level of intensity, and this competition dominates their every activity. The marginal highland peoples are more concerned with survival, and they express this concern in initiation rituals as well as in other beliefs and practices.

The joint values of strength and wealth in the highlands are demonstrated in the lavish distribution of the direct or indirect products of intensive agriculture: great heaps of vegetable foods to be given away, numerous and fat pigs, rare foods obtained by trade, game hunted in distant places, and valuables obtained in trade or purchase. Today this includes food and goods purchased with the income from coffee sales or wage labor and brought to the site by motor vehicle, and money gifts. New sources, foods and valuables have augmented the exchanges, but not changed their character.

Since 1930 the highlands have been included in the general political, economic, and social development of their region, and especially affected by the Europeans, Indonesians, and Melanesians who have come to teach and govern them. New forms of organization and activities, as well as Western manufactured goods, characterize the highlands today.

It may very well be that, from the earliest coastal contacts with the West, trade and the stimulus of new developments had an effect on the central highlands. Certainly sweet potatoes reached the highlands rapidly and became an outstanding and dominant crop, on which the large populations were fully dependent for increased food production, enlarged scale of social life, festivals, intensified exchange, and pig feasts. As a result of this growth, trade in some local products, such as stone, salt, and pigments, and the longer distance trade in shells and feathers may have increased. At the time that the highlanders were discovered, a few, tiny, worn metal blades of Western manufacture had reached the highlands through native trade routes. The islands and mainland of New Guinea were included in a complex trade network in which goods from many different areas were found in use in widely scattered locations; chemical analysis of stone, salt, pigment, and other products has made it possible to trace the source of these materials.

But until the 1930s, Western influence was indirect; it came about through trade with other New Guinea areas, rather than from direct contact with Europeans or Australians. As a result of increased Western presence in the highlands, quantities of many imported goods have been introduced. The most important was probably the steel axe, which fully replaced stone axes and adzes within a few years. With the introduction of large quantities of shell and other valuables during the 1930s, the size and frequency of exchanges expanded.

From the 1930s onward, there was a reduction in warfare because the Australian administration stopped all fights it could reach and punished the leaders when possible. An expansion of roads that were built under Australian supervision and conditions of relative peace, safety, and individual mobility facilitated more frequent ceremonial occasions. The scale of feasts was also greatly increased. With steel tools, larger garden areas could be cleared to provide more vegetables and to feed more pigs for ceremonies. Gardens were no longer overrun and destroyed by enemies.

To recapitulate, we may describe a series of major changes in the New Guinea highlands: from the original hunting, collecting, and gathering people through the development of agriculture and pig husbandry in a culture whose technology was based upon stone tools, to the introduction, several hundred years ago, of sweet potatoes, which has permitted more people and many pigs to live on higher ground, and expansion or further development of an active, competitive exchange system, and, finally, with the arrival of the Europeans, to the introduction of Western institutions and technology.

I have little information about events and changes in the western, Irian Jaya, district of New Guinea. Until 1960 the Netherlands established and maintained administrative posts, and some education and medical services were provided by mission groups. Warfare was suppressed, but political and economic development had hardly begun. Since the area came under Indonesian control, changes in the highlands area have not been publicized. The Irian Jaya highlands have certainly been affected by mining activities, missionary work, and government services, but no details are available.

The recent history of Papua New Guinea is more well known. After the first exploratory visits in the 1930s, administrative and mission posts were set up at several points in the highlands. New forms and services, with increasing technical and administrative personnel, developed in the fields of government, law, medicine, education, and agriculture, with later emphasis upon economic and political development leading to self-government and independence in the 1970s. Institutions and plans were aimed at detaching Papua New Guinea from Australian control, and providing a solid basis for an independent nation. Mission and government schools pursued the same curriculum, and an increasing proportion of children obtained elementary education and health services. High school and tertiary training in education, clerical, agricultural, medical, and other professions have been established more recently. Today there are a few highlanders holding important posts in the central government, although not in numbers proportional to their part of the general population.

Medical services are now accessible to all, and there has been a significant trend toward lower mortality rates, in infants, children, and young adults; as a consequence, population has increased. At the same time, there has been a lessening of sexual prohibitions, so that there are more frequent births and more surviving children; the age structure of the population has shifted so that now there is a higher proportion of children as well as more older people. Furthermore, young men frequently migrate for advanced training, jobs, or casual labor, putting a greater subsistence burden on the resident adults and especially the women. As there have been increasing opportunities to sell agricultural produce and coffee, subsistence foods are now only one of several garden products. Cash is used to buy food, as well as clothing, metal tools, household goods, and building materials; imported manufactured goods have almost wholly replaced some craft products. The result is a diversified and mixed cash and subsistence economy. Domestic livestock now includes chickens and cattle as well as pigs and a few other animals, which may be sold, used in feasts, or as payments. This has not necessarily improved the diet or standard of living of all, but it does seem to have resulted in a general improvement in nutrition.

The old work patterns are increasingly undergoing change as more people work for cash to buy goods that replace homemade objects. Western manufactured products are now found in every household. Most communities have some local shops, often owned by villagers, that provide some foods, clothing, tools, and household equipment. The tools, particularly steel knives and axes, make almost every job from garden work to house building easier and faster. Adults no longer spend such long hours making fiber clothing, wooden and stone tools, salt, or bark cloth. However, they do make net carrying-bags, pig ropes, and some craft goods such as arrows for their own use or sale to tourists. Wage labor, cash-crop activities, markets, schools, lamps, radios, card playing, and evening gatherings now have changed the time schedules of domestic and social life. There is some specialization of occupations – in raising cash crops, marketing produce, and raising livestock for sale.

The road system, towns, administrative and market centers, use of vehicles, and cessation of warfare have had a tremendous effect on intergroup communication. Many highlanders are employed in agriculture, industry, government, and commercial and domestic service in town and country, near or far from home. All must travel to church, school, political meetings, health facilities, markets, courts, or other town activities. Visits between communities are more frequent and there is greater participation in regional and national activities. Local isolation no longer exists, and strangers cannot be avoided. As young people have left home for school and work, their relatives have gone by road or air to visit them in distant places.

People are now involved in wholly new political and legal institutions. Until the 1960s, some men, with the titles of *luluai* and *tultul*, were appointed by the Australian officers to act as leaders, representatives, and intermediaries – stopping fights, escorting disputants to local courts, assembling the community for administrative visits and tasks, and conveying communications and requests of the administration to the people. When local government councils were established, the elected councilors and locally selected committeemen served as leaders and intermediaries between the council and the administration. Councils became minor legislative and political bodies, responsible for collecting taxes and allocating funds and tasks in their areas. More recently larger council areas and provincial area authorities have taken a greater role in local and regional affairs; local leaders have learned to use administrative procedures and political responsibilities. The provincial government, when it is established, will carry this to a higher level.

The legal aspect of development has taken a different course. The Supreme Court and district court have become dominant law agencies, to which local dispute cases not amenable to informal mediation are referred. These courts may jail or fine; their cases have predominantly concerned theft, fighting, new administrative rules and institutions, and nonindigenous persons. Councilors and committeemen mediate local disputes and take serious cases to the magistrates of local or district (now provincial) courts. A new development has been the establishment of and the appointment of local men to deal with disputes in their own tribe or clan.

The first thirty years of colonial administration introduced many new practices, and many traditional ones declined in importance. New goals were modeled on local interpretations of Western forms and values, including Christian worship, cash enterprises, manufactured goods, and governmental institutions. In many places, traditional activities were abandoned in favor of new ways of business and modernization. More recently with self-government and independence there has been a resurgence of interest in some traditional ceremonies and practices, including tribal fighting, crafts, and payments. Now, however, these are often conducted with Western-style goods and financed with the proceeds from cash crops or labor. In Chimbu the exchange system has intensified with payments in money, cartons of beer, and live cattle. The rising price of coffee in 1976 made such increased expenditure possible. Money circulates rapidly in card games, and winnings may be spent on beer for the winner and his friends. Cash crop earnings and gambling profits are not often invested in long-term improvements to homes or communities. The most desirable things, cars and trucks, are so expensive that long-term saving and cooperation or loans are needed.

Development in the highlands of Papua New Guinea has not been uniform. The places reached first, in the eastern highlands and Wahgi Valley, with low or moderate population densities, have been centers of European-owned coffee plantations and commerce. The Highlands Highway connects the seaport of Lae to the towns of Goroka and Mt. Hagen, which have become administrative and commercial centers. The Chimbu province was early recognized as too densely occupied by local people to be a source of land for outsiders for development, and the Southern Highlands and Enga provinces as well as off-highway parts of the Eastern Highlands, Chimbu, and Western Highlands provinces are still remote and less developed. The contrast is seen in the income and number of vehicles, household property, economic diversity, and development projects of the subprovinces: Goroka and Mt. Hagen are in most respects better off and more advanced than other highlands areas. In contrast, some outlying peoples see this new technological diversity only when they become laborers, and they are at a disadvantage in obtaining services. The people close to these centers have had twenty to thirty years of close contact with plantations and commercial activities, and fifteen years of local government; a generation of children have been to school. Some highlands areas that were reached only by walking paths are now approachable by rough tracks suitable for four-wheel drive vehicles in dry weather. These tracks and bridges are maintained by local voluntary labor and often become blocked by landslips. In these areas, most cash crops are carried to sale, with a lower return for time and labor. People in these remote areas are usually also far from schools, hospitals, and administrative services. They see shops, new projects, government officers, and other representatives of Western society less often than the people nearer towns and highway activities.

The highway is the commercial artery of the highlands. Okapa, Lufa, Tambul, Tari, Gumine, Kagua, Gembogl, Yalibu, and Laiagam are on spurs that will have little traffic unless they are upgraded and energetically maintained. Karimui, Telefomin, Bundi, Simbai, Wonenara, Kutubu, and some other places are still to be reached by road (see Map 1). I believe a stratification by income, opportunity, and achievement has developed within the highlands, and the less fortunate will not easily catch up. Now, the central government is limiting expenditure for education and other development programs, and there is some question whether the established programs will be maintained at the same level.

At the same time, however, there is a slowly growing sense of regional unity throughout the highlands, which may become a political force in opposition to other regional or factional groups. Some small and remote groups still hardly participate in Papua New Guinea national social, political, and economic programs. Many highland groups have had few educational or other opportunities as compared to other regions. The disadvantaged may recognize common interests. The intergroup, interclan, and intertribal competition and opposition, traditionally very strong in the highlands, continue to fragment local interests. It is mainly as an expansion of this beyond the provincial to the regional level that highland unity, as opposition to other regions, may become a political force of national significance.

References

Barth, F. 1975. Ritual and knowledge among the Baktaman of New Guinea. New Haven: Yale University Press.

Berndt, R. M. 1962. Excess and restraint: social control among a New Guinea mountain people. Chicago: University of Chicago Press.

Berndt, R. & Lawrence, P., eds. 1971. Politics in New Guinea. Perth: University of Western Australia Press.

Boserup, E. 1965. The conditions of agricultural growth: the economics of agrarian change under population pressure. Chicago: Aldine.

Bowers, N. 1968. The ascending grasslands. Ph.D. dissertation. Columbia University, New York.

Brookfield, H. C. 1962. "Local study and comparative method: an example from central New Guinea." Annals of the Association of American Geographers 52: 242–54.

    1972. Intensification and disintensification in Pacific agriculture: a theoretical approach. Pacific Viewpoint 13: 30–48.

Brookfield, H. C. & Brown, P. 1963. Struggle for land: agriculture and group territories among the Chimbu of the New Guinea highlands. Melbourne: Oxford University Press.

Brookfield, H. C. with Hart, D. 1971. Melanesia. London: Methuen.

Brown, P. 1972. The Chimbu: a study of change in the New Guinea highlands. Cambridge, Massachusetts: Schenkman.

Brown, P. & Brookfield, H. C. 1967. "Chimbu residence and settlement." Pacific Viewpoint 8: 119–51.

Brown, P. & Buchbinder, G., eds. 1976. Man and woman in the New Guinea highlands. American Anthropological Association Special Publication 8.

Brown, P. & Podolefsky, A. 1976. "Population density, agricultural intensity, land tenure and group size in the New Guinea highlands." Ethnology XV: 211–238.

Bulmer, R. N. H. 1960a. "Political aspects of the moka ceremonial exchange system among the Kyaka." Oceania 31: 1–13.

    1960b. Leadership and social structure among the Kyaka people of the western highlands district of New Guinea. Ph.D. dissertation, Australian National University, Canberra, Australia.

    1965. "The Kyaka of the western highlands" in Lawrence, P. & Meggitt, M. J., eds. Gods, ghosts and men in Melanesia, 132–161. Melbourne: Oxford University Press.

1968. "The strategies of hunting in New Guinea." Oceania XXXVIII: 302–18.

Bulmer, S. 1975. "Settlement and economy in prehistoric Papua New Guinea: a review of the archaeological evidence." J. Soc. Océanistes 31 (46): 7–75.

Clarke, W. 1971. Place and people. Berkeley: University of California Press.

Du Toit, B. 1975. Akuna: a New Guinea village community. Rotterdam: A. A. Balkema.

Gardner, R. & Heider, K. 1968. Gardens of war. New York: Random House.

Glasse, R. 1967. "Cannibalism in the kuru region of New Guinea." Transactions of the New York Academy of Sciences II: 2, 9, 748–54.

1968. Huli of Papua. Paris: Mouton.

Glasse, R. & Lindenbaum, S. 1971. "South Fore politics." in Berndt, R. M. & Lawrence, P., eds. Politics in New Guinea, 362–380. Perth: University of Western Australia Press.

Glasse, R. & Meggitt, M. 1969. Pigs, pearlshells and women. Englewood Cliffs, New Jersey: Prentice-Hall.

Hatanaka, S. & Bragge, L. 1973. "Habitat, isolation and subsistence economy in the central range of New Guinea." Oceania XLIV: 38–57.

Heider, K. 1970. The Dugum Dani. New York: Viking Fund Publications in Anthropology 49.

1972a. "The Grand Valley Dani pig feast: a ritual of passage and intensification." Oceania XLII: 169–98.

1972b. The Dani of West Irian. Warner Module 2.

Hipsley, E. 1969. Metabolic studies in New Guineans. South Pacific Commission Technical Paper 162.

Hipsley, E. & Kirk, N. 1965. Studies of dietary intake and expenditure of energy by New Guineans. South Pacific Commission Technical Paper 147.

Howlett, D. 1971. Papua New Guinea geography and change. Melbourne: Thomas Nelson.

1973. "Terminal development: from tribalism to peasantry" in Brookfield, H., ed., The Pacific in transition, 249–73. Canberra, Australia: Australian National University Press.

Koch, K-F. 1970. "Warfare and Anthropophagy in Jalé Society." Bijdragen tot de Taal-,Land-,en Volkenkunde 126: 37–58.

1974. War and peace in Jalémo. Cambridge, Massachusetts: Harvard University Press.

Lambert, J. 1975. A study of the nutritional status and economic development in the Chimbu District, Papua New Guinea from 1956 to 1975. Mimeo. Public Health Department, Konedobu, P.N.G.

Langness, L. L. 1964. Some problems in the conceptualization of highlands social structures. American Anthropologist Special Publication: New Guinea, the central highlands, J. Watson, ed., V. 66, No. 4, Part 2: 162–82.

1971. Bena Bena political organization, in Berndt, R. M. & Lawrence, P., eds., Politics in New Guinea, 298–316. Perth: University of Western Australia Press.

1973. "Traditional Political Organization," in Hogbin, I., ed., Anthropology in Papua New Guinea, 142–73. Melbourne: Melbourne University Press.

de Lepervanche, M. 1973. "Social structure" in Hogbin, I., ed., Anthropology in Papua New Guinea, 1–60. Melbourne: Melbourne University Press.

Lowman-Vayda, C. 1971. "Maring big men" in Berndt, R. & Lawrence, P., eds., Politics in New Guinea, 317–61. Perth: University of Western Australia.

McArthur, N., Saunders, I. W., and Tweedie, R. L. 1976. "Small population isolates: a micro-simulation study." Journal of the Polynesian Society 85:307–26.

Meggitt, M. J. 1960. Notes on the horticulture of the Enga people of New Guinea. UNESCO symposium, Goroka, 86–89.

1964. "Male-female relationships in the highlands of Australian New Guinea." American Anthropologist 66: 204–24.

1965. The lineage system of the Mae-Enga of New Guinea. Edinburgh: Oliver and Boyd.

1971. "The pattern of leadership among the Mae-Enga of New Guinea" in Berndt, R. M. & Lawrence, P., eds., Politics in New Guinea, 191–206. Perth: University of Western Australia Press.

1973. "System and subsystem: the Te exchange cycle amongst the Mae Enga." Human Ecology 1: 111–23.

1974. "Pigs are our hearts!" Oceania XLIV; 165–203.

Newman, P. L. 1965. Knowing the Gururumba. New York: Holt, Rinehart & Winston.

Nilles, J. 1942-5. "Digging-sticks, spades, hoes, axes and adzes of the Kuman people in the Bismarck mountains of east-central New Guinea." Anthropos 37–40: 205–12.

O'Brien, D. 1969. "Marriage among the Konda Valley Dani," in Pigs, pearlshells and women, Glasse, R. & Meggitt, M., eds., 198–234. Englewood Cliffs, N.J.: Prentice-Hall.

1974. Men named Sky: political aspects of shamanism and witchcraft among the Konda Valley Dani. Ms. Symposium on sorcery, witchcraft and magic in the New Guinea highlands. American Anthropological Association.

Oomen, H. A. P. C. & Cordon, H. 1970. Metabolic studies in New Guineans. South Pacific Commission Technical Paper 163.

Peters, H. L. 1975. Some observations of the social and religious life of a Dani group. Irian Bulletin of Irian Jaya Development, IV, 2.

Ploeg, A. 1969. "Government in Wanggulam." Verhandelingen van het Koninklijk Instituut voor Taal-,land-, en Volkenkunde 57. The Hague: Martinus Nijhoff.

Pospisil, L. 1958. Kapauku Papuans and their law. Yale University Publ. Anthrop. 54. New Haven: Yale University Press.

1963. Kapauku Papuan economy. Yale University Publ. Anthrop. 67. New Haven: Yale University Press.

Rappaport, R. 1968. Pigs for the ancestors. New Haven: Yale University Press.

Read, K. E. 1952. "Nama cult of the central highlands, New Guinea." Oceania XXIII; 1–25.

1965. The high valley. New York: Scribner's.

Reay, M. 1959. The Kuma: freedom and conformity in the New Guinea highlands. Melbourne: Melbourne University Press.

Robbins, S. 1970. Warfare, marriage and the distribution of goods in Auyana. Ph.D. dissertation, U. of Washington.

Sahlins, M. 1971. "The intensity of domestic production in primitive societies: social inflections of the Chayanov slope" in Dalton, G., ed., Studies in Economic Anthropology, 30–51. Anthropological Studies No. 7.

1972. Stone age economics. Chicago: Aldine.

Salisbury, R. F. 1962. From stone to steel: Economic consequences of technological change in New Guinea. Melbourne: Cambridge University Press.

Schieffelin, E. L. 1975. "Felling the trees on top of the crop." Oceania XLVI: 25–39.

1976. The sorrow of the lonely and the burning of the dancers. New York: St. Martin's Press.

Sinnett, P. 1972. "Nutrition in a New Guinea highland community." Human Biology in Oceania I: 299–305.

Sinnett, P. and Whyte, H. 1973. "Epidemiological studies in a highland population of New Guinea: environment, culture and health status." Human Ecology I: 245–77.

Sorenson, E. R. 1972. "Socio-ecological change among the Fore of New Guinea." Current Anthropology 13: 349–72.

Sorenson, E. R. & Gajdusek, D. C. 1969. "Nutrition in the Kuru region. 1. gardening, food handling, and diet of the Fore people." Acta Tropica 26: 281–330.

Steadman, L. 1975. "Cannibal witches in the Hewa." Oceania XLVI: 114–21.

Strathern, A. 1969. "Finance and production: two strategies in New Guinea highlands exchange systems." Oceania XL: 42–67.

1970a. "The female and male spirit cults in Mount Hagen." Man 5: 571–85.

1970b. "Male initiation in New Guinea highlands societies." Ethnology 9: 373–9.

1971. The rope of moka. Cambridge, England: Cambridge University Press.

1972. One father, one blood. Canberra, Australia: Australian National University.

Strathern, A. & Strathern, M. 1971. Self-decoration in Mount Hagen. London: G. Duckworth & Co. Ltd.

Strathern, M. 1972. Women in between. London: Seminar Press.

Townsend, P. 1974. "Sago production in a New Guinea economy." Human Ecology 2: 217–36.

Vayda, A. P. 1971. "Phases of the process of war and peace among the Marings of New Guinea." Oceania XLII: 1–24.

Waddell, E. 1972. The mound builders. Seattle: University of Washington Press.

Watson, J. B. 1971. "Tairora: the politics of despotism in a small society" in Berndt, R. M. & Lawrence, P., eds., Politics in New Guinea, 224–75. Perth: University of Western Australia.

Wurm, S. A. 1961. "The languages of the eastern, western and southern highlands, territory of Papua and New Guinea" in A. Capell, ed., Linguistic survey of the Southwestern Pacific. (revised ed.) Nouméa.

Index